The Gaze of the Listener

English Representations of Domestic Music-Making

C000025201

WORD AND
MUSIC STUDIES
10

Series Editors

Walter Bernhart
Michael Halliwell
Lawrence Kramer
Suzanne M. Lodato
Werner Wolf

The book series WORD AND MUSIC STUDIES (WMS) is the central organ of the International Association for Word and Music Studies (WMA), an association founded in 1997 to promote transdisciplinary scholarly inquiry devoted to the relations between literature/verbal texts/language and music. WMA aims to provide an international forum for musicologists and liteary scholars with an interest in interart/intermedia studies and in crossing cutural as well as disciplinary boundaries.

WORD AND MUSIC STUDIES publishes, generally on an annual basis, theme-oriented volumes, documenting and critically assessing the scope, theory, methodology, and the disciplinary and institutional dimensions and prospects of the field on an international scale: conference proceedings, collections of scholarly essays, and, occasionally, monographs on pertinent individual topics.

The Gaze of the Listener

English Representations of Domestic Music-Making

Regula Hohl Trillini

Amsterdam - New York, NY 2008

The paper on which this book is printed meets the requirements of "ISO
9706: 1994, Information and documentation - Paper for documents -
Requirements for permanence".

ISBN: 978-90-420-2489-2
©Editions Rodopi B.V., Amsterdam - New York, NY 2008
Printed in The Netherlands

For Anna Sofia

Acknowledgments

It may be that no man is an island – this particular woman researcher certainly was not one during the making of this book. I count myself particularly happy in that all the following acknowledgments come with a sense of friendship.

My warmest thanks go to Balz Engler for his generosity in every way and for fostering an extraordinarily open-minded research community at the English Department of the University of Basel. Together with Anne Shreffler, he was instrumental in convincing the Swiss National Science Foundation to support the initial research for this book with a substantial grant. Anne Shreffler's generous introductions to other Word-and-Music scholars led to many of the invaluable research contacts and friendships acknowledged below.

For fellowship, for questions, answers and ideas, and for suggesting texts 'with pianos in them', I am happily grateful to Daniel Albright, Rosamund Bartlett, Verena Binder, Werner Brönnimann, Peter Dayan, Sarah Ebner-Walton, Doris Eckstein, Sophie Fuller, Ian Goode, Anna-Patricia Hadorn, Hartwig Isernhagen, Doris Kunz Heim, Irène Kurzmeyer, Andreas Langlotz, Alex Van Lierde, Janet Pollack, Manuela Rossini, Alison Samuels, Robert Samuels, Ruth Solie, Barbara Sträuli Arslan, Antoinette Weibel, Werner Wolf, and the late Sylvia Zysset.

Ladina Bezzola Lambert, Bonnie Blackburn, Cornelia Hannah Brüllmann, Tili Boon Cuillé, Delia Da Sousa Correa, Rebecca Herrissone, Markus Marti, Andrew Shields, and Susan Barton Young have earned my especial thanks for taking the time to read and comment on portions of this book at various stages. Walter Bernhart's open-minded and painstaking editorial work has been crucial.

As trustees of the Cooper Foundation at our department, Heike Behrens and Ina Habermann awarded a generous contribution towards the publication expenses of this volume. Sympathetic and professional support in editorial, technical and administrative matters came from Kathi Bantleon, Christian Gebhard, Ruth Züllig and the staff of Basel University Library, the British Library, and the Music and Lower Reading Rooms of the Bodleian Library. The Basel Women's Association has been providing loving, professional and affordable daycare for children for over a hundred years. For their willingness to accommodate interests of mine that are only indirectly related to the teaching of English as a foreign language, I cannot thank Bruno Colpi and Sibylle Wyss-Hug of Olten Grammar School enough.

So much more than can be expressed here would have been impossible without my parents: Verena Hohl-Rüfenacht and Giovanni Hohl. Thank you.

Basel, 27 November 2007   Regula Hohl Trillini

The permission to republish material from the introduction and the first chapter which appeared in *Music and Letters* as "Shakespeare's Sonnet 128 and Early Modern Discourses of Music and Gender" in February 2008 is gratefully acknowledged.

Contents

Introduction

1. Ideals: Music and Gender

> Musicke is the princesse of delites
> and the delite of princes.
> RICHARD MULCASTER. *Positions on the Training vp of Children*

Musical performance[1] straddles the great Western divide between body and mind. 'Pure' music is divine or esoteric and maps abstract intellectual patterns or the order of the spheres. 'Pure' performance in dance and drama is suspect because it centres attention on the desired, feared and despised body. The semantic openness of music allows us to project both earthly excitement and celestial innocence onto its artefacts, but in performance, this balance is tipped: the physical presence and identity of the performers who bring forth those heavenly sounds cannot be overlooked. The separation of mind and body is suspended and deep-seated cultural anxieties are awakened. In performance, God's greatest gift becomes a "suspect and transgressive pleasure" (Leppert, 215) which inevitably provokes both fear and desire.

Gender, the other great divide, is deeply inscribed into the musical mind-body dichotomy. The enduring, abstract arts of musical theory and composition were for a long time encoded as privileged and 'masculine', while performance with its inevitable involvement of the body was closely aligned with social inferiority, the alien exotic and, most of all, women. Within the "venerable intellectual tradition that unites womanhood with music on allegorical and practical levels" (Austern, "Alluring" 344), performance attracts most of the conventional negative connotations of femininity and music. In instrumental performance, the inarticulateness and evident physicality of music-making are particularly powerful reminders of those "dis-orderly energies [...] that are constantly threatening to escape from patriarchal control, even as musical *signifiance* threatens to escape from signification, or the semiotic to erupt into the symbolic" (Dunn, 59). Theoretically exalted as the most sublime and expressive of arts, even as an instrument of

---

[1]   The term 'performance' is used throughout this book with the straightforward meaning of 'singing or playing for one or more other people present', not in senses complicated by, for instance, performative notions of gender as developed in Queer and (post-Judith Butler) Gender Studies.

redemption, music is perceived as morally equivocal as soon as it is actually performed – and never more so than when the player is a woman.

> The study of women and the ways
> in which they are affected by their musical experiences
> offers important insights on the uses and abuses of power within our species.
> CAROL E. ROBERTSON. *Power and Gender in the Musical*
> *Experiences of Women*

Despite the fears associated with female performance, it is required by many rituals in Western societies because a woman performing for a man embodies patriarchal gender relations in an exemplary way. The woman performer actively provides pleasure for the man but is also a passive object of consumption (cf. Mulvey, "Visual Pleasures" 19), and perceived as a moral threat in both roles. Performing music has come to define the players' "discursive position as feminine" (Green, 26) and their social position as inferior, which made it an unacceptable activity for men above the servant class, whom it might turn into minstrels or 'professional people'.

However, female music-making also encroaches on the male prerogatives of presence and meaningful activity: because the player's art is not detachable from her physical, sexual and social self in the way of, say, a writer's work, she cannot be easily overlooked or suppressed. The female musician must inevitably be represented as herself and these representations cannot deny her potentially overpowering attraction. This has provoked attempts at containment or denial: women musicians have been represented as visual and acoustic objects of temptation and consumption, but also as the ennobling Saint Cecilia who draws the listener towards Heaven. Just as the "psychic mode associated with women seems to stand at both the bottom and the top of the scale of human modes of relating" (Gilbert and Gubar, 19), music was considered one of God's greatest gifts as well as an enticement to perdition. The ambivalence of most representations of music's affective powers makes them emblematic of the traditional perception of woman's nature as "simultaneously more and less moral than man's" (Binstock, 125). The topoi of female musical performance are always double-minded: it cannot be done without but is always "simultaneously encoded with pleasure and anxiety" (Leppert, 64).

> The artist is male; the beautiful art-object is female.
> For a male, art is already displaced sexuality;
> for a female, art is already misplaced sexuality.
> CHRISTINE BATTERSBY. *Gender and Genius*

This double vision also informs domestic uses of music. Between the sixteenth century and the Great War, England knew one single socially respectable setting for female music in the service of male delight: courtship. For three hundred years, music featured in every plan for female education, and for three hundred years, educationalists worried about the moral threat posed by this accomplishment. Whether (male) listeners were seen as gullible victims of seduction or as unassailable controllers of command performance, the concern about the potentially negative effects of music and about the social status of those who produce such seductive sounds never went away. It resulted, from the Tudor period onwards, in increasing social restrictions on this form of physical display for men, who were constantly warned away from music as a waste of time, an enfeebling distraction, a social embarrassment or an outright danger to manhood. On the other hand, it was consistently prescribed for women, with the obvious, though not always explicit, goal of attracting suitors that had been brought up to despise the art but were conditioned to consider it an erotically stimulating spectacle.

There are more contradictions. A novel from 1693 comments on the situation of actresses "whose Reputation, as well as Person is exposed for the Pleasure, and Diversion of the Audience" (Anon., *Player's Tragedy*, 10 [sig. B5^v]). The connection between exposing 'person' and 'reputation' may not have been so close for a young bride-to-be who played "The Maiden's Prayer" in a Victorian drawing-room, but exposure was nevertheless implied. Certain 'wifely' qualities are incompatible with a willingness for physical display, but exactly that display was paradoxically used to 'advertise' girls as future wives. To fulfil its function in the courting process, music needed to be adequately seductive, but in order to ensure proper demureness, it was not allowed to be impressive in its own right. This double-bind circumscribes all women that are on musical display in social contexts; the discourse of musical accomplishment in courtship is based on the oxymoron of 'socially acceptable female performance'. In this context, Theodor Adorno's statement that 'glorification of the female character implies the humiliation of all who bear it'[2] readily translates into 'glorification of music implies the reification and humiliation of all who practice it'. In English conduct literature and in narrative constellations of courtship, music inevitably displays, exploits and contains female sexuality.

2. Practice: The Piano

> The history of the pianoforte
> and the history of the social status of women
> can be interpreted in terms of one another.
> ARTHUR LOESSER. *Men, Women and Pianos*

The piano and its ancestors (which will, in this introduction, be indistinctly called 'pianos' as long as statements are valid for all of them) are the most iconic representatives of women's domestic music and its social uses. For centuries, they were omnipresent in middle-class homes[3] and provided an indispensable setting for the enactment of social and gender roles. The price of these instruments supported the function of music in courtship because a girl at the piano not only incites her future husband's desire but also advertises the prosperity of a father who can afford tuition and a costly instrument. Moreover, this expensive and potentially prestigious activity poses no threat to male economic mastery because the music-making has no practical or commercial use. The piano greatly enhances that female task which Virginia Woolf described as providing a looking-glass "possessing the magic and delicious power of reflecting the figure of man at twice its natural size" (*Room* 35).

The physical characteristics of the piano are equally suited to the domestic instrumentalization of female musical performance, which relies both on the sexualization of music and on its domestic containment. Playing a keyboard instrument imparts disruptive power over rapt and tickled listeners, but also entails being dominated and disciplined in a very concrete and physical way: the body cannot move the instrument. Such restraint confers respectability. The piano was never as suspicious as the more obviously sensual string, wind and percussion instruments. It is not as threateningly mobile as a curvy violin or

---

[2]   "Die Glorifizierung des weiblichen Charakters schließt die Demütigung aller ein, die ihn tragen" (Adorno, 106).

[3]   The poor could afford neither pianos nor the leisure necessary to master them, and the aristocracy had less time to cultivate a truly private, domestic life.

a phallic flute but rather reminiscent, at worst, of a coffin, ideally immobilizing the woman for better use by listeners and spectators. It permits a decorous body use that can remain limited to the fingers (a frequent focus of eroticized descriptions) and avoids the 'immodest' postures demanded by 'cellos or the ungraceful wind instruments, which are "too Manlike, and would look indecent in a Woman's Mouth" (Essex, 7:84-85). To put it briefly: the piano allows visually attractive but comparatively 'unphysical' music-making.

Its mechanical sound production is a further asset. When a woman performs as a singer, her body is intimately involved and her music unmistakably and distractingly gendered; but the piano, which does not involve such intimate features as breathing or vibrato, is an almost a-physical voice and of course wordless. A pianist who is playing 'has the floor', as discourse analysis calls it, and is thus disturbing to an order in which *logos* belongs to men; but she has it speechlessly, charming by inarticulate, 'feminine' *melos*. Music-making could be domesticated and become socially acceptable at the piano because the instrument allows for an erotic stimulus which remains largely implicit. The woman pianist does not own or impose her 'voice' in the way a singer does. Being "a Kind of Musick which every one knows is a Consort by it self" (Steele, *Tatler* 2:153:361), the neutral sound of a keyboard instrument has the 'negative capability' to imitate or evoke almost all other instruments[4]. This potential for a "full music" (Pollack, 402) which needs no accompaniment, is again ambiguous: the ability to produce music for dancing single-handedly could make a company depend completely on a pianist's goodwill – but it also chained her to the instrument and prevented her from dancing herself. Like no other musician, a pianist can be seductive and reticent, overwhelming as well as chaste, indispensable yet completely subservient. The piano is an accomplice to accomplishment: it supports both the woman 'against' the male listener and patriarchal repression 'against' the woman player.

The piano does not only serve intricate mechanisms of power and complicity; it is also *represents* them in a highly significant way. Keyboard instruments are ideal touchstones for an analysis of *textual* negotiations of social and gender norms because they have no alle-

---

[4]   This was exploited throughout the history of keyboard writing, with examples ranging from Elizabethan 'hornpipes' and Scarlatti's guitar and castanet effects to Mozart's orchestral duet scoring, Liszt's transcriptions of Beethoven symphonies and the tricks of movie pianists.

gorical or symbolic potential whatsoever. Many other instruments are implicated in iconographical systems: the monochord in Pythagorean systems, lyre, flute and reed pipe in classical mythology, David's harp, Miriam's tambourines and the Last Trump in biblical narrative, the lute in Renaissance allegory, the organ in church traditions and kettledrums and trumpets in military pomp. But the virginals, the harpsichord and the piano have no part in any of these; even the earliest specimens came too late to be determined by classical or medieval iconography. They are free to reflect social uses of music-making with a flexibility and transparency that is not hampered by poetic stereotypes and handed-down metaphors. Continuously brought up to date by inventive instrument-makers, keyboard instruments have remained uniquely topical and transparent to musical innovation and shifting socio-cultural norms and practices.

With its touch of realism and contemporariness, the piano always serves as a reminder of the sexual, domestic and even financial realities that underpin musical practice. Roland Barthes uses a Flaubert passage featuring a piano in order to exemplify what he calls the "reality effect". In his analysis, the instrument is one of those "concrete details" which assume "indirect functional value in that, cumulatively, they constitute an indication of characterization or atmosphere, and so can finally be salvaged as part of the structure" (Barthes, "Reality Effect" 11). Such details are semiotically constituted "by the direct collusion of a referent and a signifier". The piano is not a symbol but represents, at most, metonymically: the "signified is expelled from the sign" (16) which stands for nothing but reality. This enables the piano to expose metaphors that eschew the reality of musical practice. When religious or mythological associations are projected from a conventional symbolic instrument such as lute, harp or lyre onto the harpsichord or pianoforte, their inconsistency with the sensual and social realities they mask becomes ridiculously obvious.

Musical metaphors *mask* ideological fault-lines so consistently that their presence practically constitutes a warning signal: it *marks* contradictions. The Victorian cliché, for example, which describes the piano as 'The Altar in the House', acknowledges the central role of the piano: it imports physical display with its implicitly troublesome erotic agenda (ultimately aiming for the marriage bed) straight into the heart of an essentially de-eroticized familial sphere. The religious metaphor 'altar' attempts to sanitize or sanctify that intrusion, while hinting, nevertheless, at its indispensable function in courtship. Most English piano scenes use this typical combination of female allure, threat and serviceability which music represents. The recognizable and representative place in English literature which domestic keyboard instruments occupy demonstrates the fascination of music as well as the anxious effort expended to contain it within the house. The English literary imagination never latched on to the modest craftsmen in chapels or theatre pits; professional musicians became fiction-worthy only when the *Geniekult* started to inspire *Künstlerromane* around figures like Beethoven, Mendelssohn, Paganini, or Liszt. Domestic piano playing, on the other hand, was so much part of the social identity of women that they could not be represented without it; but whether playing the piano is described as private solace, social routine, or reprehensible seduction, the music which women were forced to make their own is always suppressed as well as celebrated.

3. Representation: The Gaze of the Listener

The English literary history of the pianoforte (and, arguably, of music in general) is often a history of marking and masking, of mentioning yet suppressing the indispensable. Before recording technology, music needed the body to become audible: any texts which deal with it are confronted with the body and the norms that govern its social presence. Literary narratives unmask and undermine – inflect – or ignore and deny – deflect – such conventional definitions of womanhood, but many of them also reflect the suppression of musical performance. The most significant textual strategies, which function in literary and non-fictional texts alike, are the elision and metaphorization of music and the privileging of visual perception.

> Even the common words harmony and melody
> are perpetually misapplied by persons who know nothing of Music.
> JOHN BERKENHOUT. *Letters to His Son at the University*

The related techniques of metaphorization and elision are the most unobtrusive yet pervasive phenomena that will be discussed. Music is a favourite *metaphor* for all that is ordered, sacred and beautiful – 'harmonious' –, whereas representations of actual music-making – often women singing and playing the piano – usually *omit* its positive effects. Instead they exploit the sensual and sexual, quotidian and even commercial aspects of music and highlight the fact that musical performance was considered a demeaning activity for men. Texts about ideal Christian marriage or unconsummated spiritual or bridal love are full of musical imagery, but they never describe actual performances; conversely, actual descriptions frequently imply physical, corruptible love. Adultery and fornication – and ultimately any sexual activity at all – are regularly associated with seductive sounds and spectacles, whereas harmonious love, sanctioned by Heaven, is connected to a dimension of music that is theoretical, contemplative, rational and, in the last resort, inaudible and impalpable. Typically, metaphorical uses of music are hampered by their authors' limited command of technical terms, as the music-loving Dr. Berkenhout observed in 1790: "Even the common words harmony and melody are perpetually misapplied by persons who know nothing of Music […]. That Colossus in literature, Dr. Johnson, explains the word *Melody* by *harmony* of sound" (19:166). Equally, the woman evoked tends to be a mere ideal – 'Woman' with a capital letter – and her instrument often turns into a symbolic lyre or harp which may evoke antiquity or the Christian Hereafter but not the real-life habitats of parlour or drawing-room.

> Looking at angels, or indeed at people singing,
> is much nicer than listening to them.
> OSCAR WILDE. "Letter to Robert Ross"

The third textual symptom of musical unease that will be discussed is the privileging of *visual* perception which inspired the title of this book. Women, who generally "connote to-be-looked-at-ness" (Mulvey, 19), tend to be perceived as being on visual display even when they are busy producing sounds for an audience. This is a reminder of the powerful physical attraction of the musician, but it also underscores the control and detachment of the man who is an overseeing spectator rather than a ravished listener exposed to "the invasive, sense-bereaving object of the ear" (Austern, "Good Musician" 637). Like Ulysses' sailors who had nothing to fear from watching the sirens once their ears were plugged, listeners are safer when they function as viewers, and so, even in the non-visual medium of text, descriptions usually centre on the visual spectacle offered by a musician. Sound, the ostensible *raison d'être* of musical performance, is often more of "a literary idea [than] an observed phenomenon" (Hollander, *Untuning* 162), and even when this idea is expressed in representations of *performance*, it easily gives way to more pressing and accessible visual imagery.

A Victorian poem called "Marriage in Music" exemplifies the precariousness of both musical description and metaphor. The moment of real music lasts for just half a line: "When I hear music" before metaphor sets in: "I am one with thee / And one with some high heavenly life serene" (Barlow, ll. 1-2), and the extended metaphor which follows is almost exclusively visual, glossing over the musical performance that set the poem in motion:

> All sorrows vanish, – all the woes between;
> Thy whiteness leads me like a white fair star
> Rising with solemn purport from afar,
> Silver above broad endless billows green.
>
> The star of thy pure whiteness glittereth so,
> Lighting life's tideway with sweet silver glow [...]
> Life's waters all were tinged with magic gold
> When first the sun of first love rose in might. (ll. 5-10, 13-14)

Such a shift from performance to musical aspiration and visual perception is typical of the unmusical or barely trained audiences that domestic musicians so often encountered in England. Conditioned to find music undignified but sexy, and instructed to look to it for edification, male listeners in particular slip with relief into watching. Visual perception preserves and indeed enhances their erotic pleasure by giving men control over music "as something external to them, something with which they are not essentially engaged" (Shepherd, 57-58).

This transposition of the experience of an erotically interested spectator with a limited interest in music can be observed through three centuries of literature. While the additional distancing effect which turns the pure whiteness of the woman's skin into a star is typically Victorian, the gaze of the listener, of the narrator and of the implied reader is always the gaze of a male resting on the female object of his desire. Even the rare texts which represent women playing for themselves remind us that music is an opportunity for display because they usually imply an absent male lover. Evoking him as an object of the woman's nostalgia or desire, they maintain a framework of performance for a man rather than one of self-sufficient female pleasure. Conversely, representations of male players' private enjoyment are extremely rare: "the burden of sexual objectification" which is indissolubly bound up with musical performance is too much for men, reluctant as they are "to gaze at [their] exhibitionist like" (Easthope, 21).

> A woman is singing me a wild Hungarian air
> And her arms, and her bosom and the whole of her soul is bare.
> D. H. LAWRENCE. "The Piano" (notebook version)

My term for this phenomenon, 'the Gaze of the Listener', is indebted to Laura Mulvey's seminal article "Visual Pleasure and Narrative Cinema". Mulvey's use of the term 'gaze' as biological vision and

culturally conditioned perception does not refer to Jacques Lacan's
metaphor for an internalized instance, but to the (usually male) perspective which cinematic (or literary) narratives enforce on viewers of
both genders. Mieke Bal has described this model of cinematic communication as tending

> to reduce looking to power only, to an absolute subject-object relation, wherein
> the viewer / receiver has total power and the object of the look does not even par-
> ticipate in the communication. This model is in fact based on noncommunication.
> (Bal, 383)

That is intended as a critique of Mulvey's approach to film, which is
seen as too narrow; but for textual representations of music, it is truer
than Bal suspects. It is in fact an appropriate description of those
countless texts about women making music which suppress the performer's communicative and seductive powers.

One very effective way of ensuring noncommunication from
women players is the metaphorical convention of equalling them with
music, as exemplified in the *incipit* of Shakespeare's Sonnet 128
"Thou, My Music". This topos exalts and celebrates women but also
deprives them of their voice and of communicative agency. Like visual descriptions, it elides the production of physical sound, the primary source of the musician's power, and makes the woman inani-
mate and abstract. When she does no longer perform but *is* music, the
awe-inspiring Otherness of inarticulate instrumental music turns into
simple absence, into the nothingness of merely metaphorical, wordless
and ultimately soundless sound. In addition, being represented as music deprives woman of language. Instead of enunciating, she is spoken
for by the male word which reports the listener's perceptions and fantasies, and becomes the perfect erotic object, as Luce Irigaray writes:
"Subjectivity denied to woman: indisputably this provides the [...]
backing for every irreducible constitution as an object: of representation, of discourse, of desire" (133).

> Like most symbols, the piano distorts the untidiness of history.
> CYRIL EHRLICH. *The Musical Profession in Britain*

In its analysis of representations of performance, this book pursues the
double historical aim of establishing both a theme and its variations –
if I may just for this once be excused a musical metaphor. As its
theme, the study reveals a continuity of attitudes and of representational patterns that extends over more than three centuries. This history is here traced for the first time, although single aspects have been
investigated in a burgeoning but compartmentalized field of research.

I am in profound debt to the Word-and-Music scholars, but also to the Shakespeareans, Victorianists and musicologists specializing in the seventeenth century (to name but four groups) who have discussed related issues and moments before – and have thus unwittingly contributed to a larger narrative. The *variations* that can be discerned against this background concern the rationalizations of behavioural norms and the tropes and conventions as they interact with social and genre history. Some of these variations add new material or provide innovative perspectives on well-researched periods and subjects, like the norms regulating men's music-making in the Elizabethan period or the elision of proficient women pianists from Victorian novels. Others are newly established, such as the systematic differentiation between the periods that are referred to as 'Regency' and 'Victorian'. Throughout these periods, certain givens may be *variously* exploited, reflected, inflected, or subverted in representation – but they remain inescapable in negotiating the quandaries of performance.

Note: Some Historical Terms

The historical moments which the book's chapters outline bear convenient (and conventional) shorthand labels, encouraged by Paul Bové's insight that key terms are "finally more important for their function [...] than [...] for what they may be said to 'mean'" (51). So 'Elizabethan' and 'the virginals' function as common denominators for texts dating from 1531 to 1656, 'harpsichord' covers the years 1659 to 1781, and the English pianoforte's long nineteenth century is divided into 'Regency' (1785-1837), 'Victorian' (1838-1887), and 'Edwardian' (1881-1922).

Note: Citation Forms

References to literary works in prose which are divided into volumes, books, acts, scenes, chapters, letters etc., are given as "Graves, *Spiritual Quixote* 3:11:7:275" or "Lee, *Princess* 1:2, pp. 8-9". This may appear tedious, but when trying to locate a passage from a multi-volume eighteenth- or nineteenth-century novel in a modern edition with re-numbered chapters (or vice versa), I have often wished my fellow researchers had followed this procedure.

References to poems give the lines quoted as in "Whaley, 'To a Lady', l. 8", or "Thompson, ll. 5-8", while the page reference is given in the final list of cited works. References from extended verse narratives or plays in verse give act, scene and line and add the page reference at the end as in "Marmion, *Fine Companion* 4:1:164, sig. G2ʳ" or in "629-637, p. 143".

I. Sex and the Virginals
Gender and Keyboards around 1600

> Music oft hath such charm
> To make bad good and good provoke to harm.
> WILLIAM SHAKESPEARE. *Measure for Measure*

The Elizabethan period has with good reason been called the Golden Age of English Music, but writers from the period are strikingly uninterested in music itself. What was of paramount critical and moral interest were the *effects* of musical performance, while there is "scarcely a word which can be designated aesthetic criticism [among the Elizabethan] superlatives as to music" (Boyd, 34-35). The English tradition of judging music according to the behaviour and emotions which it produces (cf. Austern, "Love, Death" 19) focuses on music as a psychological, moral or medical means rather than as an end in itself. In his *Compleat Gentleman* of 1622, Henry Peacham counted music among "the fountaines of our liues good and happinesse", assuming that "all Arts hold their esteeme and value according to their Effects" (104). These effects were of great critical and moral interest in the case of musical performance, for, as Peacham says, "no Rhetoricke more perswadeth or hath greater power ouer the mind" (103). This power is explained by the fact that musical motion mirrors mental processes with its

> very standing rising and falling, the very steps and inflections euery way, the turnes and varieties of all passions whereunto the mind is subiect [...]. For which cause there is nothing more contagious and pestilent then some kindes of harmonie; then some nothing more strong and potent vnto good. (Hooker, 6:38:75)

Awareness of music's double potential for good or evil pervades all texts about musical performance, whether they ultimately focus on its beneficial potentials[5] or on the power that "stireth up filthie lust, womanisheth ye minde, ravisheth ye heart, enflameth concupiscence and bringeth in uncleanes" (Stubbes sig. D4^v).

---

[5]   Many Puritans such as William Prynne pay a token homage to the goodness of music before coming down heavily on the side of 'pestilence': "That Musicke of it selfe is lawfull, usefull, and commendable; no man, no Christian dares denie" only to go on to claim that nobody could be "so audacious as to iustifie [...] lascivious, amorous, effeminate, voluptuous Musicke, (which I onely here incounter)" (5:10:274).

In defence of music, the boundary between good and evil is sometimes drawn between the art and the practitioners, as does Richard Mulcaster, a great advocate of music in children's education:

> [I]f abuse of a thing, which may be well used [...] be a sufficient condemnation to the thing that is abused, let glotonie forbid meat [...] heresie religion, adulterie mariage, and why not, what not? [...] if either thy manners be naught, or thy iudgement corrupt, it is not *Musick* alone which thou doest abuse, neither cannest thou avoide that blame, which is in thy person, by casting it on *Musick* which thou hast abused and not shee thee. (38-39)

The anonymous author of the 1586 *Praise of Musicke* laments similarly that music "is oftentimes blemished with the faults of them that professe to have some knowledge in hir" (v). These views are refreshingly commonsensical, but it is significant that both *The Praise of Musicke* and Mulcaster's sober assessment imply the *possibility* of abuse: however godly in theory and metaphor, music is always potentially dangerous to the virtue of seduced listeners and addled performers. Careful, responsible use is of the essence.

Literary representations of women's alluring musical performances and the worries which Elizabethan conduct literature expresses about their effects are well-researched. In the following, I offer an analysis of the recommendations which normative texts give on *male* performance as a complementary mirror of the same anxieties and contradictions. This more complete frame of reference informs the subsequent discussion of the roles which music and especially keyboard instruments played in the lives of young women, and underpins the reading of the two sonnets in which William Shakespeare represents musical performance. Among the many literary texts and conduct manuals which negotiate the attendant stereotypes and norms, they stand out as particularly dense and revealing elaborations of the clichés and contradictions of this discourse.

1. "Muche musike marreth mennes maners"

Recommendations about male performance frequently negotiate the tension between praise and fear of music by the concept of moderation. In his treatise *The Scholemaster*, Queen Elizabeth's erstwhile tutor Roger Ascham mentions briefly that instrumental music, just like singing, dancing and other sports and pastimes, is "not onelie cumlie and decent, but also verie necessarie, for a Courtlie Ientleman to vse" (sig. G4^r). Nothing more is said about music. In his earlier *Toxophilus*,

Ascham quotes the Greek physician Galen as saying that "[m]uche musike marreth mennes maners"[6], comparing music to honey, which goes down well but taken in excess makes the stomach "unfit to abyde any good stronge norishynge meate" (sig. C2^r). Playing too well was considered just as undesirably excessive as playing too much; in Sir Thomas Elyot's apprehension of the dangers of intimacy with music the word 'knowledge' possibly takes on carnal overtones: "It were therefore better that no musike were taughte to a noble man / than by exacte knowlege therof he shuld haue therin inordinate delyte: & by that be illected to wantonnesse" (fol. 23^{r-v}).

A century on, in 1634, musical excellence had become even less advisable: Henry Peacham, though still considering music "worthy the knowledge and exercise of the greatest prince", yet desires that no "Noble or Gentleman should (save at his leasureable houres) proove a Master" (98) in music. The Scottish divine James Melville (1556-1614) speaks with approval of the fact that his future father-in-law "entertained maist expert singars and playars, and brought upe all his bairns thairin", including Melville's eventual wife, "a verie pleasand gentilwoman, endewit with manie guid verteus" (79), including musical skills. Yet for himself, Melville rejoiced in "the great mercie of my God that keipit me from ainie grait progress in singing and playing on instruments" because "giff I had attained to anie reasonable missure thairin, I haid naver don guid utherwayes" (29).

Sensuous 'inordinate delyte' in music could not only distract from serious duties but also tempt the over-eager musician to abandon his dignity or "grauitie" (Elyot, fols. 23^v). Thomas Becon dismisses music as "a more vayne and triefelinge science, than it becommeth a man borne & appoynted to matters of grauitie" (sig. F1^v), and James Cleland claimed in 1607 that "playing vpon instruments doth disgrace more a Noble man then it can grace and honour him in good companie [...]. For hee shoulde rather take his pastime of others, then make pastime vnto them" (fol. 229-230). It is with regard to this concept of dignity that an older courtly ideal clashes most strikingly with the ungentlemanly connotations which musical practice was assuming dur-

---

[6] The term 'marring' may refer to a specifically sexual concern: early modern physiology conceptualizes woman as an anatomically incomplete, imperfect male, lacking only heat to be transformed into the superior sex. If a man behaves in an inappropriately effeminate fashion – e. g. by performing music for the pleasure of others – he might actually become physically effeminate by the reverse process (cf. Austern, "No Women" 85).

ing the sixteenth century. In 1503, the courtship of Margaret Tudor
and James IV of Scotland involved playing lute and 'clarycordes' to
each other (cf. Stevens, 268), but already in 1534, the "open profession" of musical skill was described as being "but of a base estima-
tion" (Elyot, fol. 23^v). In 1578, Thomas Salter suggested that men
should rather "bende their eares unto Musicions and syngers, [...] then
thei them selues to be harkened unto by idle and wanton folke"
(*Mirrhor Mete* sigs. C8^{r-v}) because audiences – as Thomas Elyot
points out – tend to forget "reuerence whan they beholde [the gentleman musician] in symilitude of a comon seruant or minstrel" (fol. 24^r).
According to *The Courtyer*, that classic manual for courtly behaviour
translated from Baldassare Castiglione's Italian, a gentleman should
"shewe his musike as a thing to passe the time withall, and as he wer
enforced to doe it, and not in the presence of noble menne, nor of any
great multitude" (Hoby sig. M4^r). Music should rather be used
"secretelye, for the refreshynge of his wytte" so that no suspicion
could arise of being paid; and best of all is "to gyue iugement in the
excellencie of [musicians'] counnynges" (Elyot, fol. 23^v).

The ideal musical performance involves the Elizabethan gentleman
only perfunctorily as a player, but mostly as an expert observer, judging and savouring at aristocratic leisure while inferior members of
society are employed to provide his pleasure. This social inferiority
may lie in a player's class or professionalism but also in her gender.
As performers are increasingly objectified, performance is more and
more feminized and men established as archetypal listeners. They are
almost never represented as performing in front of others; even descriptions of the supposedly irreproachable use of music for private
recreation are very rare[7].

Of representations of solitary women players, there are a few more,
but they usually safeguard patriarchal proprieties by inscribing the
controlling male listener at least through a lament for his absence.
'Fair Annie' in the Scottish ballad, who has to serve at the wedding-
banquet of the man to whom she has borne seven illegitimate sons,
later vents her feelings in "a puir bye-chamber", taking "out her vir-

---

[7]   In Josuah Sylvester's translation of Guillaume Du Bartas's *Divine Weekes*, the
speaker gives his "weary spirits som relaxation" (320) by accompanying his own
singing of psalms and hymns with lute or virginals. One little poem by is introduced
as the "extempore" of a man "beeing desired [...] to singe some pretty song to the
Virginalles, by a Gentlewoman that he made no small accoumpt of" (Breton, epi-
graph).

ginals, / And sadly did she play" (Anon., "Fair Annie", ll. 130-132). An "unhappy verse" by Edmund Spenser addresses a beloved who is imagined pining in bed, sitting disconsolately at table or else

> playing alone careless on hir heavenlie Virginals [...]
> If at hir Virginals, tell hir, I can heare no mirth.
> Asked why? say: [...]
> that lamenting Love marreth the Musicall. ("Iambicum Trimetrum", ll. 5-12)

In both these (very different) texts, the experience of the solitary woman player is determined by the absent lover/listener. Even when she is alone, her music is coded less as the soothing leisure pursuit of an active subject, than as a spectacle for the male gaze, be it that of the 'owning' lover, the 'observing' reader of the poem, or the listener to the ballad. Desdemona's 'Willow' song in *Othello* similarly pleases the theatre audience while Emilia's sigh evokes the absent males: "Oh, these men, these men!" (4:3:60).

2. "Sweet was musig, sweeter is the layde"

While music-making was considered to endanger men's dedication to their public duties, it constituted an essential part of the educational curriculum that was to turn girls into dutiful wives. Musical 'accomplishments' were just as constitutive of Elizabethan marriageableness as playing the piano was of Victorian eligibility. This syllabus usually featured writing, reading, sewing and other needlework, playing the lute and the virginals, plus singing and dancing, as it did for Lady Anne Halkett in the 1620s and 1630s, who was "put to masters for learning [...] to write, speak French, play on the lute and virginals, and to dance; and a gentlewoman was kept for teaching them all kind of needle-work" (Anon., "Account" 2-3). The satirical *Gull's Hornbook* cites as the goals of female education "to read and write; to play upon the virginals, lute and cittern" (quoted in Chappell, 60) and to sight-read vocal music, and Margaret Cavendish's *Contract* tells of a carefully brought-up girl who is taken to additional lectures and lessons "once or twice a day, after her [daily and inevitable] exercise of Dancing and Musick was done" (26). Even an armless fairground freak (described in a comedy of 1639 along with a "hairy wench" and a camel) is described as "She that washes / Threads needles, writes, dresses her children, playes / Oth' Virginalls with her feet" (Mayne, 3:1:21 sig. H1^r).

A "song" from William Browne's *Pastorals* (1616) describes the practicing habits of a young girl (recognizable to any modern teenage music pupil's parent):

> When shee should run, she rests; rests when should run,
> And ends her lesson hauing new begun;
> Now misseth in her stoppe, then in her song,
> And doing of her best she still is wrong,
> Begins againe and yet againe strikes false,
> Then in a chafe forsakes her *Virginals*;
> And yet within an hower she tryes a new,
> That with her daily paines (Arts cheifest due)
> She gaines that charming skill. (629-637, p. 143)

The hope is that "a time will be / When merit shall be linkt with industrie" (649-650, p. 143), but genuine and lasting musical achievement was not expected. In his *Anatomy of Melancholy*, Robert Burton notes in 1621 that

> our young women and wives, they that being maids tooke so much paines to sing, play, and dance, with such cost and charge to their parents, to get those gracefull qualities, now being married will scarce touch an instrument, they care not for it. (3:2:3:1, p. 187-188)

I have encountered no literary representations of married women making music in the early modern period.

Female musical performance was socially acceptable only within a clearly defined 'window' that permitted the display of accomplishments for the purpose of lawful courtship and marriage. This is the background for the apparent non-sequiturs of the mother who is hectoring her monosyllabic daughter in Thomas Middleton's *Chast Mayd in Cheapeside:*

> Maudline. Haue you playd ouer all your old Lessons o'the / Virginals?
> Moll. Yes.
> Maudl. Yes, you are a dull Mayd alate, me thinkes you had need haue somewhat to quicken your Greene Sicknesse [...] A Husband. [...] I hold my life you haue forgot your Dauncing: When was the Dauncer with you?
> Moll. The last weeke. (1:1:1-2, pp. 2-3)

Most of the literary works that illustrate this use of domestic music explain its effectiveness by straightforward erotic appeal, but also mention its function as a signifier of an expensive education and hence family wealth. Jacobean texts make the two functions actually stand in for each other, as when the "endowments of her mind" compensate for the ugliness of a young woman in John Reynolds' moral tales of 1623. She has "an actiue and nimble wit, a sweet and sugred tongue, a rich Memory, and a powerfull and happy Iudgement, and

[is] indeed an excellent Dauncer, and Singer, and withall a most perfect and exquisite Musician" (Book 3, sig. B2^v). These accomplishments make her an agreeable companion but also confirm the fact that she is "an exceeding rich match" (ibid.). Conversely, deficient musical skills denote a lack of money or sophistication, as in this extract from a reading primer of 1631: "If her father thrive on his farme, the poore neighbours put the mastership upon him, and if she learne to play on Virginalls, 'tis thought a Courtlike breeding" (Saltonstall, sig. F2^r). Shackerley Marmion's comedy *A Fine Companion* mocks the daughter of a country knight,

> a creature out of fashion, that has [...] no manner of courtship / but two or three dances as old as Mounsier, and can play a few Lessons on the Virginalls that she has learnt of her Grandam; besides she is simple, and dull in her dalliance. (4:1:164, sig. G2 r)

In all these contexts, virgins play the virginals not so much to enjoy music or please an audience, but to play their part in the mating ritual.

> Musick beareth a swete baite.
> THOMAS SALTER. *A Mirrhor*

In order to further an acceptable courtship, music had to be attractive enough to advance the purpose, but conduct books demanded that even in this setting female skill should not draw attention to itself. Hoby's *Courtyer* demands that a lady should avoid in "playinge upon instrumentes those harde and often diuisions [virtuosic variations] that declare more counninge then sweetenesse" and refrain from 'too swift and violent trickes' (sig. Cc1^r) when dancing. The distinction between the contrasting potentials of 'sweet' feminity and 'cunning' proficiency is characteristic of the cultural practice of music in courtship: the attractiveness of music served a vital social purpose, but remained an explosive property even within such a regulated framework. Great care was taken to "separate the recommendation that women practice the art of music from any implication that they should provoke untoward affections in their enchanted listeners" (Austern, "Sing Againe" 427), even while they were attempting to provoke desirable affection in one suitable listener. Thomas Salter, whose reservations about male performance are cited above, wishes girls to refrain from music altogether since "under the shadowe of vertue [...] it beareth a swete baite, to a sure and sharpe euill" (sigs. C6^{r-v}). The 'sweet bait' may lead to matrimony as well as to illegitimate connections. In both cases, the virgin who is displayed as an erotic bait is bound to lose her virginity, whether as bride or the victim of a seducer.

The certainty that the musical metaphors of the virtuous marriage discourse are bound to become flesh by the wedding night underpins almost all literary representations of young women's music-making. The virginals, the feminine instrument by default, are consistently accompanied by crudely sexual associations. From Lewis Wager's 1566 morality *Mary Magdalene* to John Gough's tragicomedy *Strange Discovery* of 1640, 'playing the virginals' is a recognized double-entendre. The as-yet unrepentant Mary Magdalene plays virginals, recorder and regal (a portable reed organ) at the request of the allegorical characters Infidelitie and Concupiscence (Wager sig. D iii^r), and Gough briefly characterizes a secretly kept mistress as "one Arsinoe whom I think you know, she plays well on the virginals / with her he lies every night" (3:1:86-87, sig. F^2). The jealous Leontes in Shakespeare's *The Winter's Tale* coins a suggestively tactile verb for his wife and her suspected lover: "But to be paddling palms and pinching fingers, / As now they are [...]. Still virginalling / Upon his palm?" (1:2:115-116 and 125-126, p. 1571). In *The Two Noble Kinsmen*, the allusion is even cruder: "She met him in an arbor: What did she there, coz? play o' th' virginals?" The answer is: "Something she did, sir. Made her groan a month for't Or two, or three, or ten" (3:3:33-34, p. 1659).

In many allusions, the underlying sexual tension surfaces in puns on the name of the instrument[8] or its mechanism. The conspicuous bobbing of the jacks, the wooden sticks that carry the goose quills plucking the virginal strings, provoked innumerable jokes along the lines of: "This was her schoolmaister / and taught her to play upon the virginals, and still his jacks leapt up, up" (Dekker and Middleton, 1:13:[500]). In Middleton's *Michaelmas Term* a city goldsmith shoos his daughter away from his conversation with the servant Shortyard (another bawdy pun): "O my sweet Shortyard! – Daughter, get you up to your virginals" ([2:3], p. 102). The contrast between the subservience of a well-brought-up daughter and the crude innuendo which the father cannot help noticing is striking: when music, the metaphorical "princess of delite", issues from the virginals to become the real-life

---

[8]   Although the term probably derives from the Latin *virga* for 'stick' and not from *virgo* for 'virgin', there is a persisting folk etymology that the virginal is, as Dr. Johnson's Dictionary has it, "so called, because commonly used by young ladies". Ben Jonson's reference to the barber's shops that provided musical instruments for waiting clients is not overtly sexual but does suggest availability: "I can compare him to nothing more happely, then a Barbers virginals; vor every one may play vpon him" (*Every Man in His Humour* 2:3:161, quoted in Mueschke and Fleisher, 729).

"delite of princes" (Mulcaster, 37), she inevitably ministers to the concrete pleasure of any Tom, Dick and – Jack – and their 'yards'.

Yards and jacks provoke and enjoy tactile pleasures rather than seductive sounds. What is exciting is the complicated tinkling and touching, the clattering of the jacks (also a standard simile for loose teeth) and the tickly scurrying of white fingers over what used to be dark keys, the particular appeal echoing in the Italian word for brilliant keyboard pieces: toccata. The "digital scramble" of harpsichord music, as Roland Barthes calls it ("Grain" 189), was a popular erotic topos also because the focus on fingers, as opposed to arms, mouths or legs, allows representations of the sensual pleasures of music to preserve a minimal pretence of decorum[9]. A striking example is the dedication of William Byrd's *Parthenia: Or the Maidenhead of the first musicke that ever was printed for the virginalls*. This collection of virginal pieces is dedicated to a royal couple, the Elector Palatine of the Rhine Frederick and the English princess Elizabeth Stuart. Since they were only betrothed at the time, both title and text pun repeatedly – though reverently – on (male and female) virginity. Of course it is the lady who will play the pieces, and she will play for her fiancé only, respecting the performance inhibitions incumbent on her class and gender and displaying herself decorously: "If your Grace will vouchsafe to lend your white hands they will arrive with the more pleasure at the princely eares of your great Frederick" (unpaginated dedication).

3. "Thou, My Music": Shakespeare Sonnets

3.1. Mixing Metaphors / Crossing Boundaries (Sonnet 128)

Sonnet CXXVIII.
How oft, when thou, my music, music play'st
Upon that blessed wood whose motion sounds
With thy sweet fingers when thou gently sway'st
The wiry concord that mine ear confounds,

---

[9] A striking exception is Sonnet 17 from the anonymous 1595 cycle *Emaricdulfe*, which moves from the visual and tactile delight of "snow-white hands" and their "quaint dexteritie", whose touch ties the heart "in a thousand bands" to their "daintie concord and sweet musick" (sig. B4[r]) which promises heavenly bliss to the soul. This is the only example I have found of real music being credited with the effect that musical metaphors promise.

Do I envy those jacks that nimbly leap   5
To kiss the tender inward of thy hand,
Whilst my poor lips, which should that harvest reap,
At the wood's boldness by thee blushing stand.
To be so tickled they would change their state
And situation with those dancing chips,   10
O'er whom thy fingers walk with gentle gait,
Making dead wood more blessed than living lips:
       Since saucy jacks so happy are in this,
       Give them thy fingers, me thy lips to kiss.

Like the dedication to *Parthenia*, William Shakespeare's Sonnet 128 seems to be determined by sweetness and decorum right from its reverent beginning "thou, my music". However, this initial *metaphor* is immediately doubled by a *representation* of musical activity ("music play'st"). What may seem a mere jingle is in fact an anticipation of the trajectory of the whole text, which becomes, in its conclusion, literally 'hands-on' in a way that is quite exceptional in Elizabethan verse. Poetry generally favours a metaphorical discourse of music and eschews its realities, just as the Petrarchan tradition elevates woman to an unreal and unreachable degree of perfection. Actual performance with its tactile and often obscene field of associations belongs (as in the examples cited above) predominantly to drama. On the stage, partners in love can be physically present, and this presence seems to imply and invite disdain for and violation for the female musician; as has been shown, the virginals often serve as a code for such crude desire. The importation of this roughness into a love poem is only the first of a number of highly significant formal and technical transgressions in this text.

"When thou, my music" is one of the rare Shakespearean texts which represent musical performance instead of merely mentioning or stipulating it (as drama often does), and it is the only one to describe a player at the virginals; but it has been largely disregarded by both literary and musical scholars[10]. Its rare mentions in general studies of Shakespeare's sonnet sequence are all dismissive, culminating in the misogynist remark that it seems "addressed to someone not likely to read it too closely" (Wright x). But if it *is* read closely, Sonnet 128 turns out to be a uniquely dense and meaningful display of topical preoccupations about musical performance. Its manifold transgressions turn it into an exemplary embodiment of the discursive compli-

---

[10] Cf. Hohl Trillini, "Shakespeare's Sonnet 128".

cations surrounding women's music-making in the early modern period.

First of all, as mentioned, the tactile concreteness is unusual in poetry. A second transgression is found in the little crux (indeed a 'crossing'!) that concerns the erotically charged 'jacks' which 'leap'[11] inside the virginals to pluck the strings when the key is pressed down. The "gentle gait" (l. 4) of the player's fingers across the "jacks" (l. 5) seems to indicate that they rather refer to the keys of the virginals and indeed for Eric Blom "it is plain that [Shakespeare] misuses the word ['jacks'] for "keys'" (57). Plain, however, is what it is not; the indeterminate "chips" (l. 10) exhibit properties of *both* keys and jacks. Keys are in contact with the fingers, but they cannot leap (cf. Crookes and Kitson), and jacks – which do leap – could touch the player's hands only when she puts them inside the instrument to tune the strings or to loosen jacks which have got stuck. Incidentally, the warped sounds which tuning produces would be a very elegant way to construe "gently sway'st / The wiry concord" (ll. 3-4). However, in tuning one hand turns the tuning-peg inside the instrument, while the other repeatedly strikes the corresponding key to check the shifting pitch. Only if the "saucy jacks" (l. 13) were keys could the player's fingers be said to "walk" over them, and only then could they occasionally caress the exciting "tender inward" (l. 6) of the hand[12].

This ambiguity has been attributed to "the demon of inaccuracy that seems to pursue all literary men when they come to deal with musical matters" (Blom, 57). Stephen Booth dismisses the whole poem as "thwarted by the facts of harpsichord playing" (438-439). But these explanations are rather improbable. Not only is Shakespeare noted for his adept handling of technical vocabularies in many areas; the jack-key ambiguity was also generally recognized enough to serve for puns. In John Lyly's *Midas* a barber-dentist and his victim elaborate on what is obviously a stock joke:

> PETULUS. [A]ll my nether teeth are loose, / and wag like the keyes of a paire of Virginals. [...]

---

[11] 'Leaping' is another recognized innuendo, as in the extract from Dekker and Middleton's *Honest Whore* quoted above. See also Prince Hal's term 'leaping-houses' for brothels (Shakespeare, *I Henry IV* 1:2:8) or the following exchange: " [H]aue I tickled my / Ladies Fiddle well?' '[This ...] double Virginall, being cunningly / touch'd, another manner of Iacke leaps up then is now in / mine eye" (Rowley sig. F3ᵛ).

[12] Sixteenth-century keyboard technique employed the thumbs very rarely, so that the hand does not need to be cupped to help the thumbs reach the keyboard. Instead it is held quite flat, allowing the keys to touch the lowered palms.

DELLO. I cannot / tune these Virginall keyes.
PETULUS. They were the Iackes aboue, the / keyes beneath were easie" (3:2, sigs. C4ᵛ-D1ʳ).

This kind of comedy routine seems to indicate a general familiarity with the difference between jacks and keys.

Why then would Shakespeare, in all probability aware of their respective properties and functions, obscure the difference between jacks and keys through vague terms like the neutral 'chips' and by using the sexually loaded 'jacks' imprecise? I would like to argue that this openness allows the poem to maintain a complexity of metonymic meaning that attributes both the acquiescence of 'easy' keys and the aggression of 'saucy' jacks to the figure of the lover. Readings which overlook the potential significance of this doubling are inevitably reductive. This goes for a seventeenth-century manuscript which substitutes "keyes" for jacks and then omits the epithet "saucy" (cf. Robbins, 138) as much as for a recent comment which also overlooks the obscene meaning of 'jacks' and then talks misleadingly of an appreciated performance and "the poet's desire to be at the very heart of that same creative experience" (Edmondson and Wells, 86). Even the OED conforms to this pattern: it does not list 'penis' among the 39 meanings given for 'jack'[13] and consequently describes the meaning 'virginal jack' as "erron. applied to the key" (OED, online edition). Every time, Shakespeare's conception is flattened and sweetened through a too-narrow reading which conflates 'jack' and 'key'.

The mixed metaphors that tangle between player's body and instrument are a third instance of unconventional patternings in Sonnet 128. They, too, can be read either as carelessness or as a meaningful display of the tensions that determine musical performance. The metaphor "thou, my music" stakes a claim on the desired woman because it expresses the wish to approach ('finger') her erotically by turning her into a metaphorical piece of music – to be produced and consumed – or into a metonymic instrument – to be manipulated. If the woman is an instrument, the idea that she should be susceptible to erotic manipulation is of course absurd – she is never allowed to articulate her enjoyment. And yet, in a double-bind that was to continue for centuries, the passive female 'instrument' is held co-responsible for whether the resulting music is "pestilent" or "potent unto good" (Hooker, 6:38:75):

---

[13]   See Hohl Trillini, "Tom, Dick and [...] Jack".

> You are a viol, and your sense the strings;
> Who finger'd to make man his lawful music,
> Would draw heaven down, and all the gods to hearken;
> But being play'd upon before your time,
> Hell only danceth at so harsh a chime. (Shakespeare, *Pericles* 1:1:81-82)

The reference to an unlawful anticipation of sexual enjoyment implies the dilemma of music in courtship that is too successfully inflammatory: music is an enhancement of goods on the marriage market, but if it threatens to provoke early fulfilment of the promised pleasure, it jeopardizes its own legalimacy. As the woman gains sexual leverage through her music, the music itself disappears from focus: Sonnet 128, with its emphasis on the visual and tactile attractions of "sweet fingers" on "blessed wood" (l. 2-3), describes musical "concord" merely as "wiry" and "confound[ing]" (l. 4). The mixed metaphors enact the neglect of music and of the musician as a human agent which characterizes so many scenarios of a woman playing for a man.

Sonnet 128 also includes the converse scenario of a male instrument being handled by a sensual female musician, but only a part of the lover (the lips) would like to turn into a part of the instrument, and they would not like to be passively depressed keys, but virile, leaping, decidedly active jacks. In this contrast, the supposedly technical confusion between keys and jacks accrues its fullest meaning: the male instrument enjoys the caresses of the performer but remains buoyantly active while being thus used and pleasured. Machine and body fuse when dead wood vivaciously leaps to meet living fingers and is envied by living lips. Dancing 'chips' being tickled by living fingers want to kiss actively, and being dead wood is a more blessed state than being living but frustrated flesh. While "fingers walk" (l. 11) and 'reap harvest' (l. 7), lips 'blush' and "stand" (l. 8). The upheavals of passion which make human limbs and mechanical parts alike desirous "to change their state / And situation" (ll. 9-10) – status and physical location – are palpable. Although the complex mechanism of a keyboard instrument does not invite anatomical identification as readily as a sinuous lute or viol, it does evoke activity while remaining a machine, a passive object. In this way, it completes the representation of the role confusion that is inherent in the situation of a female performer before a male listener. He is being seduced by her but also is tempted to seduce her, while the woman is dangerous and victimized, man-eater and sweetmeat. In this context, also the initial doubling of 'music' takes on extra meaning: not only does it juxtapose metaphor and mimesis, it also symbolizes implicit role conflicts. In "when thou [...]

play'st" (l. 1), the woman is the syntactical subject that dominates 'music' as its dependent object; but in the appositional "thou, my music" (l. 1), the woman – although still grammatically the subject – is the object of male pleasure.

3.2. "Unions married" (Sonnet 8)

Sonnet VIII.
Music to hear, why hear'st thou music sadly?
Sweets with sweets war not, joy delights in joy.
Why lovs't thou that which receiv'st not gladly,
Or else receiv'st with pleasure thine annoy?
If the true concord of well-tuned sounds,   5
By unions married, do offend thine ear,
They do but sweetly chide thee, who confounds
In singleness the parts that thou shouldst bear.
Mark how one string, sweet husband to another,
Strikes each in each by mutual ordering,   10
Resembling sire, and child, and happy mother,
Who all in one, one pleasing note do sing:
    Whose speechless song, being many, seeming one,
    Sings this to thee: "Thou single wilt prove none."

A comparison with Sonnet 8, the musical companion piece of 128 addressed to a young man rather than a woman[14], puts these complications into sharper relief[15]. I take my cues for this cross-reading from Joel Fineman's *Shakespeare's Perjured Eye*, one of the very few studies that comment at length on both musical sonnets. The pleasant character of Sonnet 8 contrasts sharply with the crackling, concrete complications of Sonnet 128 and the other twenty-seven sonnets to the 'Dark Lady' which conclude Shakespeare's sequence. This difference has prompted Fineman to credit Shakespeare with "inventing [poetic] heterosexuality" in his depictions of a very modern "desire for what is

---

[14] The first 126 of the 154 sonnets in the first edition of 1609 are traditionally taken to address a young male friend (and possibly lover) while the remaining 28 speak to the 'Dark Lady'. This gender assignation has been questioned, but the revisionist readings remain largely conjectural (cf. Dubrow).

[15] Like number 128, Sonnet 8 is conspicuously absent from many of the studies cited above, and missing from the indexes of seemingly pertinent monographs such as Bruce R. Smith's *Homosexual Desire in Shakespeare's England* (Chicago, 1991), Gerald Hammond's *The Reader and Shakespeare's Young Man Sonnets* (London and Basingstoke, 1981), or R. J. C. Wait's *The Background to Shakespeare's Sonnets* (London, 1972). Robert Schwartz briefly derogates it for its "facile and neatly-turned phrase" (12).

not admired" (18). Conversely, the idealizing sonnets to the 'Young Man' exhibit a "specular homogeneity" that looks back to the orthodox Renaissance sonnet. When addressing the male friend, Shakespeare's language, "like the desire it mirrors, is 'fair', 'kind' and 'true'" and stresses "eroticized sameness linking idealizing lover to idealized beloved" in a kind of "homosexual truth subtending the poetics of admiration from Dante's Beatrice onward" (17).

Whatever the "homosexual truth" in Shakespeare's case, it is undeniable that the effect of identifying the beloved with music is utterly different when the person thus identified is male. The doubling of 'music' in both opening lines is striking, but, in keeping with ruling gender norms, the male addressee is a *listener*, not a performer. The total obliteration of the performer avoids the presence of a woman musician (who would be far more real and disruptive than a de-eroticized '"happy mother" [l. 11]), but also the embarrassment of a male player (who could not be completely gentlemanly). *Men's* fingers should after all not be the centre of attention, as James I explained to his son: "Delight not also to be in your owne person a player vpon Instrumentes, especially on such as men commonly win their liuing with; nor yet to be fine of any Moechanick craft; DV BARTAS saith, leur esprit s'en fuit au bout des doigts" (152). Instead of detailing a conflicted and thrilling eroticism, the poem establishes a static, almost cloying harmony[16]. Like the other 'procreation sonnets'[17], it circumvents passion, fast-forwarding to the family unit as the result of the sexual encounter. The pervasive imagery of unity and identity, sameness and likeness[18] smothers all the contradictions that trouble Sonnet 128. Instead of the tense duality of female performer and male listener, or the triangle of two jealous males and a female object of desire, the scene of two male listeners without a woman produces "the uniformly homosexual, the oddly homogeneous and purely patriarchal, composition of a family where 'one string is sweet husband to another'" (Fineman, 257) and which, "being many, seeming one" (l. 13), even evokes the doctrine of the Holy Trinity.

---

[16] See also the jingles 'sweets-sweets-sweetly-sweet' and 'sing-song-sings-single'.

[17] Shakespeare's Sonnets 1-17 are grouped under this name because they all urge the young friend to beget children and thus preserve his likeness beyond his own inevitable ageing and death.

[18] Cf. Fineman, 257. Marc Berley remarks: "The moral program of speculative music concerns some of Shakespeare's male characters, but it does not concern the bulk of them once they have seen a lady" (127).

Such 'harmonious' imagery is typical of texts about ideal married love, which abound in musical metaphors. Couples are compared to two "musicall instruments rightly fitted, that doe make a most pleasant and sweet harmonie in a well tuned consort" (Anon., *Office* 140) and love is called "the marriage vertue, which singes Musicke to their whole life" (Smith, *Preparative* 43)[19]. The favoured instruments of this metaphorical discourse are the lute or the viol (often played in 'consort', a chamber music term which easily lends itself to metaphorical use). But such images never describe actual performances. An allegorical play, "Marriage(s) of the Arts", as much as admits the incompatibility of musical ideals and marital realities. When the meek and ingenuous Musica is married off to needy Melancholico, the union does not last: she escapes to Heaven in the very last lines of the play: "Poor Melancholico has lost his wife. / For whilst within, he on the Homours tended, / Pure Musike with the Artes to Heau'n ascended" (Holyday, *Technogamia* sig. P^v).

The 'modern' virginals are never implicated in the truly harmonious love symbolized by a music so heavenly as to be, in the last resort, inaudible and impalpable. Instead, the keyboard instrument is aligned with the physical and corruptible aspects of love: with actually sounding music which "like the physical aspect of earthly love, sang vainly and emptily of a substantive reward that remained forever out of reach" (Austern, "Love, Death" 25). Conversely and significantly, the instrument in Sonnet 8 remains unspecified[20]. Moreover, every other musical term is also metaphorical, purging the conjugal love which the poem is advertising of its real, flesh-and-blood (or flesh-and-wood) dangers as if it were a Puritan marriage tract. Strings are being plucked neither by fingers nor by jacks, but 'sing', transmitting a moral message, and finally gather into an ensemble fit for a Victorian photographer or a cereal commercial: 'sire, child and happy mother'. The contrast between this heavily symbolic trinity and the surrealist cavorting of jacks, keys and body parts in Sonnet 128 could not be greater.

---

[19] Cf. these reminiscences of a happy marriage in Sidney's *Arcadia*: " [I]s a solitary life as good as this? then can one string make as good musicke as a consort: then can one colour set forth a beautie" (3:Y3r).

[20] If the phrases "by mutual ordering" (l. 10) and "by unions married" (l.6) are taken to refer to the unison tuning of adjacent strings, the lute would be implied, a specific instrument, but one that was a hugely popular vehicle for metaphors.

3.3. Silenced under the Gaze

The happy family of strings is an instance of *personification*, the turning of music, musical instruments or their parts into metaphorical persons, which is used to enhance the excessive unity of Sonnet 8. But this "most vivid form of sensualizing metaphor" (Lausberg, 252-253) also contributes to the tangles of heterosexual desire in Sonnet 128. Personification of the virginals adds a third actor to the erotic scenario of music-making, which now involves not just two lovers enjoying music and each other, but three partners who alternate roles. The emotions of the male protagonist spill over onto the virginal which is made to express, blushingly, his contradictory and indiscreet desires. He would like to leap – or have his 'jack' leap – for her, but also let her tickle him and 'walk all over him' like the boots of the lady in the Nancy Sinatra song. Man and woman seduce and are seduced, and the personified, enamoured instrument is the man's adoring and aggressive accomplice as well as his luckier rival(s) in the form of the "saucy" jacks behind whose impertinent eagerness he can hide. Thus Sonnet 128 becomes a peculiar example of the love triangles described in Eve Kosofsky Sedgwick's 1985 classic, *Between Men*: two males wooing the same woman develop a mutual bond that is stronger than the one with the object of their desire, and one rival (here the speaker) may exploit the other(s) (the jacks) in order to gain access to the woman. The personified "dancing chips" (Sonnet 128, l. 10) are fortunate enough for the speaker to wish to "change place and station with" (l. 10) them in a rather strange singular-to-plural identification, but in the final couplet a truce is suggested between the lover and his wooden rivals: "Give them thy fingers, me thy lips to kiss" (l. 14).

The complications of love embodied in the problematic choice of instrument are also underlined by a linguistic feature: Shakespeare takes recourse to several nonce-uses. Both "chips" (l. 10) and "wiry" (l. 4) occur nowhere else in his works, and neither does the plural "unions" (l. 6) in Sonnet 8. The figurative use of 'music' in both poems is also unique in the canon, whereas the word 'concord', on the other hand, is used literally only here and in *The Merchant of Venice*[21]. Everywhere else 'concord' is a (hackneyed) metaphor for friendship and peace, but in Sonnet 128 it is not only physical but even slightly unpleasant, "wiry" and 'swaying' (l. 3). This concentration of

---

[21]   In the passage deprecating "the man that hath no music in himself, / Nor is not moved with concord of sweet sounds" (5:2:83–84, pp. 280–281).

unusual lexical items and uses is symptomatic of the genre boundaries that are being crossed here: the poetic representation of real music is a near-oxymoronic phenomenon.

There is one faultline which this conflict-riddled poem does *not* cross. Like most literary representations of female keyboard playing from Elizabethan to Edwardian times, it privileges the (often visual) perceptions of the listener rather than the subjectivity of the musician, who becomes an object on display. The final tableau takes this imbalance to its final consequences. As long as music is metaphorical ("thou, my music", l. 1), the woman is comparatively in control, but as she becomes completely the performer, she ends up in a posture of almost masochistic erotic availability. The hands, fixed to the keyboard, continue to play, "tickled" (l. 9) from below by the jacks[22], and the lips are kissed, probably from above, by the man who no longer needs to envy the jacks as he stops the player's mouth with his own[23]. He turns her into what Coriolanus calls his wife: "my gracious silence" (Shakespeare, *Coriolanus* 3:1:175). The siren's disruptively attractive instrument has turned against her, immobilizing her for erotic consumption in which she simply has to 'give' her body parts.

That a woman's mouth and hands should be demanded by a *group* of males (i. e. the lover and the jacks) is yet another instance of Shakespeare putting the technical oddity of comparing a keyboard instrument to a human male to splendid account. The plurality of admirers underlines the dominance of the male listener and his viewpoint. In his fantasy, the woman who started out as the grammatically as well as pragmatically active subject, the one who plays, walks and tickles, becomes a yielding object. The listener's jealousy of the erotic bond between the woman and her music is satisfied and his fears of her dominance allayed by turning her instrument into a group of men for a sharing-out which finally manages to exploit as well as contain her erotic potential[24].

---

[22]   The line could also be construed as asking for manual stimulation of the penis(es): Give (i. e. devote to) them thy fingers; give me thy lips to kiss.

[23]   The association of kissing and silencing a woman recurs in Shakespeare's plays, see *Henry VI.2* (2:2:396), *Troilus and Cressida* (3:2:132) and, interestingly, the last scene of *Much Ado About Nothing*, where Benedick's "Peace, I will stop your mouth" (5:4:97) is traditionally taken to be followed by a kiss. Michael Friedman discusses this as the final stage of a silencing process during the courtship of Benedick and Beatrice in "Hush'd on Purpose".

[24]   Katharine Wilson blames "the looseness of the lady's morality" for the obscene fantasies of Sonnet 128 (93).

In Sonnet 128, Shakespeare uses the popular derogatory tropes associated with the mechanism of the virginals for a dense and purposeful exploration of fundamental ambiguities about female sexuality. Critics have largely overlooked this so far[25], possibly because the conventional, male perspective of the poem has prompted them to take the misogynist stereotypes on which it so cleverly hinges at face value. The consequent dismissive readings mistake ambiguities and complexities for instances of Shakespeare nodding. The sonnet which immediately follows in the sequence, the (justly) famous "Th'expense of Spirit in a Waste of Shame", has been read far more attentively, because it is less vulnerable to superficial dismissal: "To explode this world of sighing poetry-love [in 128], there follows the great sonnet of lust [129]" (Edwards, *Confines* 22). But "When Thou, My Music", is a great sonnet of lust, too. It does not explicitly denounce the shameful waste of merely physical passion, but it embodies passion's complications and the attendant cultural anxieties in its layered transgressions. It is also great because it encapsulates motifs that would remain dominant in England for the next 300 years: the visual and erotic objectification of women musicians and the concomitant lack of interest in the sounds they produce; the feminization of the keyboard instrument which immobilizes and silences them; and courtship as the dominant fictional and historical scenario of domestic music.

---

[25] Joel Fineman and Paul Innes are the only critics to have hinted at such horizons. To Fineman, Sonnet 128, "usually much maligned for 'mixing its metaphors'", represents the poetics of verbal disjunction in the 'Dark Lady' sonnets: "the 'wiry concord' of music – which, as in 'my mistress' eyes', is the auditory opposite of speech – is disjunctively collated with the poet's 'poor lips'" (Fineman, 183). Paul Innes reads Sonnet 128 as a superficially conventional sonnet which contradicts "the tenor of disruptive elements" in "an ongoing attempt to contain disjunctions" (196).

II. "Musick in the House, Musick in the Heart, and Musick also in Heaven": The Harpsichord

> The virginals, that ancient serious Matron-like instrument.
> RICHARD STEELE. *The Tatler*

Once the virginals had been superseded by the larger wing-shaped harpsichords with their more varied and brilliant sonoric possibilities, their sex appeal quickly faded. In 1710, Richard Steele called the virginals "that ancient serious Matron-like instrument" (*Tatler* 2:157:380)! Playing a keyboard instrument continued to be an essential part of the canon of accomplishments (described in Lady Ann Fanshawe's *Memoirs* as "working all sorts of fine works with my needle, and learning French, singing, lute, the virginals and dancing", 110), but as the seventeenth century wore on, the harpsichord took over, and the virginals and spinet became a code for poverty and outdatedness. Samuel Pepys's diary mentions a "short, ugly, red-haired slut that plays upon the virginalls and sings, but after such a country manner, I was weary of it but could not but commend it" (4:242, 23/07/1663). Thomas Shadwell's "silly affected Whore", Mistress Jilt, hates London and insists on the equivalent "Breeding" that she has had in the country: "[C]ould I not play, *I am the Duke of Norfolk, Green Sleeves,* and the fourth Psalm upon the Virginals; and did I not learn, and could play six Lessons upon the Viol *de Gambo* before I went to that nasty, stinking, wicked Town [...]?" (*Epsom-Wells* 3:1, p. 41). In a comedy of 1691, two sisters bewail the inadequate tutoring of an "ignorant, illiterate hopping Puppy" of a dancing-master, an old and hoarse singer, and a music-master who comes "to teach one to twinkle out *Lilly burlero* upon an old pair of Virginals, that sound worse than a Tinkers" (Shadwell, *Scowrers* 2:1:10).

Two years on, another comic character defends a lady's virtue by saying: "I believe her as Virtuous as my self; but then she Sings, and Plays upon the Virginals so sweetly, and Dances Country Dances." The doubtful rejoinder "Nay, doubtless she has all her motions to a miracle" (Southerne, 3:1:25) reveals that playing a keyboard instrument had become, within seventy years, a 'motion', genuine or not, that could signify domestic virtue even on the stage. The seventeenth century saw an emergent "redefinition of the family, which identified women as partners with their husbands in the construction of the home as a place of warmth and virtue" (Belsey, 47) and added new cultural connotations to private music-making. A newly available discourse of musical domesticity is equally remote from scenarios of convention-alized courtship or illegitimate lust.

In the emerging genres of prose fiction, particularly the courtship novel, domestic keyboard music remains erotically attractive but is also integrated into scenes of sentimental love, matrimonial affection – and matrimonial tedium. Delighted fathers and bored husbands are added to the virginals' lecherous literary audiences. In Tobias Smollett's *Humphry Clinker*, the unpleasantly patronizing husband Thomas Bullford, jolly but "of moderate intellects", derides his wife who entertains the company "with a sonata on the harpsichord [...] to admiration" (2:286). At first affecting "to be in raptures" and asking her to perform "an *arietta* of her own composing", he then falls asleep when she plays, only to wake with a snort and exclaim: "'*O cara!* what d'ye think, gentlemen? Will you talk any more of your Pargolesi [sic] and your Corelli?' – At the same time, he thrust his tongue in one cheek, and leered [...]. – He concluded the pantomime with a loud laugh" (ibid.). This mocking of gentlemen connoisseurs is character-istic of yet another seventeenth-century development: as women con-tinued to play at home, men played less and could be annoyed more intensely by what they were less qualified to appreciate. Those men who did love music found it harder than ever to justify their passion.

1. Prescriptions

1.1. "Musick not worth a gentleman's labor"

> Music is not the labour, principal attention, or great business of a people.
> ANON. *The London Magazine*

Male amateur music-making was not expected to contribute to the constitution of the newly defined domesticity. By 1650, music was no longer a subject that was taken for granted in schools, i. e. in boys' education (cf. Raynor, 141), and Obadiah Walker's 300-page *On Edu-cation* of 1673 dismisses music in two sentences:

> Musick I think not worth a Gentlemans labor, requiring much industry and time to learn, and little to lose, it. It is used chiefly to please others, who may receive the

same *gusto* from a mercenary (to the perfection of which few Gentlemen arrive) at a very easy rate. (1:10:110)

The Scottish music lover Sir John Clerk of Penicuik "bestowed a great deal of pains on the Harpsecord" (15), studied music in Leyden on his Grand Tour and had daily lessons from Pasquini and Corelli in Rome. While time was obviously no consideration, he worried about making "perhaps, more advance [in music] than became an [English] gentleman" (15, editor's note quoting MS 'Travels' 1:8), and hearing the Hapsburg Emperor play the harpsichord in public in 1697 so shocked him "that it had like to have spoiled all my inclination to performing my self" (quoted in Johnson, *Music and Society* 11). However, he continued to play, like many men who describe their struggles to keep a passion for music within acceptable bounds[26]. Samuel Richardson addresses the problem in one of his *Familiar Letters*. Arguing "Against too great a Love of Singing and Music", he asks "what glory is it to a gentleman, if he were even a fine performer, that he can strike a string, touch a key, or sing a song, with the grace and command of a *hired musician?*" (65:82), and the Earl of Chesterfield opined that playing an instrument would put a gentleman "in a very frivolous, contemptible light; bring[s] him into a great deal of bad company; and take[s] up a great deal of time, which might be much better employed" (1:170). John Locke warns of "odd company" and mentions that he has never heard "Excellency in *Musick*" commended in any man (311).

> Sir, once a time I took to fiddling;
> but I found that to fiddle well I must fiddle all my life,
> and I thought I could do something better.
> THOMAS LOVE PEACOCK. *Gryll Grange*

Such negotiations and concessions became possible and plausible once objections against music were based on common sense rather than religious misgivings. John Erskine Mar, though one of the many fathers to warn a son from playing an instrument, considers that there couldn't be "a more agreeable, innocent amusement" (186), and his term "bewitching" is a mere metaphor which does not refer to demonic powers that an Elizabethan audience might yet have feared.

---

[26] The social historian Lawrence Stone mentions a young man in a paternity suit who, while admitting regular visits to the family in question, claims that they were made to the pregnant girl's brother, "who plays upon the harpsichord, which I also play upon" (50). It is significant that this was considered an excuse worth trying!

Eliza Haywood's novel *Jemmy and Jenny Jessamy* exposes the inconsistency between overblown musical metaphor and erotic reality.
Young Jemmy, on emotional trial before marrying his Jenny, has to
resist various temptations, among them the witty and assured Miss
Chit, whose "harpsichord is never out of tune, nor her voice disconcerted with a cold" (1:13:137). Her voice "seem'd the very soul of
harmony, and when accompanied by her harpsichord, which she finely
touch'd, the mellifluous sounds had power to calm the most raging
passions of the mind" (1:12:135). Jemmy appropriately

> languished, – he died, – his soul seem'd all absorb'd, – dissolv'd in extacy; – and
> he not only spoke, but look'd in such a manner as […] might well make her be-
> lieve she had other charms for him besides those of her voice and skill in music.
> (1:13:145)

These clichés are mercilessly exposed as such when Jemmy comments
the morning after: "to deal sincerely, I like miss Chit as a musician,
but shall never think of her as a woman" (1:12:134). To Jemmy, who
is in love with someone else, music cannot compensate for the fact
that Miss Chit is 'handsome' rather than beautiful, and somewhat too
short.

So music does not so much guide male listeners towards a 'waste
of shame' as waste the time of male players. Samuel Pepys worried
about "being too much taken by musique, for fear of returning to my
old dotage thereon and so neglect my business" (4:201, 27/6/1663).
Daniel Defoe's half-proud confession in his project outline for an
English music academy treats music as a youthful folly: "I have been
a Lover of the Science from my Infancy, and in my younger Days was
accounted no despicable Performer on the Viol and Lute, then much in
Vogue" ("Proposal" 16). The understated double negative is significant: objections were omnipresent, but no longer existential. Conversely, recommendations of music as an inconsequential hobby
"when the more necessary parts of Education are finish'd" were quite
fashionable. Defoe calculates that music "saves a great deal of Drinking and Debauchery in our Sex" because the "Quality, Gentry, and
better sort of Traders must have Diversions" and would take to worse
if denied music (16-17). William Darrell's 1704 instructions to the
gentleman similarly recommend music and dancing because they
"embellish Quality, […] give a pretty turn to Breeding", and are apt to
save embarrassing conversation gaps or "relieve a drooping Discourse" (9:38). It is in such a scene that Lemuel Gulliver attempts to
show off to the royalty of Brobdingnag "with an *English* Tune upon

[the queen's] Instrument" (Swift, 2:6:126), but the undignified efforts which a "Spinet [...] near sixty Foot long" enforces serve as a reminder that music and dancing are not "firstrate Qualifications" since

> they only fit you up for a modish address, and a Female Entertainment. [...] Those Embellishments are more *noble* and *rich* that lie in the Brain, than those that sink into the Feet, or *perch* on the Finger's End. (Darrell, 9:38-39)

Irretrievable physical feminization is no longer feared from music, but finger pads, the epitome of decorous musical eroticism in women, continue to denote intellectual shallowness and effete superficiality in men (see above 27).

1.2. "All in Petticoats learn to touch an Instrument"

> Working, Dancing, Musick, Writing
> and those other necessary Accomplishments of my Sex.
> ELIZA HAYWOOD. *The Female Spectator*

For girls, on the other hand, music in the guise of performance on keyboard instruments (and plucked string instruments such as the cittern) continued to be compulsory. The purpose of achieving matrimony is implied in the familiar hints that playing usually stops after marriage: a character in a farce who hates music is nevertheless wooing a passionate music-lover because he considers it "but one of her irregular appetites of virginity". Music will pass; after all, there is no woman "so devoted to her harpsichord, but she suffered it to go out of tune after matrimony" (Colman, 6). However, conduct literature does not make this purpose explicit, but deploys a range of patently insincere reasons why every girl should play. One version is to represent the potentially embarrassing pursuit of music as ideally suited and utterly desirable to women in general:

> Ladies, as they eminently excel in the Mind, are certainly the best able to distinguish the Beauty of Harmony; and therefore, much admire the so universal Esteem which they have of *Musick*: which, by their constant Pursuits, though it serves them but for Pleasure and Recreation; yet, as it was to that charming Sex [i. e. the Muses] we owe the Invention of so noble and delightful a Science, to them I'll give the Preference; and may they be as much honour'd and revrenc'd by our Sex for their exquisite and refined Knowledge in Musick, as constantly admired and adored for their Beauty. (Costeker, 41)

This sounds as if men were simply too crude for music, whereas the ideological truth is the need to enforce an activity that lacked prestige. The patronizing pragmatism of Defoe in 1728 ("[Music] helps the Ladies off with many an idle Hour, which sometimes might probably be worse employ'd otherwise" ["Proposal" 16]) is not much better than that of Henry Home, Lord Kames, who noted fifty years later that the harpsichord "serves indeed to fill a gap in time, which some parents are at a loss how otherwise to employ" (244). John Essex, finally, piously recommends an "Entertainment without other Views, that preserves [girls] from the Rust of Idleness, that most pernicious Enemy to Virtue" (7:85).

Women authors formulated the musical imperative somewhat more sympathetically, often in a motherly voice that addresses girls directly. However, positive and convincingly stated reasons for female musical practice are lacking here, too. Hester Chapone writes in *Letters on the Improvement of the Mind* that the most important use of music is "more for yourself than others" and continues: "[I]t is of great consequence to have the power of filling up agreeably those intervals of time, which too often hang heavily on the hands of a woman, if her lot be cast in a retired situation" (2:8:118). These lame recommendations are paralleled by the slightness of the apprehended dangers. Mary Astell's hope "that Women may no longer pass for those little useless and impertinent Animals, which the ill conduct of too many has caus'd them to be mistaken for" (21) sounds like an enlightened warning of the commodification which musical performance fosters, but Astell nevertheless recommends music as a "harmless and ingenious" diversion that refreshes the body "without enervating the Mind" (16).

More interesting are the occasional gestures of individualized concern with a girl's inclinations. Hester Chapone "should be sorry to see you neglect [your] talent" (2:8:117), and Lady Sarah Pennington describes music and drawing as "well worth the trouble of attaining, if your Inclination and Genius lead to either; if not, do not attempt them, for it will be only much Time and great Labour unprofitably thrown away [...] if a good Ear, and a native Genius are wanting" (25). Even a *Tatler* item from 1710 raises the issue of individual aptitude:

> We are Man and Wife, and have a Boy and a Girl: The Lad Seventeen, the Maid Sixteen. We are quarrelling about some Parts of their Education. I Ralph cannot bear that I must pay for the Girl's Learning on the Spinnet, when I know she has no Ear. [...] Pray, Sir, inform us, Is it absolutely necessary that [...] all in Petticoats [must learn] to touch an Instrument? (Steele, 3:352:283)

Unfortunately, this interesting letter goes unanswered. The only other relevant passage in the *Tatler* is typical in its generic vagueness: "the politer Part of Mankind" supposedly thinks it "an Imperfection to want a Relish of any of those Things which refine our Lives. This is the Foundation of the Acceptance which Eloquence, Musick, and Poetry make in the World" (3:211:114). Daniel Defoe's concern with female individuals is equally sketchy. Women "should be taught all sorts of Breeding suitable to both their Genius and their Quality" (*Essay* 292). But while "Genius" can signify individual talent, "Quality" is a general social category, and the following remark is again very general: "it would be cruelty to bar the Sex of [Musick and Dancing], because they are their Darlings" (ibid.). The plural or collective terms "girls" or "the Sex" is typical of a mentality which discussed 'the Gentleman' with musical inclinations in an individualized singular as a matter of course and commonly had girls play "the harpsichord, which shows a pretty hand and a nimble finger, without ever thinking whether they have a genius for music, or even an ear" (Home, 244).

2. Representations

2.1. "Musick in the House, Musick in the Heart"

Girls were still obliged to display their pretty fingers on the keyboards, but many early novels go beyond the sexy stereotypes of Elizabethan drama and poetry to have fathers, small daughters, spouses and sentimental lovers gathering round the instrument. Edward Ward's *Don Quixote* paints an appealing idyll where a nubile girl combines homely accomplishments with musicality:

> A freckly kind familiar Lass,
> Just Rotten Ripe for Man's Embrace,
> Could Dance a *Minuet* or *a Bory*[27],
> Sing an old Song or tell a Story,
> Upon her Spinet chime the Tune,
> Of *Happy Groves*, or *Bobbing Joan*;
> And make a Pudding [that delights her uncle]. (1:147-153, p. 9)

Penelope Aubin's Charlotta "cou'd play upon the Lute and Harpsichord, danc'd finely, spoke *French* and *Latin* perfectly, sung ravishingly […] and writ delicately" (*Charlotta* 1:3) before she was ten. The same writer's Lady Lucy, an only child educated with great care, is "a perfect beauty" at thirteen, speaks French and Latin perfectly, "danced

---

[27]   Bourrée, a lively 2/4 measure.

and sung exceeding well, played on the Lute and Harpsicord [sic], and used her Needle with [...] great Dexterity", and is credited with virtue, prudence and "solid Sense" (*Lady Lucy* 1:2-5 with faulty pagination, page 5 following directly after 2). Isabella, the orphaned protagonist of Aphra Behn's *Nun*, is so well educated in a convent in languages, manners and music "[s]trangers came daily to hear [the eight-year-old] talk, and sing, and play" (214). The little girl's music, notwithstanding her numerous audience, retains that pious dignity which Elizabethan writers allowed only, and only rarely, to solitary players.

Daughters playing to their fathers belong to the same emotional climate. The most famous example is the delightful Sophia Western in Henry Fielding's *Tom Jones*, who manipulates her boorish father by catering to his rustic musical tastes although she herself is "a perfect Mistress of Music [who] would never willingly have played any but *Handel*'s". Every afternoon, she obliges this "great Lover of Music [who] never relished any Music but what was light and airy" and attempts only occasionally to "lead him into her own Taste" by suggesting alternatives to "the Repetition of his Ballads" (4:5:169). When she is asked by her friend Tom to intercede with her father for an unfortunate neighbour, Sophia plays all her father's "Favourites three Times over, without any Solicitation. This so pleased the good Squire, that he started from his Couch, gave his Daughter a Kiss, and swore her Hand was greatly improved" (ibid.). She now makes her plea on behalf of the poor gamekeeper and meets with perfect success, making sure that her father won't change his mind by repeating "Sir Simon" "till the Charms of the Music soothed Mr. *Western* to sleep" (4:5:170).

The fair Serena in William Hayley's didactic poem *The Triumphs of Temper* uses her music to less noble ends. Her father has forbidden her to go to the ball. At first, resignation to domestic pleasures prevails, expressed by harmonious playing and a smilingly improvised hymn to wisdom:

> "Let others drive to Pleasure's distant dome!
> Be mine the dearer joy to please at home!"
> Scarce had she spoke, when she with sportive ease
> Prest her Piano-forte's fav'rite keys,
> O'er softest notes her rapid fingers ran,
> Sweet prelude to the Air she thus began! (2:428-433, p. 45)

Without initially intending to, Serena reaches her ulterior aim: the Squire is so pleased that his daughter, now "conscious of her power" (2:458, p. 46), continues her strains until he "with unusual exultation prest / His lovely Child to his parental breast" (2:464-465, p. 47) and grants her permission to go to the ball.

Eliza Haywood's *Fortunate Foundlings* varies this motif by adding the perverted machinations of an evil baron who forcibly detains the heroine "under a shew of liberty". He forces her to "stay at home whole days together, and oblige her to read, or play to him on the spinnet, which frequently she did with an aking heart" (7:94). The context of an established scenario of familial affection around the harpsichord puts the villainy into special relief. In an episode in Henry Mackenzie's sentimental classic *The Man of Feeling*, the father of an eloped daughter (who is now in a brothel) remembers discovering her flight:

> Something at last arose in my mind, which we call Hope, without knowing what it is. [...] I rose and walked through the room. My Emily's spinet stood at the end of it, open, with a book of music folded down at some of my favourite lessons. I touched the keys; there was a vibration in the sound that froze my blood; I looked around, and methought the family-pictures on the walls gazed on me with compassion in their faces. I sat down again with more composure; I started at every creaking of the door, and my ears rung with imaginary noises! (29:144)

The instrument here stands metonymically for the musical services of a daughter who is remembered with more self-pity than sympathy; the father seems to be more moved by the ghostly evocation of what his daughter did for him than by her present plight or possible death. Again, the deviation from a recognized topos heightens the poignancy of the modified version.

Now that lewd associations are no longer as automatic as they were for the virginals, sensuous music and pious harmony no longer belong exclusively to either description or metaphor: musical performances can be represented as erotic *or* familiar *or* spiritual. An anecdote from Thomas Mace's 1676 lute primer *Musick's Monument* fleshes out marital harmony with an unaffected simplicity characteristic of the emerging discourse of familiar, non-erotic musical practice:

> [O]ne Rainy Morning I stay'd within; and in My Chamber, My Wife and I were all alone; She intent upon Her Needle-Works, and I Playing upon my Lute, at the Table by Her; She sat very Still, and Quiet, Listning to All I Play'd, without a Word a Long Time, till at last I hapned to Play This Lesson; which so soon as I had once Play'd, She Earnestly desired Me to Play It again; For, said She, That shall be Called, My Lesson. From which Words [...] It perfectly came into my Remembrance, the Time when, and the Occasion of Its being produced, and returned Her This Answer, viz. That It may very properly be call'd your Lesson; For when I Compos'd It, You were wholly in my Fancy, and the Chief Object, and

Ruler of My Thoughts [...]: And Therefore, ever after, I Thus Call'd It, My Mistress; (And most of My Scholars since, call It, Mrs. Mace, to This Day). (122-123)

This attitude to music is of course co-determined by the fact that it is a professional musician's, but it also represents a newly available narrative topic.

A very different text, Nathaniel Lee's extravagant tragedy *The Princess of Cleve*, brings this kind of domesticity into provocative contrast with the lewdness of some depraved French nobles. The "finish'd Fool" Monsieur Poltrot, just back from England to improve his breeding (i. e. 'study' adultery), proposes to sing some "catches and tunes" that he has picked up, including "some words of my own, that I made on my Wife before I married her, as she sate singing one day in a low Parlour and playing on the Virginals" (1:2, p. 8). He is entreated to play this in a conversation laden with innuendo:

DUKE OF NEMOURS. For Heavens sake oblige us dear pleasant Creature –
POLTROT. I'll swear I'm so ticklish you'll put me out my Lord [...] –

VIDAM OF CHARTRES. Dear soft delicate Rogue sing.

POLTROT. Nay, I protest my Lord, I vow and swear, but you'll make me run to a Whore – Lord Sir, what do you mean?
DUKE OF NEMOURS. Come then begin." (1:2, pp. 8-9)

The shock value of this passage depends precisely on the fact that indecency is no longer compulsory for the combination of woman and keyboard instrument.

The second part of *The Pilgrim's Progress* provides further alternatives. Mrs. Light-Mind, Mrs. Love-the-flesh, Mr. Lechery and Mrs. Filth meet for "Musick and dancing, and what else was meet to fill up the pleasure" (Bunyan, 18), but also the pilgrims make music to celebrate spiritual victories or refresh themselves. Christiana herself plays the viol, her daughters Mercy and Prudence the lute and virginals, respectively[28], and their welcome at the restful "House Called Beautiful" includes music:

Mercie. Hark, don't you hear a Noise? Christiana. Yes, 'tis as I believe a Noise of Musick, for Joy that we are here. Mer. Wonderful! Musick in the House, Musick in the Heart, and Musick also in Heaven, for joy that we are here (73).

---

[28] The virginals are neither old-fashioned nor dubiously tactile, and the lute is not a mere symbol: both are simply instruments to praise God with.

So unqualified a panegyric
might do for a tomb-stone.
CATHERINE SINCLAIR. *Modern Accomplishments*

Two accounts of highly talented young women from the 1660s and 1680s respectively, also combine respect for instrumental prowess and virtuous modesty. Both texts are written after the subject's death, a perspective which enhances the religious tone and the topic of virtue. Mary, the daughter of the Restoration diarist John Evelyn, died of the smallpox at eighteen and is described as a paragon: "(all partiality of relation laid asyde) [...] I never saw, or knew, her equal" (Evelyn, 4:426-429, 14/03/1685). Susanna Perwich, the young Londoner remembered in *The Virgins Pattern*, was pupil and later assistant at her mother's school, which had an orchestra and a staff of teachers including many noted professionals. Susanna "gave no ordinary hopes of proving a *very rare* Musician" (Batchiler, 2), sang, danced, composed and was so proficient on treble viol, lyra viol and lute that well-known professionals listened to her in raptures: "What curious strains! What rare divisions! / Are we not 'mong Celestial visions! / This is no humane hand" (51).

Although Susanna played "one *set* of the choisest Lessons" on the harpsichord as well as her master, she seems to have cultivated the keyboard instrument less because of its worldly associations. For despite being "compassed about with all manner of *delights* and *entertainments*, that a *carnal* mind could desire [...] yet what *dead* things were they to her, and *she* to them!" (6). Significantly, the carnality which makes Susanna prefer holiness to music (cf. fol. A 3ᵛ) is intended in the larger sense of 'worldly'. Sensuality is apprehended less than vanity and the comparative triviality of music: she "made better use of her time, at other sorts of higher Musick" (5). After the death of her fiancé, she decided to remain a virgin, and from then her music seemed "a burden to her, in comparison" to talking of Heaven. Courtship was no longer a motivation, and Susanna would have stopped playing "were it not in *conscience* to her duty of being useful by it in so *Publick* a Family, she would spend *much less* time in that" (21). There is, however, a spiritual benefit: "it helped to raise her own heart towards the *highest* Musick of all, and for *that reason* [she] practised it more than otherwise she would have done" (ibid.). This description resolves the quandary of female musicianship: Susanna is performing "as if she were not" (1 Corinthians 7, 29-30), displaying herself for listeners and for description, but completely without personal vanity or ulterior motives beyond the good of her family: "She sat so steady, and free from any the least unhandsom motion in her body, so modestly careless, and as it were thoughtless of what She was about, as if She had not been concerned at all" (4). Susanna's obituary is geared towards perfect conformity with the injunctions of conduct literature which advised "Modesty and Chastity [...] in the Exercises of Dancing, Musick, and other diversions", performance without "the leering Look, the Flirt of the Fan, and the disagreeable Motion of the Hips" (Essex, 5:47).

The diary of John Evelyn records the excellent and costly teaching which his daughter Mary received at fifteen, in "Musick of Signor Bartholomeo, & Dauncing of Monsieur Isaac; both reputed the best Masters &c." (4:271). However, her obviously brilliant progress is mentioned only once in the following three years. Only after her death, when her father's "unspeakable sorrow and Affliction" prompt an extended description of this wonder among girls, does her prowess, like that of Susanna Perwich, come into its textual own. Mary's proficiency in languages, amateur theatricals, verse writing and history are all extolled together with her beauty and piety, and her musical achievements figure prominently:

> She had to all this an incomparable sweete Voice, to which she play's a through-base on the Harpsichord, in both which she ariv'd to that perfection, that of all the Schollars of those Two famous Masters, Signor Pietro and Bartholomeo; she was esteem'd the best. (IV:421, 14/03/1685)

With similar concern for social approval, the father notes carefully that the last occasion when one of many "noble and judicious persons" to ask for her playing occurred

> at my Lord Arundels of Wardours, where was a solemn Meeting of about twenty person of quality, some of them great judges & Masters of Musique; where she sung with the famous Mr. Pordage, Signor Joh: Battist touching the Harpsichord &c: with exceeding applause. (4:420-422, 14/03/1685)

Here, too, indications of music as a 'sweet bait' are completely absent. In fact, Mary Evelyn chose to stay at home with her parents rather than to accept one of four highly suitable suitors, though "for decency, more than inclination" (IV:426, 14/03/1685). Nor did she want to be part of the "glittering scene" (IV:428, 14/03/1685) of a noble friend's house in London, although she is offered a chance to become Maid of honour to the Queen. Mary Evelyn is described as singing and playing "without any constraint and concerne", which makes her, paradoxically, "as charming to the Eye, as to the Eare" (IV:426, 14/03/1685).

In the monuments of perfect womanhood – one preachingly public, one intensely private – that are erected for Susanna Perwich and Mary Evelyn, spectacular skill nurtured by famous masters can co-exist with pious modesty. As long as Mary was alive, Evelyn had very little to say about her, but then finds that he can never "say enough, ô deare, my deare Child whose memory is so precious to me", now that he is recording "the little History, & Imperfect Character of my deare Child, whose Piety, Virtue, & incomparable Endowments, deserve a Monument more durable than Brasse & Marble" (4:429, 14/03/1685). In Susanna Perwich's obituary, a ridiculously detailed enumerative description of her beauty laments and praises veins, nails, the "marble Mount" of her nose, and of course also her "*Lilly* Hands, long *wood-bine* fingers, / Hang ever *quivering*, never lingers, / In *trembling* strokes, which always she, / Tunes into *sweetest* Harmony" (Batchiler, 45). Such seemingly prurient eloquence is safeguarded by death, which both inspires and liberates the pious historians to celebrate a music that is truly and safely 'in the House'.

> You play better sometimes, my Dear!
> SAMUEL RICHARDSON. *Pamela*

Eighty years on, towards the end of the age of familial domesticity symbolized by the harpsichord, sentimental fiction provides further examples of what could be called "Musick in the Heart". Samuel Richardson's *Pamela* details the relentless pursuit of its heroine by her employer "Mr. B". Pamela Andrews holds out until he agrees to marry her, occasioning a number of scenes which have been criticized for pseudo-pious titillation. In this context it is striking that Richardson actually elides the sexual attraction which could be engendered by its heroine's musical performances. The music which Pamela plays within earshot of her admirer Mr. B. does not enforce the blind in-fatuation which is purported to be an effect of music in conventional poems of the period (see 2.2. "And Music also in Heaven"). Her playing as well as his reaction are made to represent the perceptive sensibility of *both* partners, and his true affection for her. When jealousy of another lady player spoils Pamela's performance, the women listeners are marked as hypocritical or ignorant by their compliments, while Mr. B.'s comment exempts him from these charges, congruent as it is with Pamela's own feelings: "neither my Heart to play, nor my Fingers in playing, deserv'd their Praises. Mr. B. said indeed, You play better sometimes, my Dear!" (4:30:181).

This scene is surprisingly close in emotional tone to the works of Henry Fielding, who despised *Pamela* so intensely[29]. Fielding's *Tom Jones* describes a similar sensibility at the keyboard that is sentimental rather than erotic. Sophia Western (who manipulates her father so sweetly, see above 40) also lightens Tom's convalescence (after he has saved her in a hunting accident) by "kindly condescend[ing], for Hours together, to charm him with the most delicious Music" (5:2:205). Her "eyes, her blushes, and many little involuntary actions" (ibid.) betray the love she will not speak, and when she tries to relieve an embarrassing conversational moment, she plays "so intolerably ill" that Tom, being "not without an Ear any more than without Eyes, made some Observations; which [...] gave him pretty strong Assurances, when he came to reflect on the whole, that all was not well in the tender Bosom of Sophia" (5:2:206). Although it is shared by a couple in love, music here is not so much an erotic bait as an involuntary signal of affection picked up by a sensitivity that augurs well for Tom's and Sophia's marriage[30].

Five years after the appearance of *Tom Jones*, Samuel Richardson published his last novel, *Sir Charles Grandison*. Here, too, the musical discernment of a deserving man reveals his emotional sensibility. When 'his' Harriet is urged to play after other, impressive, lady performers, Sir Charles comments: "Fear nothing, Miss Byron [...]: Your obligingness, as well as your observation, intitle you to all allowances." Harriet treasures his compliment, paid among "a deal of silly stuff" from other admirers, and marvels at the obtuseness of a shallower admirer: "How could Sir Hargrave Pollexfen have the heart to endeavour to stop such a mouth as that!" (2:2:239). Again, a shared sensitivity to the emotional signals of music confirms the value of an affection that will outlast the courtship phase. The newly-married Sir Charles sets up a music-parlour for his wife and invites neighbouring gentlemen performers to play with her regularly. "'May I ask you, Harriet?' pointing to the harpsichord, I instantly sat down to it. It is a

---

[29] It is probably significant that *Shamela*, Fielding's merciless spoof of *Pamela*, contains no musical scenes.

[30] Such scenes enhance the brutality of William Thackeray's femme fatale Beatrix Esmond (in his historical novel *Henry Esmond*, set in the seventeenth century), who accepts another man's proposal "half-an-hour after Esmond went away that morning, and in the very room where the song lay yet on the harpsichord, which Esmond had writ, and they had sung together" (2:2:15:319).

fine instrument. Lord G. took up a violin; Lord L. a German flute; Mr. Deane a bass-viol; and we had a little concert of about half an hour" (7:5:274). Significantly, Sir Charles preserves his superior dignity by not joining in the instrumental concert[31], but proceeds to sing an admiring song that is supposed to convey "The fullness of my heart, / Pour'd out on tuneful ecstasies / By this celestial art". It concludes with a look to Heaven which has Harriet in tears of joy: "The Fair that renders earth so sweet / Prepares me for the skies!" (7:5:275).

2.2. "And Musick also in Heaven"

> But when the tuneful Keys you press,
> And Musick's inmost Pow'rs express,
> What melting Strains extatic rise,
> How ev'ry raptur'd Hearer dies.
> HENRY JONES. "To a young *Lady* on her performing upon the Harpsichord"

Most texts which take the harpsichord 'to the skies' are not novels but independent specimens of that minor genre, 'eighteenth-century harp-sichord love poem', and they address nubile girls in full seductive spate at the keyboard rather than wives. However, the share the vaguely religious rapture of Sir Charles Grandison's verse. In *The Untuning of the Sky* and *Images of Voice*, John Hollander has explored the lamentable process by which poems about music gradually detached themselves from the real experiences that are so convincingly described in fiction, to a point at which "musical epithets degenerate[d] into the emptiest sort of allusion" (*Images* 13). As Hollander explains, poets immediately took

> to the newer notions of affective music, while yet clinging to the imagery of Christian speculative music, notably that of the heavenly harmony, the singing of the angel-spheres, etc. [...] the promiscuous use of this imagery tends to trivialize all but its complimentary and decorative import from about 1640 on. (*Untuning* 202)

It remains here only to cite some keyboard poems which Hollander does not discuss as examples of how the use of the harpsichord can

---

[31] Sarah Scott's *Millenium Hall* strictly observes such gender and class reservations: the neighbours who join the ladies of the Hall for their chamber music on lute, harpsi-chord, organ and 'six-stringed bass' all fall distinctly short of hale gentlemanhood, being "a shepherd [...] with his German flute; a venerable looking man [...] on the violincello, a lame youth on the French horn, another, who seemed very near blind, on the bassoon, and two on the fiddle" (1:10).

show up the artificiality of poetic conventions. The disconcertingly mixed range of mythological and religious allusions, which obliterate rather than celebrate performers and performances, becomes downright ridiculous when connected to an unmistakeably domestic and modern instrument which is devoid of any mythological connotations.

Diana with a lute may be just tolerable as a metaphor, but not when she goes to the harpsichord in Phanuel Bacon's *The Kite*, or when personified cardinal sins and virtues sit in to admire such a performance. Seraphs and cherubs bend to listen in "hush't nature" when "Musidora [...] strikes the sounding Strings" (Baker, "On Mrs. S–", 1. 1). If the stones that Amphion moved by his singing had heard Mary Leapor's "Cloe, Playing on her Spinet", they would "surely not have stir'd for him", and Orpheus is pitied for bringing Eurydice rather than – "alas!" – Cloe back from Hades (ll. 22-23 and 27). Elizabeth Tollet crazily adds a Christian Heaven to her hyperboles on "Mrs. Elizabeth Blackler, playing on the Harpsichord":

> What sudden Harmony of Sound!
> Descending Heav'n is all around! [...]
> No mortal Touch
> Can with such Rapture strike the Mind:
> Such heav'nly Awe with Pleasure join'd. [...]
> What Praise is thine, harmonious Maid?
> What Thanks for all thy Wonders shall be pay'd? [...]
> [...] See! the Musicians of the Sky
> Descending fill the shining Air;
> And see! they hover o'er the Fair. (ll. 3-4, 6-8, 35-36, 45-47)

The 'Fair' herself is quite lost in this flutter; indeed most eighteenth-century harpsichord poems[32] are utterly remote from the experience of actual playing.

Some of these forced juxtapositions between Olympus and the parlour are intentionally comic. In John Langhorne's "To Miss. – In

---

[32] The tradition continues into the 1790s, with poems of the same kind now featuring the pianoforte addressing "elegant Seraphinas" as "Sweet Harmonist" or "Virgin Seraph", surrounded by saints, Apollo, angelic choirs, the muses, minstrels, "warbling Philomel", St. Cecilia, Orpheus with his "Prime Son" Handel, and the piano repertoire which prompts such ecstasy is represented as "dulcet strains which charming flow / From thy sweet *harp*" (Colvill, "Seraphina", ll. 15-16). In these very latest stages, irony becomes finally unavoidable as when Orpheus' art of charming wild beasts is rivalled by "Melissa's" sovereignty over her pug: "When harmony and beauty join, / What can resist the potent spell? / E'en brutal Instinct must resign; / E'en Reason ceases to rebel". (Thelwall, "On a Dog", ll. 9-12)

return for a Set of Reading-Ribbands", Mnemosyne asks her daughters, the muses, to design thank-you presents for the 'Miss'. Polyhymnia is mocked for being "lavish of her Favours, [and ...] send a Zephyr-Load of Quavers" (45-46, p. 101) when she volunteers: "Mamma, I'll tune her Harpsichord: / For Her these fav'rite Airs I'll pack, / And send Them on a Zephyr's Back" (10-12, pp. 99-100). In Richard Steele's extraordinary "To Celia's Spinet", a poem which "Old Bookwit" delivers to the young lady he is petitioning for his son in the comedy *The Lying Lover*, the male speaker asks the (male, and enamoured) "soft machine" to drive the girl to a sentimental suicide unless she accepts him:

> Tell her my Grief in thy harmonious Lay.
> To shun my Moan to thee she'll fly,
> To her Touch be sure reply,
> And if she removes it, die. [...]
> Speak in melting Sounds my Tears,
> Speak my Joys, my Hopes, my Fears.
> Thus force her when from me she'd fly,
> By her own hand, like me, to die. (ll. 1-12)

The refused lover, the beloved and the instrument are all in mortal danger – a triple 'Liebestod' compounded by the fleeting reference to Shakespeare's Ophelia, who drowns singing a "melodious lay" (*Hamlet* 4:7:182, p. 1177)[33]. These poems do not elucidate social practices or ideologies as much as exemplify absurd poetic conventions.

The power of these musico-poetical clichés obscure even the talents of poets who do have an eye and ear for the physical and emotional journey of performing. Aaron Hill's 'Bellaria' comes as vividly alive as do Sophia Western or Pamela Andrews:

> Sweetly confus'd, with scarce consenting will,
> Thoughtless of charms, and diffident of skill;
> See! with what blushful bend, the doubting fair
> Props the rais'd *lid* – then *sits*, with sparkling air,
> Tries the touch'd notes – and, hast'ning light along,
> Calls out a short complaint, that speaks their wrong.
> Now back'ning, aweful, nerv'd, erect, serene,
> Asserted *musick* swells her heighten'd *mien*.
> Fearless, with face oblique, her formful hand

---

[33]   I am indebted to Daniel Albright for the intriguing bit of information that the final section of Wagner's *Tristan* only acquired the title "Liebestod" in its later incarnation as a piano transcription by Franz Liszt.

Flies o'er the ivory plain, with stretch'd command;
Plunges, with bold neglect, amidst the keys,
And sweeps the sounding range, with magic ease. (1-12, p. 141)

However, in the following sixty (!) lines, Hill returns to meaningless classical parading (Time himself applauds in line 50), and concludes piously: "Such, and, *perhaps*, more sweet, those sounds shall rise, / Which wake rewarded *saints*, when nature *dies*" (67-68, p. 145). In Hill's "Celinda, Complaining that Her Harpsichord Was out of Tune", the girl's petulance is again very well observed:

While, with well-acted anger, you *complain*,
Still you attempt your charming task again;
And still, with lovely *petulance*, complain,
That still you strike the trembling *strings*, in vain.
Still you complain! and still my wond'ring soul
Is wildly beckon'd, by the wanton sound [...]. (1-6, p. 13)

However, cliché is not far off: "Thro' my rais'd fancy circling *phantoms* roll, / My *thoughts*, in fairy mazes, dance around!" (7-8, p. 14), and then the speaker feels himself "already die, / E'en while your *strings* you do but *try*" (13-14, p. 14). Laurence Lipking comments: "Music had lost its relation with the divine, and it had not yet found writers who could make good sense of it as something human" (*Ordering* 216).

Neither could they make good sense of the instruments played by human beings. The harpsichord usually makes a mere token appearance in titles or opening lines that sketch the occasion of a verse eulogy. In the body of the poems, apart from rare references to "flying Fingers" or "pratling Strings" (Smith, "To a Young Lady" 23-24) or picturing the girl as sitting "[b]efore your Jacks and Wire at Home" (Smith, "Jilting Mistress", l. 89), metaphorical harps or lyres immediately substitute the contemporary instrument:

Smiling, her Harpsicord She Strung:
As soon as She began to play,
Away his Harp poor Phebus flung;
It was no Time for Him to stay. (Thompson, ll. 5-8)

A third option was the lute. While the lyre has never been anything but a metaphorical entity and the harp's real-life day was yet to come, lute-playing was a practice recent yet quaint enough to heighten scenes of both contemporary and historicizing sensibility long after the seventeenth-century cosmological lute symbolism had faded from memory. Henry Brooke's *The Fool of Quality* (written in 1768, when the lute had long gone out of fashion, and set in its heyday, the seventeenth century), has a lovesick girl turning to the lute in melancholy moments ("Ah! how affectingly did the lute answer to her voice, while she gently turned her sighs to the soft and melancholy cadences", 13:187), but uses the harpsichord for humdrum scenes of female accomplishment. Henry Mackenzie employs the same differentiation in *Julia de Roubigné*. The heroine does not specify an instrument in her reminiscences of "the opinions we formed, the authors we read, the music we played together" (1:11:95) with her soul-mate Savillon. Their "story of sentiment" ended because they mistakenly believed each other married. Savillon, meanwhile, tells a friend how cold the conventional social use of the harpsichord leaves him: "I was again set next Mademoiselle Dorville, and had the honour of accompanying some of the songs she sung to us. A vain fellow, in my circumstances, might imagine that girl liked him" (2:31:71). Julia later accepts the proposal of one Montauban who saved her father from debtor's prison, but her sighs of 'Savillon' in her sleep and her tears on a music-book make her husband suspicious. The instrument that accompanies these private regrets is, appropriately, the lute.

Mackenzie introduces a third instrument for Julia's end; she is murdered by her husband, who has intercepted her letter of acceptance to a – chaperoned and innocent – meeting with Savillon, who has returned from abroad, still unmarried. Julia's melodramatic deathbed apology and Montauban's subsequent suicide are prepared by a scene in which she, already poisoned, plays the *organ* in a trance, trying to recapture a "more than terrestrial melody stole" from a dream, a music "so exquisite, that my ravished sense was stretched too far for delusion, and I awoke in the midst of the intrancement!". She gets up and

> with that small soft stop you used to call seraphic, endeavoured to imitate their beauty. And never before did your Julia play an air so heavenly, or feel such extasy in the power of sound! When I had catched the solemn chord that last arose in my dream, my fingers dwelt involuntarily on the keys, and methought I saw the guardian spirits around me, listening with a rapture like mine! (2:45:178-179)

Montauban is an unseen witness:

> [H]ow like an angel she looked! [...] she sat at the organ, her fingers pressing on the keys, and her look up-raised with enthusiastic rapture! – the solemn sounds still ring in my ear! such as angels might play, when the sainted soul ascends to Heaven! (2:46:185)

This almost Victorian saintliness is exceptional because it is a *real* performance that exhibits virtues in a performer which are usually limited to the field of metaphor. In fact the realism is limited by the organ, which is introduced to represent an emotional extreme which the harpsichord could never have hoped to be associated with; although the unsentimental and pragmatic eroticism associated with the virginals does not dominate the harpsichord quite so exclusively, it remains essential.

2.3. Pitfalls: Sex

> Music and women I cannot but give way to.
> SAMUEL PEPYS. *Diary*

Along with the new domestic and sentimental scenarios, texts continue to chart the association of keyboard music and sexual arousal. In one of her delightful letters (1727), Lady Mary Wortley Montagu reports how a friend of hers was visited by a certain Miss Leigh and was not pleased to see this "[t]all, musical, silly, ugly thing" (2:79) because she was having an intimate visitor. Eventually Miss Leigh is asked to play for the lovers. She

> very willingly sat to the Harpsicord, upon which her Audience decamp'd to the Bed Chamber, and left her to play over 3 or 4 lessons to herself. They return'd and made what excuses they could, but said very frankly they had not heard her performance and begg'd her to begin again, which she comply'd with. (2:79)

However, when the couple used this repetitio simply as "the opertunity [sic] of a second retirement", Miss Leigh, who did "not understand playing to an empty room", disgustedly ignored the request for another encore and left to spread the tale all over London. In consequence, the lover was everywhere complimented "about his third Tune, which is reckon'd very handsome in a Lover past forty" (2:79).

Such blunt testimonials to the powers of music also support various plot elements in a number of fictional genres. In picaresque narratives and episodes, music is a token of the genteel and/or sexually rewarding life which the heroines dream of. But it also functions as a factor in their downfall when the siren's skill backfires to make her the victim of the seducers she has (often unwittingly) aroused. In the collection *The English Rogue*, an old murderess recounts her childhood in her parents' Portsmouth inn, where, at age eleven, she was made "to sit in the Barr, and keep the scores":

> [M]y Father thinking it would advance his trading, bought for me a pair of Virginals; and hired a man to teach me: I giving my mind to it, soon learnt some tunes, which I played to the merry Saylers, whilst they pull'd off their shoes, and

danc'd Lustick; and sometimes I gaining a Teaster, or Groat for my Musick, was so encouraged, that I quickly took all the instructions my Master was able to give me; [...] in little time I was well furnished with [bawdy] Songs. (3:2: [21])

This ignorant enjoyment leads to early corruption: "[W]hen my Auditors laugh'd, and sometimes hug'd and kiss'd me, I had some kind of notions that were very pleasing to me; and [...] I resolved, that if it were long ere I were Married, yet it should not be so before I tryed what it was to lye with a Man". (ibid.) The heroine's apparent musical talent is instrumental to her sensual awakening and sets off her course to ruin.

For Daniel Defoe's adolescent Moll Flanders, music is similarly fatal, arousing not her own sensuality but that of her listeners. When she lives with a noble family as a teenager, she is allowed tantalizing glimpses of her foster sisters' education: "I learn'd by Imitation and Enquiry, all that they learn'd by Instruction and Direction" (ibid.). Moll's attempts on the harpsichord in the young ladies' practice intervals are so impressive that a second instrument is finally provided "and then they Taught me themselves. By this means I had [...] all the Advantages of Education that I could have had, if I had been as much Gentlewoman as they were" (42). However, these advantages also enhance Moll's natural assets of beauty and a good voice, and "that which I was too vain of was my ruin" (43) – both her foster brothers seduce the obviously attractive girl and she is ignominiously dismissed. Genders are reversed in successful (though married) womanizer Monfredo in the anonymous 1693 novel *The Player's Tragedy*, who is "Handsom, cou'd Sing, Dance, and Play on the Musick", displays "a smattering in Poetry", combines "a Manly presence" with "a soft Effeminacy in his face, that cou'd not but render him agreeable to the wanton dalliances of the Fair" (6 [B3^v]) – and is finally killed by a jealous rival.

Untoward musical attraction surfaces in many teacher-student episodes. A 'catch' from 1710 puns obscenely on the 'shakes' which Celia's spinet tutor demands of her[34], and in Joel Collier's parody of Dr. Burney's travelogue, student and teacher elope to Scotland (85).

---

[34] "When Celia was learning on the spinnet to play, / her tutor stood by her to show her the way." When criticized for neglecting to add a 'shake' (i. e. a trill) to a long dotted note, Celia promises "I will shake it when I com to't again", a promise which is transformed to "tis a long prick – I will shake it" (Chocke [n. p.]) if the 'catch' is performed as a three-part canon.

The hero of Tobias Smollett's *Ferdinand Fathom* sings and plays the violin to the daughter of a rich host and then "upon divers occasions, gently squeezed her fair hand, on pretence of tuning her harpsichord" and is "favoured with returns of the same cordial pressure" (1:12:48) until she gives in to him "before her passion could obtain a legal gratification" (1:12:50). In Eliza Haywood's *Female Spectator*, the music-master plot is given an educational twist. Young Celemena falls so violently in love with Mr. Quaver that her parents decide to let her marry him to save her health. Their assumption that "the musician would receive an offer of this nature with an excess of humility and joy" (2:7:51) is, however, mistaken: "Sir, I live very well as I am on my business, and will not sell my liberty for twice the sum" (2:7:53). When the offered dowry *is* doubled to 10,000 pounds, he asks for 15,000, otherwise "I am your humble servant"; Celemena overhears this interview, is disgusted and cured, and Quaver goes away "justly mortified, and ready to hang himself for what he had lost by his egregious folly" (2:7:55-56).

The ridicule heaped on Quaver is typical of the lighter attitude towards musical men that had developed by the mid-eighteenth century. In Charles Shadwell's 1773 comedy *The Fair Quaker*, we find the effete, yet successful musical womanizer: the "sea-fop" Captain Mizen, "only fit to seduce [his] brother officers' wives" (1: [1], p. 5), boasts of his elegant cabin, which sports carpets and wall-linings, candle-lit mirrors "and the best pictures of Venus and Adonis; and a forte piano also; on which, and the guittar, I pass my hours at sea". Another character comments: "A guittar! ye divinities! I begin to agree [...] that the service is in danger, when sea captains thrum the guittar" (1: [1], p. 8). George Colman's farce *The Musical Lady* adds a national aspect. Honest, unmusical George Mask is courting Sophy who is music-mad and enthusiastic for all things Italian. His motivation for pursuing Sophy despite her annoying fixation amusingly perverts a hackneyed poetical metaphor: "mistress's lyre is strung with gold" (6). He finally wins her by pretending to be the Italian music enthusiast 'Masquali': "I won't shock your ear with the English sound of Husband – Take [me] for your *sposo*! – your *caro sposo*" (22). After the wedding, Sophy is enlightened and admonished: "And now, dear Sophy, do but cheerfully resign this one foible [i. e. music], we will be the happiest couple in Great Britain" (40).

All these womanizers and foreigners[35] make it obvious that being attracted to a musical man cannot but be an emotional error of judgment, even if it does not involve the class transgression of the music-master episodes. Frances Sheridan's heroine Sidney Bidulph refuses 'the love of her life' to marry a man who plays the harpsichord "ravishingly" enough to make her envious:

> I had taken a sort of dislike to him when he first came in, I cannot tell you why or wherefore; but this accomplishment has reconciled me so to him, that I am half in love with him. I hope we shall see him often; he is really excellent on this instrument, and you know how fond I am of musick. (*Sidney Bidulph* 1:64)

This initial reaction is eventually vindicated by her husband's betrayal, but forgotten in the sensual and emotional confusion which music was obviously thought capable of producing. In Henry Fielding's *Amelia*, the unfortunate Miss Mathews, who tempts the heroine's weak husband in prison, has herself been undone through music. Hebbers, her seducer, is an extremely attractive and polished friend of the family, whose remarkable musical skills recommend him to her father, "a most violent Lover" of the art and therefore an unreliable parent. Young Miss Mathews has made only "very slender Progress" (1:7:49) in her unavoidable harpsichord lessons and dislikes being asked to play for Hebbers, until he manipulates the fact that her sister is thought of very highly as a performer to manipulate her into jealous, spiteful ambition.

> He took great Pains to persuade me that I had much greater Abilities of the musical Kind [...] and that I might, with the greatest Ease, if I pleased, excel her; offering me, at the same time, his assistance, if I would resolve to undertake it. [...] To my Harpsichord then I applied myself Night and Day, with such Industry and attention, that I soon began to perform in a tolerable manner. [... and began] to love *Hebbers* for the Preference which he gave to [my skill]. (1:7:49)

When Miss Mathews finally falls in love, Hebbers claims an unhappy previous engagement, and then 'undoes' her at her sister's wedding, taking advantage of the effects of "Music, Dancing, Wine, and the most luscious Conversation" (1:7:53).

---

[35] Professionalism signifies class inferiority even in *Paradise Lost*, where Milton's Satan, disparaging the unfallen angels, contrasts his notion of liberty with the musical servility of "the minstrelsy of Heaven" (6:164-168).

2.4. Pitfalls: Class

Seventeenth- and eighteenth-century literature not only underscores the class aspect of musical seduction, but also the dangers of mere musical ambition. Henry Fielding's Tom Jones describes a destitute potential bride as "in herself a fortune" because she is "so beautiful, so genteel, so sweet-tempered, and so well educated, [...] sings admirably well, and hath a most delicate hand at the harpsichord" (*Tom Jones* 14:8:684), but he is a warm-hearted and notoriously incautious lad. Most other texts are remarkably wary of such social mobility. Sarah Robinson Scott's educational utopia *Millenium Hall* even forbids music to lower-class girls because proficiency can be dangerous.

> [I]t might induce a young woman of small fortune to endeavour at mending her circumstances, by performing in public or at best introduce her unto company of a far superior rank, who would think her sufficiently rewarded for the pleasure she gave them by the honour of their acquaintance though the experiences attending it must ruin her fortune; and as soon as her distresses should be known, her music would lose its charms, and neglect or insult become all her portion. (2:7:95)

This brief hint from 1762 anticipates a motif which became endemic in the last quarter of the eighteenth century, where a spate of cautionary tales dramatizes the fate of families ruined through musical ambition (sometimes combined with an unsuitable romantic attachment).

Earlier texts tend to underscore the importance of music as a class marker in stories that invert Scott's plot and describe musical skill as a marker of a girl's essential gentility that is temporarily obscured by unfortunate circumstances. In the inserted tale of "the fortunate Isabella" (a re-working of the biblical Book of Ruth) in Richard Graves's *Spiritual Quixote*, a young squire notices Isabella gleaning in his fields because she puts on her simple clothes "so cleverly, that every thing became her" and because of the "genteel shape and elegant motions" (3:11:7:209) which contrast with her humble occupation. The incongruence is even greater when he follows Isabella to her simple home and is

> surprized to see an handsome harpsichord, which took up half the room, and some music-books lying about, with other books proper for young Ladies to read. [...] his curiosity would not suffer him to rest till he had made some enquiries about her; as there was something in her manner, that convinced him she must have had a different education from what usually falls to the lot of young women in that humble sphere of life. (3:11:7:211-212)

Mother and daughter turn out to be gentlewomen reduced by misfortune, and Isabella "after a decent parley, with gratitude surrender[s] her charms to so generous a lover" (3:11:7:215), retrieving her former station partly thanks to her harpsichord's function as a class marker.

A harpsichord not only marks financial prosperity, but also enables finer distinctions of taste. Superior performance skills in a girl who couldn't ever own a harpsichord give her an air of gentility over people who are merely trying to buy class by music. When Samuel Richardson's Pamela is finally married to her Mr. B. (see above 45), Mr. B's uncle, Sir Jacob Swynfort, refuses at first to be introduced to the ex-servant whom his nephew has married and has to be tricked into meeting and appreciating the charming Pamela under a false name. When the truth comes out, he penitently and automatically assumes that such a paragon must also be musical: "Will you let a body have a Tune or so? My Mab can play pretty well, and so can Dolly: – I'm a Judge of Musick, and would fain hear you." Pamela complies impressively:

> Od's my Life, said he, you do it purely! – But I see where it is – My Girls have got *my* Fingers! And then he held both Hands out, and a fine Pair of Paws shew'd he! – Plague on't, they touch two Keys at once; but those slender and nimble Fingers, how they sweep along! My Eye can't follow 'em – Whew – whistled he – They are here and there, and every-where at once! (*Pamela* 3:33:389-390)

The conclusion is inevitable: "Why, Nephew, I believe you've put another Trick upon me. My Niece is certainly of Quality!" (3:33:390)

Sir Jacob's good-natured vulgarity and the fat red fingers that run in his family indicate the limitations of his taste and elegance, as does the fact that he measures music mostly by money: "[Y]ou know not the Money they have cost me to qualify them[36]; and here is a mere Baby to them, outdoes 'em by a Bar's Length, without any Expence at all bestow'd upon her" (ibid.). Inferior or limited performance skill characterizes the vulgarity of the *nouveaux riche* or the lacking urbanity of country-bred girls. Tobias Smollett's Launcelot Greaves despises girls who clumsily ape "the dress and manners of the gentry" for their "raw red fingers, gross as the pipes of a chamber-organ, which had been employed in milking the cows [...] being adorned with diamonds, were taught to thrum the pandola, and even to touch the keys of the harpsichord" (*Launcelot Greaves* 1:3:22-23).

---

[36] Maybe the misses Swynfort didn't practice enough, like the two ladies in Francis Coventry's *Life and Adventures of A Lap-Dog* who have "just finished their Breakfast by Twelve o' Clock after travelling; Aurora was then sitting down to her Harpsichord, and reading the Play-bills for the Evening" (2:4:159).

> Excelling in Musick [...] is no great Commendation.
> ANON. *The Whole Duty of a Woman*

The quality of musical performance skills is a reliable class marker in seventeenth- and eighteenth-century fiction, but like in Elizabethan times, excessive skill tips the social scales. The anonymous *Whole Duty of Woman* reminds girls that dancing lessons mainly serve the end of knowing "how to move Gracefully" – "for when it goeth beyond it, one may call it *Excelling in Musick*, which is no great Commendation" (48) – and then practically quotes *The Courtyer*'s reservations about music for men (see above 16): "the easiest and safest [!] Method is to do it in Private Company amongst Particular Friends, and then Carelessly, like a Diversion, and not with Study and Solemnity, as if it was a Business, or yourself overmuch affected with it" (49). 'Business' (though not musical busy-ness) is for men; girls have to beware of vanity and class transgression. "Masters indeed are procured [...] and the young ladies may unfortunately excel in a minuet, on the harpsichord, or with a pencil; this I call unfortunate, because it only served to lay them open to flatterers" (Scott, *Ellison* 2:6:92). Charles Allen cautions the 'Polite Lady' against "the highest degree of perfection": "It is no shame to a young lady to be outdone [by a professional]. Perhaps, on the contrary, it would be a shame for her to be equal to any of these in their respective arts[37] [because it implies neglect of] all the other parts of a *complete education*" (21-22).

These are the fears that inspire a conscientious father in Henry Brooke's novel *The Fool of Quality* to limit his daughter's musical training and complete her education within the family circle:

> My daughter is now drawing to woman's estate, and should learn something more substantial than needle-work, and dancing, and harpsichords, and Frenchified phrases. I therefore propose to take her home, where, by the help of our cook and housekeeper, she may be taught how to make a Sunday's pudding and to superintend a family. (13:183)

This will make the girl "rather [...] happy than great" (ibid.) and avoid the fate of girls whose boarding schools acquit them with little more "than a little bad French, a smattering of music, [dancing] a tolerable minuet, a great deal of low pride, much pertness, intolerable vanity, and some falsehood" (Scott, *Ellison* 2:6:92-93). John Fordyce's *Ser-*

---

[37] Cf. Henry Home, Lord Kames: "I find no reason for degrading young women of condition, to be musicians more than painters. Such laborious occupations [...] are proper for those only who purpose to live by them" (244-245).

mons warn that music can be "degraded into an idle amusement, devoid of dignity, devoid of meaning, absolutely devoid of any one ingredient that can inspire delightful ideas, or engage unaffected applause" (6:256).

Yet however great the dangers, music did not go away. The complicated negotiations of recommendation and warning are almost comic at times. Charles Allen discusses the two or three daily hours spent in "revising all the different parts of your education" with a profusion of concessive markers that betray his ambivalence: "Now, *tho'* I would by no means have you to neglect [music and dancing], *but on the contrary* to be daily improving in them; *yet* I think you ought to apply your chief attention to [useful accomplishments]" (127-128, my emphases). Hester Chapone assumes that the average girl is basically "labour[ing] to enrich [her] mind with the essential virtues of Christianity". But neither should "the dear child"

> neglect to pursue those graces and acquirements, which may set her virtue in the most advantageous light, adorn her manners, and enlarge her understanding [...] in the innocent and laudable view of rendering herself more useful and pleasing to her fellow-creatures, and, consequently, more acceptable to God. (2:8:93-94)

Contradictions are thick on the ground. Music is called into service as a class signifier and for decorative purposes, but also for the advantageous display of virtue – which is obviously not expected to be its own reward. Not numbered among the essential "virtues of Christianity", being "pleasant to one's fellow-creatures" is nevertheless elevated to a condition of acceptability to God in the concluding sentence – with intellectual growth ("enlarge the understanding") added as an unexpected and implausible bonus.

2.5. Standardized Subversions

> People who perform music
> also perform their gender and class,
> but never in an unambiguous way.
> RICHARD LEPPERT. *The Sight of Sound*

The uneasy dance of concessions in which accomplishments are credited with adding to virtue, personal adornment, intellect, usefulness and godliness is also apparent in fiction where it conflicts with the blueprints that govern the descriptions of heroines, inevitably presented as pretty and musical. Borrowing an originally heraldic term from Julia Kristeva, Katherine Sobba Green calls these introductory passages, which combine normative "taxonomy and monetary exchange" (72), 'blazons'. She comments: "Much as women have internalized a male scopic perspective, so female novelists internalized this form of tropic commodification" (79). This includes token gestures of praise for musicality. While the financial and family situation of fictional heroines can vary within a certain range of possible plot twists, the personal attractions of beauty and 'accomplishment' are a standardized shorthand code for the desirability that comes with being a literary protagonist.

However, music is problematic even in such a standardized context. All blazons confirm that women must be musical, but not *too* musical. A heroine without musical accomplishment is inconceivable, but amatory fiction from the mid-eighteenth-century onwards regularly downplays these skills to focus instead on intellectual and moral qualifications, which seem to be a contrast[38]. Music is always simultaneously mentioned and suppressed. A character in Penelope Aubin's *Charlotta* is brought up by a morally corrupt mother who provides entertainment and "had me taught to Dance, Sing, and Play on the Spinnet: in fine, she took Pains to make me agreeable, but none to Instruct me in Virtue and Goodness" (22:254). Charlotte Lennox's *Female Quixote* evidences the superior intelligence of its heroine by her indifference to the inferior music of a silly tinkler. The city girl Miss Glanville is disconcerted to find the country-bred Arabella "perfectly elegant and genteel" (1:2:7:118), while her own conversation reveals such profound ignorance that her brother feels the need to intervene by turning the discussion "upon the Grecian History". He manages to engross Arabella's conversation "for two Hours, wholly to himself; while Miss Glanville (to whom all they said was quite unintelligible) diverted herself with humming a Tune, and tinkling her Cousin's Harpsichord" (1:2:7:124).

Miss Turner, one of the seven virtuous and learned wives which the hero of Thomas Amory's eccentric *John Buncle* marries and loses, is "good-humoured, sensible, and discreet", but also "well acquainted with the three noblest branches of polite learning, antiquity, history, and geography". The statement that she "likewise understood musick, and sung, and played well on the small harpsichord", is finally and

---

[38] George Sewell uses cheap over-played music as a metaphor for jaded emotions which are just indolent enough "to move / To *Sing-song, Ballad*, and *Sonata* Love" (10-11).

Figure 1: Franz Kotzwara, "Word of Command", Battle of Prague (1788).

and the attack which occurs after various bugle horn calls and "Signal Cannons" is another piece of F major unworthy even of a Clementi sonatina:

Figure 2: Franz Kotzwara, "The Attack", Battle of Prague (1788).

No wonder that the whole eight pages became a byword of annoying noise; *Punch* cites the piece in an 1842 illustrated series of "Social miseries" (cf. Burgan, 49) and William Henry defined torture as having to hear it "most unmercifully crucified by one of these expert daughters of Euterpe, who is not only devoid of *taste* but *ears*" (note to 21:4, p. 87). Such cheaply effective music enabled the untalented or lazy as well as the more industrious young women to exhibit "floridity of style" and "dexterity of execution". The "endeavour to approach as nearly as their opportunities will permit to professional excellence" made the middle-class "British Female Dilettanti [...] universally acknowledged [...] to have surpassed, in their exquisite execution upon keyed Instruments, all their competitors" (Burgh, vii). The adjective 'exquisite' is somewhat misleading, though. Rather than the new tonal 'delicacies' which could have served an intimate style of music-making suited to the ideals of rational and affectionate companionship, the essential currency on the marriage market consisted of spectacular runs, Alberti basses and octave passages. It is the near-industrial rattle of showy accomplishment that resounds loudest both through Regency fiction and the turn-of-the-century debate about female education.

1. "Accomplishments have taken virtue's place"

> Demosthenes being asked,
> what was the grand essential of eloquence, replied,
> "action, action, action".
> And thousands of parents,
> with regard to the education of their daughter, would say,
> "accomplishments, accomplishments, accomplishments".
> THOMAS BROADHURST. *Advice to Young Ladies* [40]

The cheapness of popular music went hand in hand with the "phrenzy of accomplishment" which was now beginning to rage "with [in]creasing violence" (More, *Strictures* 48[41]) and caused intense concern over the moral and intellectual damage it was thought to do to young women. The British-American novelist Susanna Rowson rhymed "A girl that is once thought a beauty, / Scarce ever hears of virtue, sense or duty" ("Women as They Are", 9-10, p. 105). Virtue, sense and duty – translatable as morals, intelligence and good housekeeping – are regularly played off against showy accomplishments, of which music was considered the most damaging, thanks to the sharply increased practice load demanded by the new pianoforte music. For ladies "of fortune and polite education", ornamental accomplishments still functioned as positive class signifiers, but a middle-class woman was now supposed to "hardly find time to apply" to the piano (Hanway, *Thoughts* 63). She risked being considered "deficient in female qualities, if she, like the aristocratic woman, spent her time in idle amusements [...] aimed at putting the body on display" (Arm-

---

[40]   Cf. the financially troubled father who plans to "Educate, educate, educate" his daughters until there isn't "a girl in Tavistock Square that can beat Polly [...] at the piano" (Trollope, *Last Chronicle* 32:280-281).

[41]   The intensity of the debate is also indicated by the fact that More's *Strictures* went through eight editions in two years.

strong, "Rise" 114). The contrast between such sobriety and the hectic practising (everywhere cautioned against and everywhere imposed) on girls before marriage is typical of the debate of the time.

1.1. Rattling and Piano-forting

> Lorsque le pouvoir veut faire taire,
> la musique est reproduite, normalisée, répétition.
> JACQUES ATTALI. *Bruits*

After the 'tinkling' of the harpsichord, 'rattling' became the new keyboard catchphrase. It went with a new literary stereotype: the excitable, voluble "Miss Rattle", who represents frenetic over-accomplishment in Hannah More's inverted courtship novel *Coelebs in Search of a Wife*. Such girls are "never tired of pleasure", and can always be found "*galloping* over a concerto*" (Hanway, *Ellinor* 1:9:115) or tirelessly "rattling about" (Gore, *Armytage* 1:15:99). Their music often functions as a mere noise, "that general extinguisher of light – 'a little music!'" (Gore, *Cecil* 311). Mr. Darcy in *Pride and Prejudice* is glad of such an extinguisher once he has begun "to feel the danger of paying Elizabeth Bennett too much attention" (Austen, 1:11:64), and in Mary Shelley's *Falkner* the purpose is made explicit: "I hear him coming. Do play something of Herz.[42] The noise will drown every other sound, and even astonish my father-in-law" (1:15:90).

'Noise' refers not so much to the sound volume of early pianofortes (which were hardly larger than concert harpsichords) as to the newly attained maximum figures for notes per minute. Listeners lamented the "crashing, thundering sonata, of the high-pressure instrumental school [...] [with its] astounding rattling of keys and chaotic confusion of sharps, flats and naturals" (Gore, *Cecil* 321-322). All these notes did not come in handy bursts as in a baroque toccata but in sustained, mechanical sequences (see the extract from the "Battle of Prague" above). The incipient industralization furnished apt metaphors for those rushing semiquavers: "[Fashion] has converted the pianoforte into a velocipede, and reckons her success by the number of miles which she can traverse in an hour, not regarding the awkwardness or ungracefulness of her method of travelling" (Anon., "On Church Music" 178). To enable speedy musical journeying, industrial

---

[42] Henri Herz (1803-1888), a French pianist and composer of virtuosic though mostly shallow piano pieces.

practice methods implemented a new hidden agenda of 'quantity over quality'. Czerny, Cramer, Clementi and many others wrote (literally) hundreds of etudes each, and monotonous scales instead of figured bass exercises constituted the bulk of any practice session (cf. Gellrich). The metronome was patented in 1815 and left many young girls (as described in Frances Gore's witty novel *The Désennuyée*) "backboarded, metronomed, and mazurk'd into a most cadaverous complexion [after] their disastrous London campaign" to get husbands (96). Figures of four to eight hours of piano practice a day are cited, and Hannah More calculated that by practising daily (except on Sundays and thirteen travelling days a year) from age six to eighteen, a girl would total 14,400 hours of piano practice (cf. *Strictures* 55). The ambitious mother in Maria Edgeworth's *Practical Education* considers turning her daughter into an "automaton", eight hours a day for fifteen years: "For one [private] concert [...] I think it would be too high a price. Yet I would give anything to have my daughter play better than any one in England" (3:2:5). No wonder some educationalists warned that accomplishments should "be restrained within a proper subordination to those pursuits, which are superior in their nature and consequence" (Wakefield, 76).

The obsession with quantity that determined instrumental writing and practice regimes is also evident with regard to instruments. Wind and bowed stringed instruments were still considered unsuitable for women, but a handbook for governesses lists "piano-forte, harp, guitar, harmonica, harp-lute, castanets and tambourine" while wondering "what advantage to her domestic character as a daughter, a female, a member of Society, a friend to the poor; or to her character as a human being and a Christian" could derive from being obliged to dip into "three, four or five" of these (Appleton, 189). A silly fictional lady practices even less dignified instruments on an admirer, whom she pesters with "sentimental billets" or makes listen "to her guitar, or flageolet, or Jew's-harp or accordion, or some such trash, merely that his cabriolet may be seen waiting at her door" (Gore, *Désennuyée* 6). Pianos themselves became trashy as mass-production techniques began to meet the increasing demand: cheap instruments imitated the look of costlier pieces with stamped and nailed-on brass ornaments. Audiences, instruments and saleable repertoire alike, whether child-

ishly simple[43] or emptily virtuosic, demonstrate the paradoxical phenomenon of widespread musical practice and a general lowering of
musical standards in Britain after 1780 (cf. Johnson, *Music and Society*).

Teachers and pupils begin to appear in fiction. In Fanny Burney's
novel *The Wanderer*, Juliet Ellis, a refugee from revolutionary France,
is forced to use her "superior talents" to teach[44] and is confronted with
a wide range of mostly obnoxious students. The realistically observed
types clearly reflect Burney's experience of growing up as the daughter of a professional musician. There is the talented but lazy girl's
"haughty indifference about learning", which derives "from a firm
self-opinion, that she excelled already"; although she is hardly able to
read music and incapable of going through a complete piece, she despises her teacher's model performances as "a mere mechanical part
of the art, which, as a professor [she] had been forced to study"
(2:3:24:237-238). There are also self-styled enthusiasts and stingy
mothers, who consider "superior merit in a *diletante* [sic] a species of
personal affront" (2:3:21:208) but nevertheless cadge free instruction
from the impressive teacher by arriving early or asking to be played to
(cf. 2:3:24:233-234). A wealthy grocer invites Juliet to give his
daughter "as much of your tudeling as will come to [five guineas].
And I think, by then, she'll be able to twiddle over them wires by herself" (2:3:24:239), while a well-travelled art connoisseur, who consid-

---

[43]   Cf. titles such as Nicola Sampieri's *Pleasant Variety of Little Sonatinas set very
easy for the Piano Forte on purpose to encourage the young ladies to play this fashionable instrument* (1795), *Young Ladies' Delight. Progressive and Miscellaneous
little Pieces; Chiefly intended for the Improvement of the Fair Sex* (1805) or *A
Christmas Box, for Young Ladies, Being a Valuable and Useful Collection of the most
admired little Pieces properly arranged for the Piano-Forte, with additions intended
and calculated for their Improvement, by Signor Sampieri* (1805; all published in
London).

[44]   Mrs. Elton's patronizing recommendation of Jane Fairfax' talents hints at an even
darker perspective in *Emma*: "Your musical knowledge alone would entitle you to
name your own terms, have as many rooms as you like, and mix in the family as much
as you chose; – that is – I do not know – if you knew the harp, you might do all that, I
am very sure; but you sing as well as play; – yes, I really believe you might even
without the harp, stipulate for what you chose" (Austen, 2:17:326). Jane Fairfax famously considers this selling herself in the "governess-trade" and is not sure whether
it does not cause "greater misery of the victims" than the slave trade (Austen,
2:17:325).

ers her "more divine than any thing that he had yet met with on this side the Alps", forces his ill-mannered and lazy sisters to take lessons from "The Ellis". However, their "weariness, that a dearth of all rational employment nurses up for the listless and uncultured" prevents success: "I can't bear to be long about any thing: there's nothing so fogrum" (2:3:24:230-232).

Most girls were forced to be so 'long about' the piano that their practising became a nuisance not only for themselves. Coleridge bemoaned the "piano-fortery, which meets one now with Jack-o'lantern ubiquity in every first and second story in every street" (*Letters* 136, 2:159), and Frances Gore's witty 'Désennuyée' considers that "the party-wall of a London house ought, by act of parliament, to be two bricks thicker" because within twenty-four hours of her new neighbours' arrival she hears "a harp twanging in the front drawing-room; the footman play[ing] the fiddle in the pantry, and three children and a teething infant". To crown it all, "a piano was rattling in the back dining-room" (28).

Such descriptions bear witness to what the *Westminster Review* called the "depreciating influence upon taste" of the popular piano repertoire. Such music was accused of perpetuating "the reign of what is tawdry and false and fashionable among these, whom other nurture might have rendered capable of relishing thoughts as well as sounds, and expression yet more than finger-gymnastics" (H. F. C., 341). However, the worry that "modern music", which mirrored modern life's tumultuous and meaningless activity, would "damage the individual's moral fibre" (McVeigh, 66) could not prevent the tediously repetitive practice routines which paradoxically contributed to a progressive deprecation of musical women and ultimately to their – though not yet the piano's – silencing. Derision determines many accounts of fashionable enthusiasts, who were described as sitting at concerts "with their mouths open to catch the music; like unfledged sparrows ready to be fed" (Austen, *Persuasion* 2:9:209), or advised "to be silent, and not feign raptures they do not feel; for nothing can be more ridiculous" (Wollstonecraft, *Thoughts* 42-43).

The worst are untalented but enthusiastic players which make listeners "writh[e] in excess of torture" by "barbarously murdering" beautiful music "without feeling one *pang* of remorse". One lady, full of "coolness and intrepidity", "*executed* [original emphasis] the '*dove sei*' of Handel, in the strains of a raven in an ague fit" (Hanway, *Ellinor* 2:6:110). An ugly and ostensibly pious, but vain amateur "of the first note" can "make the jacks of her harpsichord dance so fast that no understanding ear could keep pace with them" (Holcroft, *Hugh Trevor* 2:4:114). The "understanding ear" of the narrator, who accompanies her in a piano concerto, gives her away throughout an extended description. She silences her meek father at the 'cello with a dictatorial "piano!" before, in order to attack a solo section, she "heaved up an attitude with her elbows, gave a short cough to encourage herself, and proceeded". When "[t]ime, tune, and recollection" are lost at the first difficult passage, she reprimands her accompanist[45] but continues until the ensemble manage to "find one another out at the last bar, and g[i]ve a loud stroke to conclude with; which was followed by still louder applause. It was vastly fine! *excessive* charming! Miss was a ravishing performer, and every soul in the room was distractingly fond of music!" (2:4:115-6) This enthusiastic audience (including mamma) has been chattering loudly during the whole performance – Thomas Hood's ironic "Ode for St. Cecilia's Day" certainly had a point when it implored female amateur musicians to remember "that the Saint has wings" and not to "thrum the strain, / As if you'd never rise again" (ll. 45-47).

1.2. "Addressed to the eye"

> In the present mode of educating females, the useful is entirely neglected,
> for the more ornamental and superficial accomplishments.
> SUSANNA ROWSON. *Mentoria*

Piano practice, although frequently denounced as a less than nurturing activity, had supplanted earlier educational preferences for "what was merely useful" in an "almost exclusive" preference for "what is merely ornamental", as Hannah More put it in 1799 (*Strictures* 77). Since instrumental performance involved "an exhibition of the person" (Darwin, 1:12), it was classed as an "external" skill and as such became virtually synonymous with accomplishment in general, being visually more attractive than drawing yet seemingly more decorous

---

[45]   This is done by exclaiming: "Lord, Sir! I declare, there is no keeping with you!" The blame can also be shifted wordlessly: one player has learnt "from some lady players of her acquaintance, when she had put them all at *fault*, to frown, shake her head, and attempt to mark the time, [...] making her audience believe, that they misled her, instead of she them, in this musical *chase*" (Hanway, *Ellinor* 1:14:178).

than dancing[46]. Catherine Sinclair describes an unhappy society hostess whose "conversation, her music, her dress, and her smiles, were all put on, like her diamonds, for public display" (*Modern Accomplishments* 1:3). What is striking about the discursive negotiations of this shift is the lack of positive arguments for musical training. Its social necessity is taken for granted and it was assumed "unreasonable" to expect "that young ladies should deem the acquisition of knowledge a matter of primary importance"; although the mind "in its turns, [should] have a fair chance for improvement", accomplishments should be pursued "with a proper degree of ardour, and with the wish to arrive at excellence" (Broadhurst, viii-ix). Such advice implies that mental improvement was not even expected from music. It is no longer recommended for any supposed emotional or intellectual benefits, but merely advertised as harmless and "if properly directed, capable of being eminently beneficial" *ex negativo* i. e. because it prevents girls from reading too many of the novels "which are hourly sapping the foundations of every moral and religious principle" (Burgh, vii). Fordyce's popular *Sermons* typically recommend practising music, but "with more discrimination than the rest" (6:256).

> Accomplishments have taken virtue's place,
> And wisdom falls before exterior grace.
> WILLIAM COWPER. "The Progress or Error"

Critics who looked further staged a veritable campaign against the exaggerated weight of 'decorative' accomplishments, which disparaged the piano's role in particular. People as diverse as the spinster novelist Maria Edgeworth, the unconventional Mary Wollstonecraft, the pious educationalist Hannah More (who had vowed never to read Wollstonecraft's *A Vindication of the Rights of Women*) or James Fordyce (whose *Sermons* are a principal target of *Vindication*) all worried about music occupying "such a gulph of time, as really to leave little room for solid acquisition" (More, *Coelebs* 23:111). The historian Catherine Graham Macaulay, who insisted on seeing women "in a higher light than as the mere objects of sense" in her challenging *Letters on Female Education*, characteristically uses an anecdote about

---

[46] Jane West does not mention music under "Female Employments and Studies" in her *Letters to a Young Lady*, but her argument for pursuing needlework is worth recording: "I think the goddesses all excelled in the arts of female industry, except the hoyden Diana; and you know she *always* continued a *spinster*" (417)!

Alexander the Great to comment on a girl's brilliant musical performance: "the many hours which must have been daily devoted to the
frivolous task of modulating air into sound [... inspire] sentiments of
the same nature with which Alexander's dancing inspired Philip of
Macedon" (62-63). The word 'frivolous' indicates concern over the
triviality of music but also over the vanity which it stimulates. Thomas
Gisborne writes:

> Not that the pupil [...] is expressly instructed that to acquire and to *display* orna-
> mental attainments is the first business of life. Quite the contrary. [... She is
> taught] not by express precept, yet by daily and hourly admonitions, which could
> convey no other meaning, that dancing is *for display*, that music is *for display*,
> that drawing and French and Italian are *for display*; can it be a matter of aston-
> ishment, that during the rest of her life she should be incessantly *on the watch to
> shine* and to be admired? (75 and 78-79 [my emphases]).

Once again the no-longer-quite-so-hidden agenda of accomplishment
creates its double-bind, explicitly demanding musicality from the girls
which it traps, and implicitly insisting on the morally deleterious
privileging of visuality.

Many didactic courtship novels make the conundrum explicit, too.
Hanway's *Ellinor* criticizes the ridiculous diversity and superficiality
of a modish education which enables girls to read French novels, "de-
cypher" and write love letters and "totter a minuet, rattle the keys of a
piano-forte, twang the strings of a harp, scream an Italian song, daub a
work-basket, or make a fillagree tea-caddie", while remaining as ignorant "as a native of Kamtschatka" about English literature, laws, history and politics (2:15:306-307). In George Croly's *May Fair* this
sounds as follows:

> A half De Staël, half Eloise,
> To trample the piano's keys –
> To blot black beetles upon paper –
> To light the 'Muse's midnight taper';
> [...] To dream of 'Marquis Romanzini',
> (You'd buy the scoundrel for a guinea;)
> To heave the breast, and roll the eye,
> And lisp, "Di tanti palpiti!" (4:99-108, p. 154)

The last line very cleverly ridicules the typical combination of silli-
ness and ostentation enforced by such an education. While the speaker
rhymes 'Romanzini' and 'guinea' with Byronic cheek but near-cor-
rectly, the rhyme of 'eye' and 'palpiti' in the following couplet signals
the finishing-school belle's outrageous ignorance of Italian. What she

does understand is that visual effects ("To heave the breast, and roll the eye") are essential to the success of musical performance.

> The music, the ostensible cause of the assembly,
> is wearisome to the last possible degree to the spectators,
> for auditors they cannot be called.
> ANON. "Private Concerts"

> Though every body seems to admire,
> hardly any body listens.
> FANNY BURNEY. *Evelina*

Vicesimus Knox remarked that "music seems of late to be addressed to the eye as well as to the ear. Dexterity of execution, the wonderfully expeditious motion of the fingers, the hand and the arm, cause an equal share of applause with the tones of the instrument" (*Essays* 78). 'Equal share' may be an optimistic estimate of the importance of sound – only an unusually informed music-lover like Thomas Love Peacock would identify music first of all with *sound* when summing up female education as "sound, colour and form: music, dress, drawing, and dancing" (*Melincourt* 150). Although "not so happily adapted to grace" (Anon., *Mirror of Graces* 195) as the highly fashionable harp[47], "one of the most elegant objects to the eye" (Busby, 128), the piano continued to lend itself to visual display. Susanna Rowson's fashionable belle "Miss Tasty" fascinates with extensive movements: "Plac'd at the harpsichord, *see* [my emphasis] with what ease / Her snowy fingers run along the keys; / Now quite in alt, to th'highest notes she'll go; / Now running down the bass, she falls as low" ("Women as they are", 83-86, p. 110). William Henry's *Modern Ship of Fools* complains that "the body's decoration / Employs one half of this great nation" so that the fools who teach music see to it that "Miss" should know "lessons, airs, duets, in plenty, / And play the

---

[47] The harp is a frequent attribute of superficial and seductive characters such as the spoilt Lady Juliana in Susan Ferrier's *Marriage* or Mary Crawford in *Mansfield Park*, while Fanny Price, characteristically, has never heard a harp before coming to live with her rich relatives (cf. Austen, *Mansfield* 1:6:69). Other ladies take up the instrument merely because their target males maintain that "nothing added so much grace to beauty as playing upon the harp" (Burney, *Wanderer* 2:3:24:235) and then direct their whole mind to imitating a teacher's manner of holding the harp or "her way of curving, straightening, or elegantly spreading her fingers upon the strings; and in the general bend of her person" (2:3:24:229-230).

octave of Clementi" (21:11-14, p. 88) to exhibit their wrists flying in spectacular passages.

Frances Gore's Cecil is susceptible to visual attraction but not impressed by piano gymnastics. On being forced to listen to a sonata "of the high-pressure instrumental school" (*Cecil* 321), he dreams of murdering a fellow listener who is beating time in ecstasy and even of attacking the pianist herself, were it not for her "azure eyes and floating ringlets" (323). Robert Colvill's "Extempore at a Concert" celebrates a musician's visual appeal both in its verse and the Latin motto "Virtute et ingenio in forma, admodum venusta, Nihil amabilius": "O form divine! Which Venus self might wear! / That Elegance of mind her best Compeer! / That Syren Harmony inshrin'd! to grace the tuneful sphere" (ll. 7-9). "Elegance of mind" is just a token concession to educational concerns; the main point is that 'siren harmony' be "inshrin'd" in an attractive body. In Colvill's "To the Elegant Seraphina", the spectator's visual interest is tempered by the word "chastest", but the essential financial aspects are also introduced: "Thy silver flying fingers, deck'd with gold, / Roll back the tides of chastest Harmony" (37-38, p. 98). Even the educationalist Erasmus Darwin slips into voyeuristic considerations just as he warns girls of vanity: "[Music is] liable to be attended with vanity, and to extinguish the blush of youthful timidity; which is in young ladies the most powerful of their exterior charms" (1:12). In another classic double-bind, Darwin registers irony or scorn for girls who have lost the charm of innocence, while appraising them as a spectator. This is what Maria Edgeworth's heroine Helen distances herself from when a spiteful rival belittles the unselfish patience with which she has been playing dance music for hours. The lady disparages Helen's modesty both by a commercial metaphor and a visual allusion: "Our musician has been well paid by Lord Estridge's admiration of her white hands". In order to avoid further insults, Helen vindicates her own less meretricious nature by dancing the next evening with "a boy partner, whom nobody could envy her" (*Helen* 2:6:174).

1.3. Punishment by Plot

Its function as a demeaning vehicle for physical display was not the only problematic aspect of the piano: it also occupied time which middle-class girls should have used to better purpose. Edward Lyte describes a perfect country squire's wife, who is "accomplished, man-

nered, lady-like and fair" (31, p. 93), yet lacks the obnoxious manner-
isms of a city lady ("she read few novels, seldom screamed, or
fainted" (33, p. 93)). Music and manicure are the essential antonyms
of useful work:

> [She] thought her hands were made for something more
> Than nursing up in kid [gloves], or running o'er
> Piano keys. She could both mend and make,
> Wash and get up small linen, boil and bake. (35-38, p. 93)

Charles Dibdin's didactic poem *The Harmonic Preceptor* features
sisters of whom one studies things such as chemistry, geography and
drawing, while another 'fags' at music "without taste or an ear / And
over the *keys* of the harpsichord flirts, / With those fingers that ought
to mend stockings and shirts" (103-106, p. 10). The conclusion is that
girls should leave "to fine ladies the Italian shake [trill] / And learn –
their husbands' shirts to mend and make!" (Anon., *New Female Instructor* 7:55).

The picture was different in the case of upper-class girls, for whom
accomplishments are considered "absolutely necessary [to ...] filling
their respective characters with propriety" (Rowson, *Mentoria* 2:6:91).
Their occupations could afford to be useless; it did not matter whether
they "sang, played, drew, rode, read occasionally, spoiled much muslin, manufactured purses, handscreens, and reticules for a repository
[or] transcribed a considerable quantity of music, out of large fair print
into diminutive manuscript" (Lister, *Granby* 105). The snobbish or
mean hostesses on whom Juliet Ellis depends for a large part of *The
Wanderer* (see above 69) all want their daughters trained by this outstanding musician, but are simultaneously indignant about Juliet's
accomplishments: "And pray where might such a body as you learn
these things? – And what use can such a body want them for?"
(Burney, 1:1:8:75-76). Great skill is inappropriate for such a stranded
creature because musical skill signifies "a degree of leisure which
belongs exclusively to affluence" (More, *Strictures* 49).

However, the difference between being accomplished enough to
mark gentility and accomplished enough to seem a professional must
be observed. Juliet's proficiency discredits the romantic hypothesis
that she might be a princess in disguise and encourages people to treat
her as a servant who is always ordered to perform. Lord Byron,
groaning at "long evenings of duets and trios" (*Don Juan* 16:45:1, p.
633), complains that amateur playing becomes a "sort of half profession / When too oft displayed" (16:44:398-399, p. 633), and in Fanny

Burney's *Cecilia* a mother is asked: "Your ladyship surely would not have her degrade herself by studying like an artist or a professor?" (310). For the gentry, it was "almost a maxim [...] never to do anything 'like an artist'. Thus they seldom do any thing well" (Anon., "Private Concerts" 296)[48].

Girls from very modest families, on the other hand, should not even "be placed at a school where [ornamental] arts are taught" lest they be caught up in the musical mania which had infected "all but the humblest rank of persons" (Cockle, 241), and develop tastes incompatible with their "future allotment" (Wakefield, 58). A "butcher's wife will [not] serve her husband's customers, [n]or a moderate farmer's daughter manage the dairy or the poultry-yard with more adroitness, for knowing how to walk a minuet, or to play upon the harpsichord" (Wakefield, 62). "To cultivate tastes of which the enjoyment is precluded by circumstances may often become dangerous, by opening the avenues of temptation, or at least by inducing a dislike, if not a culpable neglect of necessary duties" (Wakefield, 58). The anonymous manual *The New Female Instructor* states the danger of musical class transgression unequivocally: "If people will step out of their sphere, and act in a character foreign to that for which they were designed [...] many [...] become the victims of their own [...] conduct" (7:55). Didactic fiction dramatizes such tales of victimization in standardized storylines which usual blame benighted parents for the ensuing ruin.

> Sometimes, 'tis the mother; whose dear only child,
> Out of love, is infallibly ruined and spoiled.
> CHARLES DIBDIN. *The Harmonic Preceptor*

In a cautionary tale by Susanna Rowson, the trouble starts with "an industrious tradesman's" affluence and mamma's decision "that Miss must be genteelly educated". Numerous useless and badly taught accomplishments, including "the very fashionable one of jingling the keys of the harpsichord, with great velocity, though perhaps out of time and out of tune", secure the spoilt girl a husband, but she makes a "wretched figure" as the mistress of her family (*Mentoria* 2:6:86). Her

---

[48]   Cf. the awful snob Lady Catherine de Bourgh in *Pride and Prejudice*: "There are few people in England, I suppose, who have more true enjoyment of music than myself, or a better natural taste. If I had ever learnt, I should have been a great proficient." (2:8:194)

husband starts drinking, ruin ensues, and in the end the accomplished young lady cannot even feed her children. Hannah More even brings death on carelessly brought-up girls. Farmer Bragwell's daughters have become "too polite to be of any use"; when their mother requests their assistance in making pastry for a grand dinner, they ask disdainfully

> "whether she had sent them to Boarding school to learn to cook; and added that they supposed she would expect them next to make puddings for the hay-makers." So saying they coolly marched off to their music. [...] They spent the morning in bed, the noon in dressing, the Evening at the Spinnet and the night in reading Novels. (*Farmers* 11)

The old-fashioned "Spinnet" is an additional signal that the sisters are acting out a lifestyle above their station. In Hector Macneil's verse narrative *Bygane Times*, the "vain vaunter" Wat Linkit holds "himsel up aboon his station, / Wi' brag, and shew, and affectation" (318-320, p. 21). Seconded by a thoughtless wife, he has his daughter Myzie sent to schools with "fashion'd fools; / Gat Maisters in, albeit she saw na / The use o' French or the Piana" (336-338, p. 22). Garish finery, evening parties and private balls finally leave "sweet Myzie" pining "wi' sorrow and vexation, / Mourning a blasted reputation" (381-382, p. 25). She dies, leaving her family without "a hame, or friendly shelter!" (310, p. 20).

Apart from class issues, piano-induced misery can also include the consequences of a deficient education which neglects moral and intellectual instruction through an unreasonable insistence on music and other accomplishments. The heroine of Mary Wollstonecraft's early novel *Mary* is a gentle, impressionable girl with no opinions of her own, "educated with the expectation of a large fortune" and no sense of duty. Her "years of youth [were] spent in acquiring a few superficial accomplishments, without having any taste for them", and so she "of course became a mere machine" (1:1-2) – a memorable phrase evocative of mechanical piano practice. Once Mary is married to the "vicious fool" (1:2) her parents have chosen, excessive novel reading and the perusal of sentimental pictures enhance the character weakness which leads to neglect of her own daughter and an untimely death. In Catherine Sinclair's *Modern Accomplishments*, the unhealthily music-crazy Lady Fitz-Patrick is punished by the callousness of a daughter who takes after her. Dragged everywhere to show off her proficiency on harp and piano, Elinor finally loses all appreciation for good music, condemning composers such as Handel and Corelli[49], who are unsuited to her own hyperactive style, "to oblivion as antediluvians" (9:176). When the mother falls sick (having hastened her own death by foolishly attending a concert), Eleanor refuses even to read aloud to her because she needs to practice the harp. Her mother complains that "every chord will go through my brain like a knife" but finds no pity: "Excuse me, mamma! It is really impossible! I have never practised my part on the harp for that duet [...] tomorrow" (12:263).

In Susanna Rowson's collection *Mentoria*, a mind "entirely uncultivated" at the expense of decorative accomplishments leads to an unsuitable marriage. "There had been no pains taken to instil into [Celia's] mind a true knowledge of what religion meant; she had not been taught to keep her passions under the controul of reason" (2:6:51). When Celia's mother dies rather early and her father decides to remarry in the interest of his daughter, the girl's emotional immaturity has disastrous results. She "called her father cruel, unjust and unfeeling, and vowed she would die sooner than call Miss Nelson mother" (2:6:53). Miss Nelson, though a paragon of virtue, is unable to conciliate Celia and dies of grief when the girl elopes with an unsuitable husband. The young couple are eventually reconciled to the father, but it is too late: "Neglected, nay despised, by her husband, [Celia] launched into every species of dissipation, and was in a few years reduced to a state of absolute penury [and remorse]" (2:6:61). To avoid even less suitable potential partners, Priscilla Wakefield recommends female music instructors because "the fascinating tones of music [are] as dangerous as the graces of dancing, in exciting the tender emotions" (51-52). Monsieur Gentil in Theodore Hook's farce *Music-Mad* in fact hates "de music, – de scrape, and de scratch" because his wife has run away with her music-master (9), and in *Coelebs in Search of a Wife*, a girl is blamed for "her own infatuation" that made her admit her Italian instructor "when her friends were excluded" (More, 23:113).

Against this background of horror stories, Elizabeth Inchbald's bestseller *A Simple Story* sets out to demonstrate what can "be hoped from [...] A PROPER EDUCATION". Lady Matilda's mother care-

---

[49] Disdain for the baroque composers of 'Ancient Music' usually signals the stupidity of chattering music enthusiasts who cannot appreciate such 'old-fashioned' music: "Handel, Corelli, and Pergolese, horrid!" (Edgeworth, *Patronage* 2:23:336).

fully instructs her in ornamental arts, but dies young after being cast off for adultery, and after finishing school, "all the endless pursuits of personal accomplishment" have left Matilda's mind "without one ornament" (1:1:5). Fortunately, an able tutor is able to redeem Matilda through more intellectual pursuits, and "the pernicious effects of an improper education" are relegated to the subplot concerning the destiny of "the unthinking Miss Milner" (4:12:337-338). In Thomas Holcroft's *Anna St. Ives,* the news of an elopement with "a man of uncommon learning, science, and genius, *but a musician*" (2:40:124, my emphasis) works as a deterrent which strengthens the heroine's resolution to marry a suitor of her (sensible) parents' choosing.

2. Courtship Narratives

> Female accomplishments have increased,
> are increasing and ought to be diminished.
> THOMAS LISTER. *Granby*

The manifold objections against music in general and pianomania in particular, which range from educational and social preoccupations to simple tedium, only serve to accentuate the paradoxical importance which accomplishments had as currency on the marriage market. A hectic and impersonal kind of music-making seemed indispensable for the clinching of any middle-class marital union. The obvious contradictions between music as a fraudulent, soulless screen and the true communication that is desirable in companionate marriage were not only discussed in conduct manuals and educational fiction but dominate a wider range of courtship plots as well as the description of any of their heroines. The practice is routinely ridiculed and satirized, but instead of liberating or questioning, such criticism often stabilizes the feminization of the piano, belittling both the rattling girls and the new instrument which had brought their musicianship so much prominence, and certainly cementing the notion that music-making, particularly at the piano, is less than perfectly appropriate for men. As in the two previous chapters, I will therefore outline the contemporary discourse on music for men as a background for the following discussion of musical courtship and its representations.

2.1. "The ladies at the harp, piano, the gent the violin"

> The declining prestige of music as a masculine pastime
> is more than matched by the rise of music
> as an accomplishment for women.
> HOWARD IRVING. "Music as a Pursuit for Men"

Instrumental and particularly keyboard performance continued to be considered as beneath the dignity of male amateurs, a harmlessly eccentric relaxation at best. Even the keen amateur violinist Dr. Berkenhout recommends careful balancing lest the "relief which was at first admitted as a handmaid to Study" should turn into "her mistress: nay, the baggage has sometimes been so insolent as to turn her mistress out of doors" (19:185). This metaphor marginalizes music-making not only as feminine but also as socially inferior, even illegitimate: the very delightfulness of music makes it "very improper for those who have no time to spare" (19:184). Only if scholarship and musicianship are each "kept in its proper place [...] the union is applauded and desired" (Jarrold, 12). To this end, rather than "excel [...] as a gentleman performer" (Berkenhout, 19:165), men should learn instruments such as the cello, the flute or the viola ('tenor'), which demanded "good judgment" instead of "great execution" (and hours of daily practice), and were, moreover, suitable for the intellectually more prestigious "ancient" (i. e. baroque) music (cf. Irving, 137)[50]. Dr. Berkenhout describes how a gentleman, passing the window of the room where he sat playing the harpsichord, exclaimed: "I hate to see a man at the harpsichord!" and comments: "I had never before annexed the idea of effeminacy to that instrument, but from that moment, I began to be of that gentleman's opinion" (19:189). Lord Byron reports from a party where

> a man with a flute played a solemn & somewhat tedious piece of Music – well – I got through that – but down sate Lady Anne to give evidence at the Pianoforte with a Miss Somebody (the "privy purse") in a pair of spectacles – dark green – and these & the flutemen – & the "damnable faces" (as Hamlet says) of the whole party threw me into a convulsion of uncourtly laughter. (*Letters* 4:104, 25/04/ 1814)

---

[50] The passionate flute-playing of Anne Lister (1791-1840), a lesbian Yorkshire-woman who appropriated the masculine persona of an upper-class landowner to the point of being called 'Gentleman Jack' by her Halifax acquaintances, may be considered complementary evidence (cf. Lister, *Heart*).

It seems that the acceptable flute offered pitfalls of its own to male dignity.

In fiction, hardly any men practise music outside sentimental courtship scenes (described below), and if they do, it is counted against them. The hero of Lord Bulwer-Lytton's *Pelham*, who relies on "a piano-forte in my room, and a private billiard-room" (2:6-7) as his only resources from the beer-swilling vulgarity of Cambridge student life, was described by Tennyson as a "rouged and padded fop" and *Fraser's Magazine* called him a "silver fork polisher" in February 1931 (quoted in Sadleir, 35). In Maria Edgeworth's *Belinda*, Lady Delacour's praise of her husband's flute playing significantly focuses on connoisseurship (knowledge rather than skill): " [H]e has really a very pretty taste for music, and knows fifty times more of the matter than half the dilettanti who squeeze the human face divine into all manner of ridiculous shapes by way of persuading you they are in ecstasy!" (2:20:294-295). In Catherine Sinclair's *Modern Accomplishments*, the rich arts enthusiast Sir Philip Barnard is "killing time in the mornings at the gallery, and murdering his music master at home" (10:191), and a young aristocrat's education which includes some feminine skills is described as "more brilliant than solid" in Mary Hanway's *Ellinor*: "[H]e did not think it necessary to be a profound scholar, he rode, fenced, and danced *à la merveille*, spoke French and Italian fluently, could draw prettily, accompany a song with his violin decently, and get through his part in a quartet party with tolerable precision" (3:12:205). However attractive, this young man does not get the heroine, and neither does the eminently unsuitable Henry Neville, who woos the semi-orphan Maria in Jane West's *The Advantages of Education*. One of his songs informs "Queen Nature" that Love has led him back to her, and the "masterly manner" in which he accompanies himself at the harpsichord is rewarded with a silent smile. Cue narratorial warning: "Attentions of this delicate kind were, to a young woman of Maria's sentimental way of thinking, infinitely more dangerous than the most passionate address" (1:17:165-166). Indeed she should be performing for him.

> She would be a match for any man,
> who has any taste for music!
> MARIA EDGEWORTH. *Practical Education*

Men should not go far beyond a 'pretty taste' for music: it is women's musicality that remains central to marriage transactions. A large repertoire of piano duets or piano pieces with easy accompaniments for flute or violin gave men the opportunity to perform in a manner consistent with gender norms (cf. Irving, 137). It is certain that in the "tête-à-tête at the piano with Miss Celandina [Paperstamp]" (Peacock, *Melincourt* 309), which confirms that Mr. Derrydown has given up on Anthelia, the bookish heroine (who hates music), and proposed to a more conventional and financially more appealing girl, would have seen him playing the less showy secondo part. This is also true when musical campaigning is ultimately unsuccessful. Glorvina O'Dowd in *Vanity Fair*, "[u]ndismayed by forty or fifty previous defeats, [...] laid siege to Major Dobbin". She sings "at him unceasingly" and insists on duets when she finds out that "our honest and dear old friend used to perform on the flute in private". However, the Major is unmoved: "Bah! [...] she is only keeping her hand in – she practises upon me as she does upon Mrs. Tozer's piano, because it's the most handy instrument in the station" (43:419-420).

Women take the musical even in plots which represent music-making as a sentimentally shared activity; Frank Churchill's providing "a second, slightly but correctly taken" to the proficient Jane Fairfax in *Emma* (Austen, 2:8:245) is the perfect example. In Ann Radcliffe's *Sicilian Romance*, Julia's incipient love for Count Hippolitus de Vereza makes her so restless that her "lute and favourite airs lost half their power to please" (1:1:48), but later that day, her piano performance at an aristocratic private concert is a great success[51]. When Vereza is asked to accompany her in a duet, Julia's "pride of conscious excellence" lends a simple air "those charms of expression so peculiarly her own". After resting exquisitely on a sustained note, her voice proceeds "with such impassioned tenderness that every eye wept to the sounds" and the "breath of [Vereza's] flute trembled" (1:1:50). Silently, his eyes communicate his love to Julia in a rare instance of non-verbal musical communication which prefigures marital harmony.

Robert Bloomfield's verse narrative "May-Day with the Muses" enacts the same scenario as a rural idyll. Young Jennet, "all that Heaven could send" (914, p. 178) to her ageing father, finds her husband in Alfred, the noble-minded and musical son of the neighbouring squire. Alfred is a proficient pianist despite his blindness, but Jennet

---

[51]   As in *Julia de Roubigné*, the lute functions as a code for romantic solitude while the pianoforte is the locus of social encounters, even if Radcliffe's *Sicilian Romance* is set "towards the close of the sixteenth century" (1:1:5).

keeps her skill in singing a secret as their acquaintance progresses. Finally Alfred's playing inspires her to sing with "such a voluble and magic sound" (1027, p. 185) that it brings tears to her own eyes while he continues to play though trembling "to his fingers' ends" (1031, p. 185), and proposes fifteen lines later: "Up sprung the youth, 'O Jennet, where's your hand?'" (1046, p. 186) Again, the empathy expressed by shared music-making promises well for a shared future, reinforced by the fact that the husband's disability excludes superficial visual attraction.

Page-turning is an even more subordinate form of pre-marital musical co-operation, granting the enjoyable proximity of chamber music-making to gentlemen of minimal musical literacy. In Peacock's *Crotchet Castle*, two young ladies are at music at harp and piano, with men turning pages. One of them does it "with so much more attention to the lady than the book, that he often made sad work with the harmony, by turning over two leaves together" (7:695), but in the end, both duets turn into matrimony. In Peacock's *roman à clef, Nightmare Abbey*, Scythrop (modelled on the poet Shelley) becomes nail-bitingly jealous of Marionetta (modelled on his first wife, Harriet Westbrook) when he observes her at the harp, where the Honourable Mr. Listless [!] is engaged in the "delightful labour" of page-turning. This musical promiscuity is symbolic of Marionetta's oscillation between affection and chilling indifference; she also torments Scythrop musically "by striking up some Rondo Allegro, and saying, 'Is it not pretty?'" in the middle of a pathetic speech of his "till he would start away from her, and enclose himself in his tower, in an agony of agitation" (5:373).

In Thomas Lister's *Granby*, page-turning sustains a little intrigue masterminded by a clever man who does, of course, not perform himself. The cynical society lion Trebeck charms Caroline with his conversation, but makes her uneasy by his tacit enforcement of complicity in a practical joke against a less astute suitor. He casts the infatuated Lord Chesterton as Caroline's assistant when she is preparing to play a piece from memory – though with an open music book lying on the piano. Pretending to leave the office of page-turning to Chesterton with regretful courtesy, Trebeck leans on the piano, "fixing his eyes upon [Caroline] with a look of peculiar meaning". Caroline is embarrassed and lowers her eyes, whereupon "Lord Chesterton thinking that she had got to the bottom of the page, took the hint, and turned over the leaf". Caroline looks up to undeceive him, but meeting "the quick, penetrative glance of Trebeck", she looks down again and is rewarded with another unnecessary page-turn. This is repeated until his Lordship departs "in the persuasion that he had gracefully rendered an acceptable service". When another guest enlightens Chesterton, Trebeck covers Caroline's embarrassment by trapping him into a worse admission: "All my fault, I assure you [...] – Chesterton, you saw through it all, I'm sure, and only shammed ignorance, to humbug me in my turn." Lord Chesterton is weak enough to claim that he "did entertain a considerable suspicion [...] of the little stratagem which was intended to be practised" (179-181). Caroline is annoyed with Trebeck and herself, and being a perfect heroine, she marries neither the foolish lord who cannot page-turn nor the musically too knowledgeable man of the world.

2.2. "Mere musical dolls set out for sale"

> In the education of females
> an advantageous settlement in marriage is the universal prize,
> for which parents of all classes enter their daughters.
> PRISCILLA WAKEFIELD. *Reflections on the Present Condition of the Female Sex*

As a rule, Regency fiction is extremely unsentimental about the economics of match-making. It is the period that coined the expressive term '40,000 pounder' for a girl with this amount of fortune (Bage, 8:26) and described the marriage-market as "overstocked with accomplished young ladies" (Edgeworth, *Helen* 2:3:150) who are turned into "mere musical dolls, to be set out for sale in the great toy-shop of society" (Peacock, *Nightmare Abbey* 1:358) "to be disposed of to the highest *bidder*" (Hanway, *Ellinor* 4:1:13). Money and accomplishments are partly interchangeable:

> When I have enumerated her accomplishments, who would believe, that a diminution of a single cypher in her fortune – a simple taking away of 0 from 5000 l. – should change the hearts of men [... The girl is beautiful, well-read and able to] perform several songs upon the piano forte, very much to the envy of her less accomplished companions. [... and yet] must money be added to all this? Heavens! what things are men (Bage, 1:5).

But a girl tutored in piano, harp and singing "[t]o give her beauty consequence" (Combe, 105) could still hope to capture a wealthy suitor, "Who, without asking for a Dower, / Would lead her to the Nuptial Bower" (ll. 114-119).

This function of music is underlined by the fact that the multitude of subjects, skills and employments taught by "dancing-masters, mu-

sic-masters and all the tribe" (Edgeworth, *Helen* 2:3:157) were reduced to the most immediately erotically attractive ones at a girl's
coming out. Busy, hyper-fashionable Miss Rattle learns French, Italian and German, paints flowers, shells and views of "ruins and build-
ings" which her tutor, "a good soul", usually finishes for her. "I learn
varnishing, and gilding, and japanning [...] modelling, and etching,
and engraving in mezzotinto and aquatinta, for Lady Di Dash learns
etching, and mamma says, as I shall have a better fortune than Lady
Di, she vows I shall learn every thing she does." Masters for piano,
harp, singing and dancing ("I can stand longer on one leg already than
Lady Di") leave only "odd minutes" for history, geography, astron-
omy, grammar, botany, chemistry, and experimental philosophy
(More, *Coelebs* 23:108). And yet: "I shan't have a great while to work
so hard, for as soon as I come out, I shall give it all up, except music
and dancing" (23:107). Both the pious Hannah More and the revolutionary Mary Wollstoncraft denounce music for its part in a "Mahometan" educational agenda which "consists entirely in making woman
an object of attraction" (More, *Coelebs* 14:67). Wollstonecraft, who in
her *Vindication of the Rights of Women* denounces Milton for depriv-
ing "us [women] of souls" and his Eve for insinuating "that we were
beings only designed by sweet attractive grace, and docile blind obedience, to gratify the senses of man when he can no longer soar on the
wing of contemplation" (2:33), comments: "Surely these weak beings
are only fit for a seraglio!" ("Introduction" 9)

> We have heard Miss That or This, or Lady T'other,
> Show off – to please their company or mother.
> LORD BYRON. *Don Juan*

In Regency courtship novels, it is mostly dominant mothers or aunts
who shoulder the task of preparing their daughters 'for sale'. Some
careless or evil ladies use practising as a routine excuse to get rid of
their daughters – Jane Austen's evil Lady Susan, in order to meet a
lover, forces her fifteen-year-old daughter into a small room with a
piano for most of the day for "practising as it is called". The narrator,
who only rarely "hear[s] any noise", wonders: "what she does with
herself there I do not know. [...] Is it not inexcusable to give such an
example to a daughter?" (Austen, *Lady Susan* 17:45-46[52]) –; but most
fictional mothers are in deadly earnest about rearing accomplished

---

[52]   Cf. also Edgeworth, *Belinda* 2:14:76.

daughters. These efforts meet with distinct narratorial disapproval, but as long as class boundaries are respected, 'punishment by plot' is limited to failure for marital schemes (see above 75).

Maria Edgeworth's *Patronage* contains a wonderful portrait of a scheming mother. Mrs. Falconer makes sure that there is no party without her daughters: "Miss Falconers must sing – Miss Falconers must play – [...] No piano, no harp could draw such crowds as the Miss Falconers" (1:9:98). Preparing for a party and discussing absent friends "in various tones of ecstasy and of execration", Miss Georgiana Falconer coyly admits to fear of the Misses La Grande, in whose presence she absolutely refuses to play:

> I can never bring out my voice before those girls – If I have any voice at all, it is in the lower part, and Miss La Grande always chooses the lower part – Besides, Ma'am, you know she regularly takes 'O Giove Omnipotente' from me – But I should not mind that even, if she would not attempt poor 'Quanto Oh quanto è amor possente'[53] – There's no standing that! Now, really, to hear that so spoiled by Miss La Grande. (2:23:337)

Silent reserve greets the Misses La Grande's final arrival "after the first forced compliments", and now Mrs. Falconer, "superior in ease inimitable" among agonizedly rivalling mothers, makes everybody sing and play until "the admiration and complaisance of the auditors" are exhausted. Georgiana's younger sister having refreshed the audience with "some slight things [...] such as could excite no sensation or envy" (2:23:338-340), Georgiana herself finally gets to perform her favourite warhorse in the presence of the target Count:

> "[I] could not ask Miss Crotch to play any more, till she had rested [and so] Georgiana! for want of something better, do try what you can give us – she will appear to great disadvantage of course – My dear, I think we have not had O Giove Omnipotente." "I am not equal to that, Ma'am," said Georgiana, drawing back, "you should call upon Miss La Grande." "True, my love, but Miss La Grande has been so very obliging, I could not ask. [...] Try it, my love – I am not surprised you should be diffident after what we have heard [...] but the Count, I am sure, will make allowances". (2:23:342)

However, the Count's predictable enchantment is to no ultimate avail: "Though every where seen, and every where admired, no proposals had yet been made adequate to [Mrs. Falconer's] expectations" (2:23:247).

---

[53] "Giove Omnipotente" (correctly 'Onnipotente') is a popular, frequently-arranged cavatina from Peter von Winter's long-forgotten *Ratto di Proserpina* (1804); "Quanto Oh quanto" a once famous trio by the same composer.

The Miss Falconers are at least allowed to achieve another girl's conventional (though not emotionally promising) marriage by roping in an unattractive aristocratic suitor for lovelorn Miss Hauton. She is profoundly depressed after her beau has been shipped off to the West Indies, but it takes just a fortnight of "flattering, pitying, and humouring"

> to recover the young Lady from this fit of despondency, and produced her again at musical parties. She was passionately fond of music; the Miss Falconers played on the forte piano and sung, their brother John accompanied exquisitely on the flute, and the Marquis of Twickenham, who was dull as "the fat weed that grows on Lethe's brink," stood by, – admiring. (1:9:87-88)

The result is, inevitably, that Miss Hauton lets herself "be led, in fashionable style, to the hymeneal altar by the Marquis of Twickenham" (1:9:92), an implicit debunking of accomplishment the erotic attraction of which is shown to be largely a conditioned reflex: Miss Hauton's own playing is never described and only a stupid man could be caught by a merely imagined shared fondness for somebody else's music. Music is made to succeed 'technically', but still fails emotionally.

The quiet glee of Maria Edgeworth's narrator is typical of the period, and it is one of the distinctions of William Thackeray's *Vanity Fair* as a historical novel that it (written in 1848) represents this 1810s' attitude so precisely. Becky Sharp's musical campaigning for Joseph Sedley is suitably unsuccessful, while the despicable marriage of George Osborne and Amelia Sedley originates in a sentimental piano scene. George, smitten, asks to "have some music, Miss Sedley – Amelia" and as they go "off to the piano, which was situated, as pianos usually are, in the back drawing-room [...] Miss Amelia, in the most unaffected way in the world, put her hand into Mr. Osborne's" (4:28-29). Afterwards Amelia feels obliged to ask Rebecca to sing, who "exerted herself to the utmost, and, indeed, to the wonder of Amelia, who had never known her perform so well". Joseph Sedley, "fond of music, and soft-hearted", is "in a state of ravishment during the performance of the song, and profoundly touched at its conclusion" (4:31-32) – but does not have the courage to propose.

2.3. "The net of courtship and the cage of matrimony"

> Music is universally admired even by those
> who have the misfortune to have no taste for it.
> MARIA EDGEWORTH. *Practical Education*

Courtship novels with their specific focus on the emotional pitfalls and opportunities of choosing partners are particularly sensitive to the absurdity of training girls to an art that functioned so briefly and deceptively at the crucial moment of choice. A vulgar matchmaking aunt in Edgeworth's *Belinda* complains about her ungrateful niece:

> There's your cousin Joddrell refused me a hundred guineas last week, though the piano forte and harp I bought for her before she was married stood me in double that sum, and are now useless lumber on my hands; and she never could have Joddrell without them, as she knows as well as I do. (2:16:126-27)

Music was necessary to *get* Mr. Joddrell, but not to keep him; very probably he does not like music. The zealous governess Miss Marabout in *Modern Accomplishments*, who oversees Eleanor Fitz-Patrick's disastrous accomplishment gathering, obviously distorts the facts when she complains that her best pupil gave up music after marrying. "It was a sad mortification to me, and must disappoint her husband extremely, as he is distracted about music; but we might have expected it, as really no young ladies ever keep up accomplishments after they marry". (Sinclair, 7:149)

The accomplishment trap worked the better because their lack of musical training made men more likely to fall for the "decorated screen" of accomplishments, "behind which all defects in domestic knowledge, in taste, judgment, and literature, and the talents which make an elegant companion, are creditably concealed" (More, *Coelebs* 23:111). A worldly-wise young Lady in Fanny Burney's novel *Cecilia* knows that

> not a creature thinks of our principles, till they find them out by our conduct: and nobody can possibly do that till we are married, for they give us no power beforehand. The men know nothing of us in the world while we are single, but how we can dance a minuet, or play a lesson upon the harpsichord. (310)

No wonder people spoke of a "matrimonial lottery" (Edgeworth, *Practical Education* 3:20:6). A husband in Thomas Love Peacock's *Nightmare Abbey* comments: "It is only after marriage that they shew their true qualities, as I know by bitter experience" (1:358).

A converse real-life example of seeing through the screen is furnished by John Keats's first description of his fiancée Fanny Brawne.

He ironically ticks off items from an imaginary list of standard requirements:

> She is about my height – with a fine style of countenance of the lengthen'd sort –
> […] her Arms are good her hands badish – her feet tolerable – she is not seven-
> teen – but she is ignorant – monstrous in her behaviour flying out in all direction,
> calling people such names that I was forced lately to make use of the term Minx –
> this is I think not from any innate vice but from a penchant she has for acting
> stylishly. I am however tired of such style and shall decline any more of it – […].

Particularly tiring, it seems, was Fanny's rattling: "she plays the Music [i. e. the piano] without one sensation but the feel of the ivory at her fingers – she is a downright Miss without one set off". It took the conventional praise of a bystander to shake Keats out of the routine of deprecating the girl for her accomplishments: "Miss B – thinks her a paragon of fashion, and says she is the only woman she would change persons with – What a Stupe She is superior as a Rose to a Dandelion –" (*Letters* 2:13-14).

> How wretched, how deplorable his fate,
> Who gets this fluttering insect for a mate.
> SUSANNA ROWSON. "Women as They Are"

If John Keats refused to prize Fanny Brawne by her fashionable musical skills, others went as far as to regard them as an obstacle. John Moore's caustic Mordaunt would willingly relinquish half the fortune of any accomplished lady he might marry, "on condition that she would renounce her painting, and never attempt to speak French, nor to play on the piano-forté, in my hearing" (*Mordaunt* 1:21:101-102). This comment reflects the additional objections to noisy and excessive musical practice which arose with the emerging ideal of companionate marriage. An article on "Music as a Pursuit for Men" advocates shared music since the nation's pleasures have become "more domestic and more dependent upon the choice of such employments as are alike interesting to both sexes" ("Vetus", 8); but fiction more realistically sees music as an impediment to such exchanges. The hero of Thomas Lister's *Granby* comments:

> [L]adies spoil their natural gifts by loading them with artificial ones. Those who
> have many accomplishments, are seldom so pleasant as those who have few. […]
> I wish the thousand shining qualities, which of course no lady can ever be with-
> out, to appear at her tongue's end, and not at her finger's. (122-123)

True companionship requires a wife educated enough to "comfort and counsel" a "man of sense": "it is a companion he wants, and not an artist […] not merely a creature who can paint, and play, and dress, and dance" (More, *Strictures* 72). Hannah More's inverted courtship novel *Coelebs in Search of a Wife* warns extensively of educational patterns which threaten domestic happiness instead of helping to "form a friend, a companion, and a wife" (23:113). The scenario which Susanna Rowson paints of women "as they would be" if they were treated as reasonable beings, not as fools "whose only joys / Are plac'd in trifling, idleness and noise", is obviously Utopian. If women were allowed to, "whilst inspiring love, [...] keep respect" then men would "meet the sweet reward of all your care; / Find in us friends, your purest joys to share" ("Women as They Are" 190-192, p. 115).

Literary representations of married couples share Rowson's implicit pessimism; they hardly ever allow music to support rational companionship. The most optimistic description occurs, characteristically, in a *poem*, George Dyer's "Two Amiable Young Women Playing Successively on the Harpsichord", in which two girls are not erotic rivals, but distinguished for the "[s]implicity of virgin hue, / Freedom, and truth, and honour true" (ll. 20-21) of their playing. Dyer contrasts this favourably with more sensuous "Arabian delights" (see above 86), and the conclusion projects this scenario forward onto married life: "When each sweet girl becomes the tender wife, / Who such musicians hear, who such may love thro' life!" (ll. 28-29)[54]. In novels, which would have offered the space to elaborate such scenarios, music is usually represented as unnecessary or even detrimental to wedded happiness. Even if Maria Edgeworth achieves reconciliation between the oafish Lord Delacour and his witty estranged wife by making Lord Delacour perform ("much to his own satisfaction"), it is Lady Delacour's young friend Belinda who plays *with* him.

> He played on the flute, he told the story of Studley's original Titian [...]. The perception that his talents were called out, and that he appeared to unusual advantage, made him excellent company: he found that the spirits can be raised by self-complacency even more agreeably than by burgundy. (*Belinda* 2:20:296)

Jane Austen's Sir Thomas Bertram similarly has to rely on his daughters for the music which an indolent wife cannot be expected to pro-

---

[54] In "The Charm of Music", Dyer depicts an even quieter scene in which two ladies play by turns "to sooth their friend in pain, the author going to pay a last visit to an esteemed friend before her death". Far from provoking erotic intensity, their music is disinfected by the painful context, the rivalry to please being played out at the sickbed, "When at still of eve you sooth your friend, / Striking by turns the keys" (25-26).

duce and which merely serves to "conceal the want of real harmony" (*Mansfield Park* 2:2:224) in the company.

Lord Belfield in *Coelebs* is at pains to stress that his wife is musically educated and that he appreciates it as he should ("I am fond of [music] myself, and Lady Belfield plays admirably"). But he adds immediately that she, with "her duty [to] so many children", has very little time to play, nor he to listen.

> But there is no day, no hour, no meal in which I do not enjoy in her the ever ready pleasure of an elegant and interesting companion. [...] In a mere artist [could I] reasonably look for these resources? A woman, whose whole education has been rehearsal, will always be dull, except she lives on the stage, constantly displaying what she has been sedulously acquiring [while ...] well chosen books, do not lead to exhibition [but afford a] gratification [which] is cheap, is safe, is always to be had at home. (More, 23:111-112)

The consistent theatrical metaphor in this passage underlines once again the danger of display, of visual exhibition, which is paradoxically the greatest danger of music.

3. Counter-Narratives

> A musical girl should diffuse harmony and enjoyment
> of the most intellectual kind to her own beloved family.
> WILLIAM PINNOCK.
> *The Young Lady's Library of Useful & Entertaining Knowledge*

Erasmus Darwin suspected that "great eminence in almost anything is sometimes injurious to a young lady" (10) because "a great apparent attention to trivial accomplishments is liable to give a suspicion, that more valuable acquisitions have been neglected" (1:12). In fiction, several kinds of what I would like to call counter-narratives give converse evidence of what was apprehended from the exhibitionist 'rattling' enforced by the marriage market. Fashionable music is contrasted with desirable simplicity, as are the love songs for which simple accompaniments are written and exchanged. On the other hand, music in platonic relationships and the intimacy of the family circle counterpoint the courtship scenario, most obviously so when daughters play to their fathers, since fathers must be left behind when daughters marry.

3.1. Simplicity

The first alternative trope to be discussed is the taste for musical simplicity, for that "Chaste, correct, and emphatic Performance" which was being crowded out by mechanical "all but impossibilities". A "craving after pungent means of excitement" characterizes "'the Multitude' with whom Celerity, Noise, Shakes in abundance, and manual efforts of various kinds, pass as proofs of excellence" (Anon., "Desultory Remarks" 181) and who is "incapable of being satisfied with that quiet enjoyment which so fully gratified our predecessors" (Anon., "A Sketch" 244). Such quiet enjoyment of "the most rational and delicate pleasure" of music is advertised with pious thankfulness in Mary Wollstonecraft Shelley's *Thoughts on the Education of Daughters*. This early text is less sweepingly critical of music than *A Vindication* and foregrounds performance quality and depth of musical knowledge as viable alternatives: " [I]f a young person has a taste for [the arts ...] do not suffer it to lay dormant. Heaven kindly bestowed it, and a great blessing it is; but, like all other blessings, may be perverted: yet the intrinsic value is no lessened by the perversion" (42). Wollstonecraft professes to prefer "expression to execution" and notes that "the sublime harmony of some of Handel's compositions"[55] requires "sense, taste, and sensibility, to render their music interesting. The nimble dance of the fingers may raise wonder, but not delight" (43-44). Simple music clearly symbolizes emotional and moral health; in her *Wrongs of Woman*, Wollstonecraft describes a highly fraught situation in which the heroine plays "a favourite air to restore myself, as it were, to nature, and drive the sophisticated sentiments I had just been obliged to listen to, out of my soul" (2:7:73).

The mistrust of sophistication and what it implies is also evident from those sincere characters who do not only incline to simple performances but are downright *unable* to play more difficult music. Fashionable dexterity is irreconcilable with the true, modest musicality which does not only encode rural (Scottish) backwardness for Walter Scott and others, but also naturalness, intelligence and moral strength. Consider Miss Rose in *Waverley*, who can just accompany her own singing:

---

[55] Probably not one of Handel's virtuoso harpsichord suites or set of variations, but an aria in a keyboard transcription.

> To make amends, she sung with great taste and feeling, and with a respect to the sense of what she uttered that might be proposed in example to ladies of much superior musical talent. [...] [Her] sensibility to poetry [...] gave more pleasure to all the unlearned in music, and even to many of the learned, than could have been communicated by a much finer voice and more brilliant execution, unguided by the same delicacy of feeling. (1:13:59)

Similarly, Lucy Bertram in Scott's *Guy Mannering,* who "sings her native melodies very sweetly", is liked "more than for the accomplishments she wants, than for the knowledge she possesses" (1:29:157). Allan Cunningham's "Fashionable Sin" compares sweet Scottish Nancie favourably to a society belle in all details of attire, skin, language and music: "My Lady plays on her spinnet, / But, Nancie's like a mavis lilting; / My Lord adores her folding song, / When from the grass her coats she's kilting." (ll. 29-32)

In Mary Hay's *Victim of Prejudice,* a country curate's wife plays "with more feeling than skill", and has a voice that is "sweet, but without compass". This is not irony but real praise for a family full of taste, modesty and affection, who is able to enjoy a repertoire of "simple canzonets, impassioned airs, or plaintive ballads" (1:9:111). Conversely, Thomas Love Peacock describes a governess as "[p]erfectly cold-hearted, and perfectly obsequious [...], a very scientific musician, without any soul in her performance". The lady is employed by the soulless and aptly named Dross family, characterized by "arrogance, ignorance, and the pride of money" (*Melincourt* 175). Maria Edgeworth quotes the "celebrated Madame Roland", who hoped that her daughter would not become "a performer [but would] above all other things, love the duties of my sex". To that purpose, the ability "to accompany her voice agreeably on the harp" and to "play agreeably on the piano-forte" (*Practical Education* 3:20:14) are sufficient – a desideratum which echoes Elizabethan warnings against the virtuosity of "harde and often diuisions" (see above 19).

Musical virtue and vice are often juxtaposed in parallel characters. The 'silver spoon' novelist Frances Gore, who was very knowledgeable about music, contrasts the silly and modish (if warm-hearted) Marion Armytage with her more serious sister-in-law in a series of highly topical contrasts and allusions to contemporary musical life. Sophy, who sings "a little" and calls herself "no great performer", has nevertheless had lessons from Giuditta Pasta[56], whereas the gushing Marion ("I doat upon music!") is more up-to-date: "Oh! Pasta's style is quite gone by, now. [...] Grisi[57] is twice as popular" (*Armytage* 1:16:236). Sophy favours pianos by the classical English maker Broadwood, who in 1818 had furnished Beethoven with a complimentary and much-appreciated instrument, while Marian enthuses about fashionable gadgets: "Oh! Don't expect me to like [a Broadwood]. I can't bear any instrument but Herz's or Petzold's! – Petzold's last, with the organ stop and flageolet, and drums for military symphonies[58], are the most perfect in the world" (1:15:100-101). Marion's playing has "a proficiency which must have cost [her] so much time and diligence to acquire" and which her husband feels bound to commend – but he dearly wishes "that her performance had not so much resembled the gabbling of a parrot". The narrator endorses this critique of artificiality by calling her "by art – strictly by art – a brilliant musician" (1:7:44).

Marian Armytage's "honest and endearing" character is ultimately vindicated, but her musical tastes represent a serious lack of emotional refinement. Ann Radcliffe's *Mysteries of Udolpho* describes a similar contrast between the unassuming protagonist Emily and "a scientific performer", the Countess Lacleur, who also organizes concerts at her house. The Countess has "passed the spring of youth, but her wit has prolonged the triumph of its reign" – a wit which the pious narratorial voice is at pains to qualify as "brilliant, rather than just". In fact, every admirable or interesting trait of the Countess's personality is balanced by a flaw, not the least of which seems to be her virtuosity. Valancourt, the hero, is impressed, but always remembers "with a sigh the eloquent simplicity of [his] Emily's songs and the natural expression of

---

[56]   Guiditta Pasta (1797-1865), an Italian soprano, who gave her London operatic début in 1818, was legendary for her accomplished and natural acting and individual timbre.

[57]   The Italian soprano Giulia Grisi (1811-1869), who made her London début in 1834, was an impressive singing actress, though without Pasta's genius.

[58]   Such military pieces often imitated Ottoman regiments. The craze for all things Turkish inspired gadgetty piano stops with tambourine and jingle effects for pieces like Mozart's Rondo "Alla Turca". Marion also mentions a "new man's" "Dance of Death" symphony "with accompaniments of pick-axes and spades. Never was any thing so amusing!" (Gore, *Armytage* 1:16:237)

her manner, which waited not to be approved by the judgment, but found their way at once to the heart" (2:8:294).

The fact that simple music is not subject to critical "judgment" also has the advantage of achieving "all the great purposes of music, those of moving the passions in the cause of virtue, and of exciting sentiments of manly pleasure" with reduced practice requirements, whereas "the stupendous excellence of rapid execution, requires the unremitted labor of a life" to satisfy listeners whose "natural feelings [are] superseded by acquired taste" (Knox, *Essays* 82). The John Mordaunt who intends to forbid hectic music-making to a potential wife (see above 90), is glad to have a lady love with modest musical pretensions because he is convinced that a girl who "attempts nothing more than simple airs on the harp or piano-forte, which she accompanies with her own delightful voice", "has spent her time to better purpose" (Moore, *Mordaunt* 3:109:467). The somewhat self-righteous heroine of Thomas Holcroft's epistolary novel *Anna St. Ives* claims: "I should laugh at all the world were it to tell me it is more difficult to prevent the beginning, growth, and excess of any passion, than it is to learn to play excellently on the piano forte" (2:30:98-99). Her simultaneous dismissal of passion and hard-won musical proficiency betrays both a certain emotional immaturity and a laudable anxiety not to be thought of as a soulless rattler.

3.2. Sentiment

> A love complaint –
> scribbled by him, and set and sung by her!
> THOMAS HOLCROFT. *Anna St. Ives*

Anna St. Ives's dismissal of passion is soon put to an ironical test which embodies another recurrent counter-motif to accomplished rattling: the susceptibility to songs which are copied, practiced or even commissioned as love tokens. This well-established topos occurs twice in Charlotte Turner Smith's *Emmeline*. Fredrick Delamere, coming upon the manuscript of a song "which he had a few days before desired her to learn", tries to read Emmeline's partiality from her handwriting: the song "seemed to have been just copied [...], and he fancied the notes and the writing were executed with more than her usual elegance" (1:16:114-115). He even finds his portrait under the music, but later, Emmeline breaks the engagement off, later marrying a less highly-strung man who has his melancholy at her absence "soothed yet encreased" by asking his sister to sing "the verses he made; and he would sit hours by her *piano forté* to hear repeated one of the many sonnets he had written on her who occupied all his thoughts" (3:11:328). This is the situation which tests Anna St. Ives's immaturity. Her indulgence of adapting a melody to an intensely admiring poem which has been left on her music desk and repeatedly singing it to her own accompaniment is analyzed from the point of view of no less than three characters in this multiple-perspective epistolary novel.

Anna is restless because filial obedience urges her to accept the rakish Coke Clifton, while she cannot forget the deserving Frank Henley who wrote the poem she set to music. When Frank overhears Anna singing his song, "[h]is whole soul seemed absorbed [...]. Satisfaction, pleasure, I know not whether rapture would be too strong a word for the expressions which were discoverable in his countenance." Scrupulous Anna herself fears to have thoughtlessly fostered "a belief that I mean to favour a passion which I should think it criminal to encourage" (Holcroft, *St. Ives* 1:35:113); Frank in his turn claims to have left his verses inadvertently and to have overheard Anna by accident. Nevertheless, he wonders about her feelings:

> [S]he had been setting my verses! [...] It was impossible she should have sung as she did, had not the ideas affected her more than I could have hoped, nay as much as they did myself. She knew the writing. [...] – She sung as if she admired [...] *She could love me if I would let her!* (2:35:110)

Anna then reports the tenderness with which Frank requests his song again, which "almost struck me to the heart. He laid the song upon the music desk, and looked – No no – I will not attempt to tell you how! Words were needless; they could not petition with such eloquence – A barbarian could not have refused." (4:76:251-252)

However, at this point Coke Clifton enters, recognizes Frank's handwriting and, in yet another reading of the song, explodes into sarcastic rage when asked for his musical opinion.

> Oh! Exceedingly! – It was very fine! – Very fine! The words are Mr. Henley's. I imagined as much, madam. I thought them expressive, and amused myself with putting a tune to them. [...] How did you like the subject? What subject, madam? Of the words. I really don't know – I have forgotten – Nay, you said you thought them very fine! Oh! Yes! – True! – Very fine! – All about love – I recollect. Well, and having so much faith in love, you do not think them the worse for that. Oh, by no means! [...] Love in a song may be pardonable. Especially, madam, if the song be written by Mr. Henley. (4:76:252-253)

After adding a pious disquisition on the need to trust a future wife, Clifton leaves Anna to worry whether she has "entirely acted as I ought" (4:76:254). His subsequent description of the episode (in a letter to a friend), obsessed with the idea of catching out a guilty pair, makes his reading of their musical intimacy even more obvious:

> So barefaced! – So fearless! – So unblushingly braved! – Fairfax, I came upon them! – By surprise! – [...] There they sat! – Alone! – She singing a miserable ditty, a bead-roll of lamentable rhymes, strung together by this Quidam! – This Henley! – Nay! – Oh! – Damnation! – [...] Set by her! – Ay! – A ballad – A love complaint – [...] scribbled by him, and set and sung by her! – By her! – For his comfort, his solace, his pleasure, his diversion! – I caught them at it! (4:76:254-255)

After roughly another thousand words, Clifton decides to rape Anna in revenge[59], although the novel concludes with his conversion through Anna and Frank, who then get married[60].

Also in other narratives, the incendiary potential of love songs is ultimately contained. In Mary Wollstonecraft's *Mary*, music raises a young girl's hopes about a neighbouring gentleman: "It is true, he never talked of love; but then they played and sung in concert [...] while she worked he read to her, cultivated her taste, and stole imperceptibly her heart" (3:18-19). He leaves and forgets, though, and she is left to play his favourite tunes "by way of relaxation" (5:34). The narrator of Robert Bage's *Hermsprong* becomes inconclusively infatuated with the sweet Miss Campinet, who eventually marries the hero:

> I loved her! – yes, I loved her! But if there be a spiritual affection, such was mine. I thought of her, as of an angel [...] With my violin, I have been permitted to accompany her at the piano forte. She has condescended to accept the loan of my books and music. I have been honoured with hers. But [...] there was about her a dignified reserve, – a guarded propriety in her most engaging sweetness. (5:16-17)

---

[59] The association of innocent female performance with attempted rape is a favourite motif of Susanna Rowson's. A heroine soothing herself by singing the song that accompanied her first love encounter ends "her amusement" in tears: "[she] was shutting the book, when [Lord Ossiter] laid hold of her, [...] clasped her rudely in his arms and snatched a kiss." The rakish lord then adds insult to injury by offering the girl to "furnish you a house, keep you a chariot, and settle five hundred a year" (*Fille* 17:80-81). The scene at the moonlit organ mentioned above ends in a similar way (cf. *Trials* 3:47:108 and 3:42:41-42).

[60] *Anna St. Ives* also contains a far less emotionally involved poem, a routine effort typical of the continuing tradition of religiously mixed poetic metaphors which jar with the pianoforte as much as they did with the harpsichord.

In Fanny Burney's *The Wanderer*, the only people who enjoy Juliet's playing – who are "almost dissolved with tender pleasure" (1:2:13:116) – without envying her skill or considering it socially unsuitable are the Lord Melbury and Lady Aurora, who turn out to be her brother and sister, and the man who will eventually marry her. He muses: "[w]hy, thus evidently accustomed to grace society, why art thou thus strangely alone [...]?" (2:1:11:102)

The most significant (and most frequent) version of 'music in the heart' is of course the daughter playing for her father, the archetypal counter-narrative to courtship. The Scottish rector keeping the *Annals of the Parish* relies on his daughter's tunes on the spinet when he is "troubled with low spirits" and his wife "busy with the wearyful booming wheel" (Galt, *Annals* 33:128). Cherry, 'The Heroine', despises the concept: "Such an insipid routine, always, always, always the same. [...] After tea I am made sing some fal lal la of a ditty, and am sent to bed with a 'Good night, pretty miss,' or 'sweet dear.' The Clowns!" (Barrett, 1:30). In William Godwin's *Caleb Williams*, the familiar motif is played out with a twist in the ambiguous relationship between the orphaned Emily Melvile and her cousin and guardian Tyrrell. Habit has rendered her indispensable to him, although "Emily's want of personal beauty" and the fact that they are cousins "prevented him from ever looking on her with the eyes of desire". She regularly plays for him and even has "the honour occasionally of playing him to sleep after the fatigues of the chace; and soothe him by their means from the perturbations of his recurrent depression" (1:7:47-48). When Emily falls in love with his aristocratic neighbour Falkland, Tyrrell is enraged and tries to force her to marry an uncouth acquaintance. Emily is advised to plead with him 'pathetically' and uses music to advance her purpose. His "untuned" mind prevents him from taking his customary pleasure in her playing of his favourite tunes; but "her finger was now more tasteful than common", so that he cannot bring himself to leave and ends up in a nearby chair, watching Emily closely: "The furrows into which his countenance was contracted were gradually relaxed; his features were brightened into a smile; the kindness with which he had upon former occasions contemplated Emily seemed to revive in his heart" (1:8:57-58). However, the stratagem ("Now have not I done it nicely? [...] Formerly you said you loved me. [...] You would not make me miserable, would you?") does not work; Tyrrell continues to exert pressure to the point of having Emily sent to prison, where she falls ill and dies.

3.3. "Most impassioned when alone"

> I have thought that she is most impassioned when alone,
> and perhaps all musicians are so.
> THOMAS HOLCROFT. *Anna St. Ives*

Emily's lonely death, removed from father and prospective husband alike, takes sentimentality to an extreme. It is also the lonely player who uses the piano – which "could not qualify for the auditory attention of the Romantic imagination in England" (Hollander, *Images* 5) – in its few Romantic representations. Scott's *Antiquary* illustrates a sensibility which prized only the outdoors 'music of sound'. Lovel, the hero, is dreaming a "strain of delightful music", and when he wakes, the music is "still in his ears, nor ceased till he could distinctly follow the measure of an old Scottish tune" (1:10:79). When he identifies, through the open window, "the same music which had probably broken short his dream", it has "lost much of its charms – it was now nothing more than an air on the harpsichord, tolerably well performed" (1:10:80). To preserve dreamy delights, the piano has to be taken outdoors or substituted by a more Romantic instrument.

Shelley's "Julian and Maddalo" takes the piano outdoors as far as possible, to an open window on a Venetian island where salty wind and spray are coming in to a madman "sitting mournfully / Near a piano, his pale fingers twined / One with the other". He does not play, but sits with his head "leaning on a music book, / And he was muttering, and his lean limbs shook" (273-279, pp. 191-192). Domestically rattling scales and chords would endanger the romance of the madman, who instead makes poetry of music by reading it while the piano is silent. The harp is easier to transport[61]. Peacock's Anthelia, whose "first music of [...] childhood" were murmuring brooks, spends entire days of "captivity" with an unwelcome suitor "near the window with her harp, gazing on the changeful aspects of the wintry sea" and composing a "wild and impassioned" (*Melincourt* 18) air to express herself. Mary Shelley's Matilda takes the harp outdoors as her companion, "sweet soother of feelings" and "only friend" (*Matilda* 2:13; cf. also Hanway, *Ellinor* 4:6:115). The harp-playing of the impover-

---

[61] This romantic, open-air appeal combined with fashionable charm to make the harp a Regency favourite before it went out of fashion in the mid-nineteenth century when "the piano coped far more readily with the ever increasing chromaticism which spelt the progress of bourgeois music" (Scott, *Singing* 50).

ished "syren Princess of Innismore" in Lady Morgan's *Wild Irish Girl*
has infinitely more "soul seizing charm" than the conventional skills
of a conventional family employed "at the piano [... or] reading;
mamma at her knitting, and the pretty little duenna copying out music" (26:84 and 82). Susanna Rowson, ever inventive, uses an organ to
contrive a romantic outdoor effect with the moon "veiled in a fleecy
cloud" and a "gentle zephyr whisper[ing] through the trees" on a fine
evening. A forgotten workbag leads the heroine to a garden house,
where the moon is now shining "full upon an organ which was placed
there for me to entertain myself with, and as I am fond of solemn music, the stillness of the evening and the serenity of every surrounding
object inspired me with a wish to touch the instrument" (*Trials*
3:47:106-107) – a wish which is of course indulged.

Conduct literature and the realistic fictions which face the reality of
domestic keyboard instruments are more modest in their claims about
the emotional relief which music offers. Educational tracts such as
Maria Edgeworth's *Practical Education* simply state that accomplishments serve to keep daughters "out of harm's way, they make a
vast deal of their idle time pass so pleasantly to themselves and others!" (3:20:6) or recommend, more sympathetically, women's private
playing as a resource against "ennui" because it would be cruel to
limit the number of female employments which "the customs of society" restrict so noticeably (3:20:7). Novels provide almost mechanical
lists of elegant and rational recreations that inevitably include music:
"the pursuit of knowledge, and [...] the attainment of elegant accomplishments" which mark the passing of time "only by improvement"
(Radcliffe, *Sicilian Romance* 1:1:31-32). Consider two lady friends in
Susanna Rowson's *The Fille de Chambre*:

> Mrs. Barton [...] was fond of reading, drawing, music, and fancy works; in these
> she discovered Rebecca's taste and knowledge, and many was the heavy hour she
> beguiled in joining the labours of her lady, improving her judgment, and with the
> sweetest diffidence and humility correcting her errors. (18:101)

Fanny Burney's Cecilia amuses herself with walking and reading, the
pianoforte, "fine work" and the conversation of a companion, "a
never-failing resource against languor and sadness" (*Cecilia* 460).
When a real man is in the picture, the piano may not be enough:

> Frightened at her own tenderness [... Camilla] took up a book; but she could not
> read [...] She went to her piano forte; she could not play: 'Too – too amiable
> Edgar!' broke forth in defiance of all struggle. Alarmed and ashamed, even to her-

self, she resolved to dissipate her ideas by a long walk. (Burney, *Camilla* 1:2:14:156-157)

The virtuous, serene Emily Fitzhenry in Mary Shelley's *Lodore*, who is "cheat[ing] the lagging hours of the morrow [...] with her painting and music" also finds the piano not potent enough as a consolation. When she begins to realize that her departed lover may have been heroically serious in his vow never to see her again because he is too poor to marry, her music-making takes on a different colour: drawing or escaping "from her aunt's conversation to the piano; but these were no longer employments, but rather means adopted to deliver herself up more entirely to her reveries" (2:8:152-163).

Mary Shelley's mother, Mary Wollstonecraft, has a far more revolutionary scene in her programmatically titled novel *The Wrongs of Woman*. The heroine is about to leave her violent husband and is improvising after a night on the sofa while her spouse is feigning indifference.

> My spirits were all in arms, and I played a kind of extemporary prelude. The cadence was probably wild, and impassioned, while, lost in thought I made the sounds a kind of echo to my thinking. [...] Mr. Venables [...] gathering up his letters [...] said, "That he hoped he should hear no more romantic stuff, well enough in a miss just come from boarding school;" and went [...] to the counting-house. I still continued playing; and, turning to a sprightly lesson, I executed it with uncommon vivacity. (2:7:73-74)

Maria's animation increases when she realizes that her husband must have returned to listen at the door. Her music does not only solace her but express emotional defiance – a purpose that was not to reappear in fiction before the 1890s (see below 193).

The tall dark Lady Geraldine in Maria Edgeworth's *Ennui* fascinates Glenthorpe, the depressive protagonist, with her indifference to opinion and flattery: a "slight degree of fear of [her] powers" (6:133) "first awakened my dormant intellects, made me know that I had a heart, and that I was capable of forming a character for myself" (19:196). Typically, Lady Geraldine refuses orders to play in company by feigning tooth-ache and rebuffs even Glenthorpe's pleading "with the air of a princess":

> "Excuse me: I am no professor – I play so ill, that I make it a rule never to play but for my own amusement. If you wish for music, there is [devoted and fawning] miss Bland; she plays incomparably, and I dare say will think herself happy to oblige your lordship." I never felt so silly, or so much abashed, as at this instant. (6:134-135)

Not much later, Glenthorpe marries a conventionally demure girl, demonstrating again that musical independence represents a degree of emotional self-determination incompatible with conventional wedded bliss.

3.4. Heroines, Blazons and Jane Austen

> Accomplishments are the only criterion
> by which a girl's education is ever appreciated.
> CATHERINE SINCLAIR. *Modern Accomplishments*

Like the works of earlier decades, Regency novels introduce their heroines by standardized paragraphs of praise. However, Regency blazons ignore the difficulties and ambiguities associated with music; the delicate balance of intellect, skill and morals which educationalists worried over is levelled into the block entity 'accomplishments'. No girl is ever introduced, for example, as excelling at music while being a totally untalented draughtswoman and a conscientious though mediocre needle-worker; but neither is music downplayed separately. We hear summarily of an "excellent education" which provides both "accomplishments and elegance of manners" and "a firm sense of duty" (Edgeworth, *Helen* 1:1:7) or are provided with a list. Such a list can be perfunctory ("she was fond of reading, drawing, music, and fancy works" (Rowson, *Fille* 18:101) or elaborate, detailing a "great taste for music, and a dawning of genius for drawing", mastership "of the fine arts [...] and painting", needlework skill and some knowledge "of history and natural philosophy" (6:22).

The praise remains stereotyped even when the narrative voice assumes the perspective of a suitor impressed with "innumerable" – though strictly regulated – "charms": "She performed on the harpsichord with great taste and execution, had a soft melodious voice, and sung with judgment. Her mind had been carefully cultivated, which rendered her a well informed rational companion" (28:138). In Mary Hays's *Emma Courtney,* the "feast of reason, and the flow of souls" originate indiscriminately in "music, in drawing, in conversation, in reading the *belles lettres* – in –" (1:22:71), but despite the endless abundance suggested by the final dashes, this list is a mere token of a fixed model. The only apparent gestures towards differentiation occur when sisters or friends are grouped into collective displays of model femininity, in which the individual girl represents a mere sample. Of the three sisters in William Godwin's *Fleetwood*[62], the first

> applied to the art of design [...] The second daughter had chosen music for her fa-
> vourite pursuit; and her execution, both on the piano forte and in singing, was not
> inferior to that which her elder sister had attained on canvass. The youngest was a
> gardener and botanist. (2:13:192)

Mary Hanway's Ellinor shows her family feeling through needlework: she works a waistcoat for her guardian and her sister Augusta is seen "practising a sonata of Haydn's; while Lady Fanny Flutter was lolling on a *duchesse*, playing with an Italian greyhound, ennuied to death to know how to dispose of [her] time" (*Ellinor* 2:10:182). Augusta, the more light-weight, but redeemable daughter, plays the superficial piano, but music of superior quality, while the aptly named Lady Flutter has none of these resources; but every character takes one single emblematic skill. These lists replicate the effect of compulsory accomplishments in real life: one girl seems "pretty nearly as good as another, as far as any judgment can be formed of them before marriage" (Peacock, *Nightmare Abbey* 1:358).

Such a degree of standardization was bound to attract parody and subversion. After the eighteenth-century strategy of "praising with faint damns" – circumscribing a heroine's musical skill to avoid suspicion of superficiality – Regency blazons may operate with self-referential and often explicitly subversive irony. In Jane West's *Advantages of Education*, the narrator is warned by a friend that information about the heroine's beauty and accomplishments is compulsory: "You may put your manuscript in the fire, [...] not a soul will read it; who do you think will be interested in the fate of a girl, whom they do not know to be handsome and elegant?" (1:1:1-2). More pithily, Thomas Love Peacock's bookish Anthelia comments: "In our sex a taste for intellectual errors is almost equivalent to taking the veil; and though not absolutely a vow of perpetual celibacy, it has almost always the same practical tendency" (*Melincourt* 150)[63].

---

[62] Godwin's novel is subtitled *The New Man of Feeling*; the shift in sentiment indicated in this reference to Henry Mackenzie's 1771 novel is also reflected in the different use which these books make of music.

[63] The Mary Wollstonecraft figure in Amelia Opie's *roman à clef Adelina Mowbray* furnishes more evidence: she reads history, biography, poetry and novels and improves her French and Italian with her lover but refuses to marry on principle. Art and music are never mentioned.

By 1813, Eaton Stannard Barrett's spoof *The Heroine* was recognizable as such by its very title. Its novel-crazed protagonist Cherry Wilkinson renames herself Lady Cherubina de Willoughby, which may be a reference to the romantic rake in *Sense and Sensibility*, published three years before, and is aware enough of blazons to despise musical accomplishments as far too domestic. She defends the irresponsibility of novel heroines by saying that being a heroine is better

> than remain a domesticated rosy little Miss, who romps with the squire, plays an old tune upon an old piano, and reads prayers for the good family – servants and all. At last [...] she [...] educates the poultry, and superintends the architecture of pies. (12:113)

Cherry is as dismissive of old-fashioned domestic playing as she is of eighteenth-century literature (the allusion is to Sophia Western, see above 40): the music she herself prefers would definitely rattle.

> We neither of us perform to strangers.
> JANE AUSTEN. *Pride and Prejudice*

The most famous parody of heroine blazons has so far gone unmentioned: the ironic method of *The Heroine* is echoed in *Northanger Abbey* by Jane Austen, who had probably read the earlier book when revising her first novel for publication in 1818. *Northanger Abbey* debunks not only the popular reception of Gothic novels[64] but also opens with a classic anti-blazon, which differentiates the heroine's seemingly indispensable qualifications to an unprecedented degree. Catherine Morland is introduced as the quintessential anti-heroine in looks (too bad), mental and physical health (too good) and femininity (lacking). While her French, drawing, reading and account keeping are "not remarkable", she is simply hopeless at music: "At eight years old, she began. She learnt a year, and could not bear it; [...] The day which dismissed the music-master was one of the happiest of Catherine's life" (1:6). These unobtrusive differentiations are remarkable in the

---

[64] This is actually anticipated in a piano scene in *The Heroine*. On an exploratory night ramble through a mansion where she is a houseguest, Cherry finds an old piano. Although she fancies herself pursued by murderers, her first thought is the stereotypical gesture of an introductory 'rattle': "Intending to run my fingers over the keys of a piano, I walked towards it, till a low rustling made me pause. But what was my confusion, when I heard the mysterious machine on a sudden begin to sound [...] as if all its chords were agitated at once, by the hand of some invisible spirit" (Barrett, 22:176-177). Cherry screams, is discovered and ridiculed – the piano harboured no Romantic ghost but a very domestic mouse.

standardized contemporary context. The description of Catherine as a teenager is already more satirical at the expectations which the older girl now has to meet:

> [S]he came on exceedingly well; for though she could not write sonnets, she brought herself to read them; and though there seemed no chance of her throwing a whole party into raptures by a prelude on the pianoforte, of her own composition, she could listen to other people's performance with very little fatigue. (1:8)

Catherine is a listener, a bored recipient of accomplishments – almost a masculine-encoded figure. With the singular economy that is characteristic of her use of contemporary musical tropes, Austen's text uses, modifies and derides a social nuisance and a literary stereotype simultaneously.

It is only in Jane Austen's later novels that these set pieces undergo the subtle development for which Julia Kristeva appropriated the phrase 'blazon' in the first place. Kristeva notes how the blazon in medieval French novels "lost its univocity and became ambiguous; praise and blame at the same time, [...] the nondisjunctive figure par excellence" (53). Such ambiguity is typical of Austen's work in general but is particularly remarkable in the field of music, which is so riddled with both social and literary conventions. After the demonstrative parody of *Northanger Abbey*, Austen's mature works question representational conventions more subtly by unmasking clichés through the words of her characters rather than the didactic narratorial voice of a blazon proper.

When the sharp, worldly Mary Crawford in *Mansfield Park* is enquiring about a neighbouring family, she stops herself to comment:

> But it is very foolish to ask questions about any young ladies – about any three sisters just grown up; for one knows without being told, exactly what they are – all very accomplished and pleasing, and one very pretty. [...] It is a regular thing. Two play on the piano-forte and one on the harp – and all sing – or would sing if they were taught – or sing all the better for not being taught – or something like it. (Austen, 2:11:335)

These remarks represent the problematic superficiality of accomplishment and its social uses so transparently that the text can dispense with the didacticism of the average courtship novel. Moreover, it exposes the speaker's own ulterior motives through her own words: Mary is a consummate exploiter of the potentials of accomplishment, who defies the logistic difficulties of harvest time to have her harp transported to the Mansfield parsonage and stages her own playing for the eyes of Edmund Bertram, and here she is worried about potential rivals in the game. The remark quoted above comes immediately after the following conversation:

> "How many Miss Owens are there?"
> "Three grown up."
> "Are they musical?"
> "I do not at all know. I never heard."
> "That is the first question, you know," said Miss Crawford, trying to appear gay and unconcerned, "which every woman who plays herself is sure to ask about another." (2:11:334-335)

Again, a social mechanism, a literary cliché and a scheming character are all unmasked in a few concise lines.

This sophisticated economy prevails in musical scenes throughout Austen's work. Her narratives contain all the stock motifs of music in fiction around 1800 but transcend the typical caricatures of contemporary texts: pushy mothers, obnoxious overachievers, romantic excess at the keyboard, the accomplishment-into-marriage plot and its attendant money calculations. The topic of women giving up music after marriage is combined with subtle variations on the relative importance of musical accomplishment for very rich girls (the 'ten-thousand-pounder'), and the ignorance and indifference of people who insist mechanically and absurdly on their own fashionable enthusiasm is contrasted with sensible, quietly appreciative listeners. Austen also has all the counter-narratives in place: sentimental love songs used to unfortunate effect, charmed fathers, the diligent and unselfish playing of modest young women and, as described above, the anti-heroine[65]. All these scenarios are memorably incarnated in her novels. Every reader remembers Mary Bennett's tedious earnestness, the disparity between Emma's talent and her lack of application, Jane Fairfax's uncanny proficiency, the mystery surrounding Frank Churchill's distressing gift of a beautiful square piano, and Marianne Dashwood's self-indulgent "nourishment of grief" (*Sense and Sensibility* 1:16:96) at the piano after the rakish Willoughby has abandoned her.

However, the very popularity of Austen's figures has had a certain limiting effect on scholarly insights into her treatment of music. Studies of music and gender in *Victorian* fiction have been including her six completed novels for discussion almost as a matter of rou-

---

[65] Maybe Austen figured herself as musical anti-heroine; even the hagiographical "Biographical Notice", in which her brother Henry credits Austen with all imaginable virtues, has to admit that "[h]er own musical attainments she held very cheap" (xi).

tine[66], and since she is the only novelist from the Regency period to command anything like the popularity or canonic status of the great Victorians, the temptation to subsume her texts under 'Victorians and music' rather than to discuss *Pride and Prejudice* along with *The Wanderer* or *Camilla* is understandable. However, a thorough understanding of Austen's sophisticated and topical use of music is only possible against a historical background of concerns that she shares with her fellow novelists. This discourse of music is very different from that in the nineteenth-century canon of familiar masterpieces by Dickens, George Eliot, or Hardy. Austen's plots and characters are not limited by the repressive Victorian strategies of representation that are outlined in the following chapter, but encompass the wide range typical of Regency concerns and techniques and work out topical contemporary concerns with an unprecedented level of subtlety and textual self-awareness. There is no space here for a thorough discussion, which will have to be published separately; I will just sketch one more example which represents the general problems of performance in a way that is representative of its own period.

The objectification entailed by musical command performance is denounced most explicitly by Elizabeth Bennett and Mr. Darcy in *Pride and Prejudice*, two consummate *verbal* performers of intimate repartee. After Mr. Darcy has been listening to Elizabeth playing for another man with "a full view of the fair performer's countenance" (2:8:195) for a while, she steps out of her position as doubly observed and mute player into that of a *speaker*:

> "You mean to frighten me, Mr. Darcy, by coming in all this state to hear me? But I will not be alarmed though your sister does play so well. There is a stubbornness about me that never can bear to be frightened at the will of others. My courage always rises with every attempt to intimidate me. [...] Well, Colonel Fitzwilliam, what do I play next? My fingers wait your orders." (2:8:195-196)

Elizabeth's use of the hackneyed metonym 'fingers' playfully accuses Colonel Fitzwilliam of several stereotypes at once, hinting as it does at mindless keyboard rattling and the male 'listener's' primarily visual perception. Her seemingly conventional remark to a second man who is conventionally *watching* her implicates Darcy in the solidarity of seeing through such clichés and intimates that it is merely her fingers

---

[66] Cf. the articles by Lustig, Losseff, Vorachek, Plantinga and Burgan. Ruth Solie's *Music in Other Words* does not mention Austen but illustrates a mostly Victorian chapter on "girling at the parlor piano" with an 1818 drawing by Dominique Ingres.

that are at Fitzwillam's command. A similar dissociation from her own physical attributes occurs when Elizabeth explains musical limitations by laziness, whereas Darcy had first attributed his own reluctance to perform to lack of talent:

> My fingers [...] do not move over this instrument in the masterly manner which I *see* [my emphasis] so many women's do. [...] But then I have always supposed it to be my own fault – because I would not take the trouble of practising. It is not that I do not believe my fingers as capable as any other woman's of superior execution. (2:8:197)

These words take on their full strength in dismissing a belittling and demeaning tradition if read against the background of the intense contemporary worries that excessive practising might stint intellectual development. In fact, the moment when Darcy feels that he has "never been so bewitched by any woman" (1:10:57) and when Elizabeth is puzzled to feel that she is "an object of adoration" (1:10:56) to a man she believes to dislike her, is *not* musical. Instead, these insights come after a verbal altercation between the pair, which is silenced by the request for music from a third party. *Not* performing frees the couple for solidarity: this is the constellation which one of the best musical moments of Regency fiction represents. Darcy says of Elizabeth: "No one admitted to the privilege of hearing you, can think any thing wanting. *We neither of us perform to strangers*" (2:8:197, my emphasis). With the frankness that is typical of her period and the economy that is so much her own, Austen conveys the way in which this proud and exceptional couple preserve their intimacy and dignity in a claustrophobically curious and musically shallow society. Thirty years on, this openness had given way to a dense and coherent set of suppression strategies.

IV. "Glorious disability"
The Piano and the Mid-Victorians

> Music, and music alone, enjoys the glorious disability
> of expressing a single vicious idea.
> ANON. *Eliza Cook's Journal*

The chapter on music in Thomas Ward's *Survey of Fifty Years of Progress* for the 1887 Jubilee is typical of the ambiguities and fears that came to determine Victorian attitudes to music. It is the last and shortest contribution in the book; the author is one of just four out of 28 that lack an academic or aristocratic title; and its account of musical progress through the middle of the nineteenth century is riddled with concessive elements, double negatives and circumlocutions. Of the musical 1840s, "it cannot be said that music was flourishing in this country [despite ...] signs of vigorous musical life" (594) and in the late eighties music is "no longer regarded by thinking men merely as the most expensive of noises, or as a means of obtaining pleasurable sensations" (619). The 'noise' of music had indeed become much less expensive, but the fact that pianos were getting within the financial reach of colliers and farmers (cf. *Musical Times* August 1873, 175) did not do music any good. Literary representations usually disparage such associations[67] or use them in still-popular narratives of misguided social ambition[68]. After 'fifty years of progress', in which the social

---

[67] In *Far from the Madding Crowd*, Gabriel Oak woos Bathsheba Everdene with musical promises: "You shall have a piano in a year or two – farmers' wives are getting to have pianos now – and I'll practise up the flute right well to play with you in the evenings." (Hardy, 1:4:65) The villagers are sceptical: "I wonder what a farmer-woman can want with a harpsichord, dulcimer, pianner, or whatever 'tis they d'call it. Seems her old uncle's things were not good enough for her." (2:15:133) In George Meredith's *Ordeal of Richard Feverel*, a thirteen-year-old farmer's niece is "as good as the best of [ladies and] strums to me of evenin's" (8:61), yet "did not seem happy at the farm" (20:161).

[68] A modest tutor in *The Mill on the Floss* goes into debt for "handsome furniture [...] a stock of wine, a grand piano, and the laying-out of a superior flower-garden" (2:1:142). Thomas Hardy's Grace Melbury, so fatally alienated from her country origins that she refuses the honest farmer Giles Winterbourne to marry a philandering doctor, dreams herself back into her finishing school "in the fashionable suburb of a

standing of musicians was improving, people flocked to hear (mostly foreign) virtuosos and the standards in amateur music-making were slowly rising, the social and moral role of music was still not uncontested. Around 1800, very few people had harboured either illusions or fears about the social uses of music. By mid-century, denial, praise and metaphor flourished as fear and ambiguity were rising.

> Music is, in her health, the teacher of perfect order
> and the voice of the obedience of angels;
> and in her depravity she is also the teacher
> of perfect disorder and disobedience,
> and the Gloria in Excelsis becomes the Marseillaise.
> JOHN RUSKIN. *The Queen of the Air*

Anxiety about music was becoming so pervasive as to be shared – or at least pandered to – even by professionals. Arthur Sullivan echoes Richard Hooker (see above 13) with his statement that the "countless moods and richly varied forms [of music] suit it to any organization", but then suggests a highly characteristic exception: music "can convey every meaning except one – an impure one". What used to be called the 'pestilent' effect of music is now not warned of but simply declared nonexistent, and the limitation made constitutive of music's superiority. Painting and sculpture "may, and indeed, do at times, suggest impurity" (Sullivan 285) through "material images" or "definite thoughts" (Southgate, 28), and so Sullivan is moved to "thank God that we have [in music] one elevating and ennobling influence in the world which can never, never lose its purity and beauty" (285). Music was called "pure to all" because only "the listener's mind colours the musical impressions made on it with *his own* thoughts and feelings" (Southgate 39). This kind of whistling in the dark ("never, never"!) makes it obvious that music, like sex as described in Michel Foucault's *History of Sexuality*, had become

---

fast city" where tastefully dressed girls play on the lawn with "notes of piano and harp trembling in the air from the open windows adjoining" (Hardy, *Woodlanders* 6:43-44). In William Cox Bennett's "Tale of Today", a miller's only daughter commits suicide after being seduced by a "titled slip of lordly blood" (31). Her cottage parlour "With little comforts brightened round, / [...] Where bookcase and piano well / Of more than village polish tell" (13-18) possibly speaks of exaggerated social ambition that may have helped to ruine the girl, but the authorial voice, outraged at "the suicide's seducer", is remarkably sympathetic to her.

an object of great suspicion; the general and disquieting meaning that pervades our conduct and our existence, in spite of ourselves; the point of weakness where evil portents reach through to us; the fragment of darkness that we each carry within us. (69)

Aspects of 'darkness' obviously continued to "reach through" even as music was officially sanctified.

The second important analogue between Victorian attitudes to music and nineteenth-century constructions of sex according to Michel Foucault is that the discursive suppression could never be complete.

Those who believe that [it] was more rigorously elided in the nineteenth century [...] through a formidable mechanism of blockage and a deficiency of discourse, can say what they please. There was not a deficiency, but rather an excess, a re-doubling, too much rather than not enough discourse. (64)

Discursive excess resides in harmonious metaphors and pious injunctions, in the musical encounters that drive so many marriage plots and even in musical heroes and heroines. Victorian fiction and conduct literature cannot do without music, but they continuously contain and weaken musical harmony 'in action'. The rapture of music is never fully shared with the reader, not even when occasions of performance and enjoyment of domestic music-making are completely blameless by the most conventional standards.

1. Gender and Courtship

> Men misapprehend women, both for good and evil.
> Their good woman is a queer thing, half doll, half angel;
> their bad woman almost always a fiend.
> CHARLOTTE BRONTË. *Shirley*

What could be called the 'Closing of the Victorian Mind' was particularly thorough with regard to musical gender norms. After the comparative laxity of the turn of the century, they turned extremely rigid, and by 1839 it was recognized that "the present unequal diffusion of music among the sexes" had proceeded far enough to be considered, "in itself, an evidence of [music's] degradation" (H. F. C., 307). The scenario of charming woman player and unmusical male listener was so set that metonymic "small fingers" floating over "keys" and a nameless speaker's inability to read music are enough to evoke it in Dante Gabriel Rossetti's poem "During Music":

I lean o'er thee to scan
The written music cramped and stiff;
– 'Tis dark to me, as hieroglyph
On those weird bulks Egyptia' (ll. 5-8).

The faultlines are clearer than ever: music seems familiarly conventional ("cramped") and cosily erotic ("I lean o'er thee") but also
"weird" and as deadly as an inscription on a sarcophagus – the an-
tithesis of rational, interactive speech. A women's magazine spells out
the gender implications:

> It is only by a marriage with words that *she* [i. e. music, my emphasis] can be-
> come a minister of evil. An instrument which is music, and music alone, enjoys
> the glorious disability of expressing a single vicious idea, or inspiring a single cor-
> rupt thought. (Anon., *Eliza Cook's Journal* 7 [1852] 96)

The oxymoron "glorious disability" is a near-perfect Victorian definition for both music and women. Both continue to signify each other
(witness the female pronoun and the term 'marriage') and renew their
ancient double meanings of sacredness and vulgarity, divinity and
physicality. This double potential continued to be exploited in courtship[69] and ensured the piano its place right at the heart of the patriarchal family. As the middle-class drawing room took over from the
Regency 'assembly rooms' and balls and became an "idealized refuge,
a world all its own, with a higher moral value than the public realm"
(Sennett, 20), the piano became the "family orchestra" (Hullah, *Music*
24) or the 'Household God', omnipresent in educational recommendation, its problematic aspects driven underground by persistent denial.

Countless monograph titles of the type *Woman and the Demon*,
From Slave to Siren, *Nobody's Angel*, *Fallen Angel* or *No Angels in
the House*[70] demonstrate the scholarly interest in the intense contradictions surrounding Victorian women – even a fictional academic,
Robyn Penrose in David Lodge's *Nice Work*, publishes a book called
Domestic Angels and Unfortunate Females (1:2:52). Analogous titles
such as *Angelic Airs / Subversive Songs* (Clapp-Itnyre) reflect the parallel discursive complications about music which have been studied
with similar concentration. However, much of this scholarship has
focussed on authors with a discernible interest in music or on sub-gen-

---

[69] Calling the piano as "an altar devoted to saint Cecilia" (*Chamber's Journal* 1881
quoted in Pearsall, 74) may carry overtones of a marriage service.

[70] The references are to Auerbach, Janson, Langland, Mitchell, and Peterson.

res such as sensation fiction and *Künstlerromane*. 'George Eliot and music'[71], or 'Thomas Hardy and music' are topics which each have accumulated a substantial individual research bibliography. While some of the evidence analyzed in these studies is indeed of general relevance to the period, it is important to remember that the perspective of the passionate music-lover – whether writer of, or character in, fiction – is fundamentally marginal to the Victorian mentality. The 'excess of discourse' which Michel Foucault describes is characterized by a highly consistent use of certain narrative strategies in that majority of texts which do not have a particular musical agenda. Against what practically amounts to a collective text, private acts of subversive re-definition such as Elizabeth and Darcy's joint refusal to perform become almost impossible. Music-loving writers and characters are fundamentally exotic exceptions in a highly restrictive and centralized general narrative of music, gender and society.

1.1. British Masculinity

> Frenchmen may learn to play the piano,
> but men in this country have something else to do.
> WILLIAM BLACK. *A Daughter of Heth*

In the mid-nineteenth century playing a musical instrument was "virtually forbidden to boys of 'good family', particularly if they betrayed signs of talent or serious interest" (Ehrlich, 71).

> [W]hile every English girl has been tormented into an aimless knowledge of the practical difficulties of the pianoforte, any one of her brothers who [...] addicted himself to any musical instrument whatsoever, or showed the smallest zeal for the art [... risks being] laughed at as an effeminate 'milk-sop' [...]! (H. F. C., 307)

George Grossmith, the comic recitalist and Savoy Opera star, remembers ladies commenting in his 1870s childhood: "How odd it seems to see a boy playing" (36). In Mary Coleridge's *Lady on the Drawing-room Floor*, a little boy manages to pick out a tune on the piano and announces delightedly that he wants to learn to play: "The look of utter astonishment on my father's face alarmed me even more than the frown that I had looked instinctively to see" (219). The Scottish boys in William Black's novel *A Daughter of Heth* find "the notion of a

---

[71]   The footnotes to pp. 153-186 in Solie, *Music* constitute one example of such a bibliography for George Eliot, though without mention of Delia Da Sousa Correa's *George Eliot and Music*.

boy being able to play on the piano [...] irresistibly ludicrous. [...] 'We dinna learn music at the schule, ye gowk.'" (1:5:6)

In grown men, even a theoretical acquaintance with music was considered embarrassing: Arthur Sullivan noted "a curious affectation of [musical] ignorance on the part of many men of position", who – in board meetings concerning musical institutions! – "deprecate any knowledge of music with a smug satisfaction like a man disowning poor relations" (273). Francis Hueffer describes a meeting of Royal College of Music trustees who "almost without exception prefaced their remarks upon music by saying that they knew nothing about music" (2-3). The total feminization of musical performance dispensed with practical or pious explanations of its unworthiness as a male pursuit. It is simply a given, inescapable in fiction, too, where male music lovers and amateur players are invariably off-key: foreign, evil, effeminate, childish or any combination of these. No decent and manly Englishman is allowed to love music passionately, and the new-gained strength of this taboo is evidenced in the near-obsessive frequency and diversity of negative examples.

Musical foreigners, with very few exceptions[72], live on a continuum ranging from likeably eccentric through ridiculous to sinister. Will Ladislaw's Polish grandfather is of the first kind (Eliot, *Middlemarch* 4:27:401). Thomas Love Peacock's dilettante Mr. Trillo, who is rumoured to have been born O'Trill and faking attractive foreignness by taking "the O from the beginning, and put[ting] it at the end" (*Crotchet Castle* 5:682) is a harmless caricature, as are Monsieur Quatremains and Signor Twankeydillo in Thackeray's *The Newcomes*. The chef Alcide Mirobolant in *Pendennis* is more elaborated: "adorned with many ringlets and chains", he takes up a new post with his library, pictures and a piano and invariably warms up at the instrument before composing a menu: "Every great artist, he said, had need of solitude to perfectionate his works." (Thackeray, 23:211-212) In George Meredith's *Diana at the Crossways*, the ridicule is reserved for the lady who praises a newly famous pianist's pieces as the "most Aeolian thing ever caught from a night-breeze by the soul of a poet", only to continue more pragmatically: "The above, by the way, is a

---

[72] Such as the impressive German Jew Julius Klesmer in *Daniel Deronda* or the Belgian teacher Monsieur Joseph Emanuel in *Villette*, who fascinates the poor governess Lucy Snowe: "What a master-touch [...]! In what grand, grateful tones the instrument acknowledged the hand of the true artist!" (Brontë, 28:400)

Pole settled in Paris, and he is to be introduced to me at Lady Pennon's" (2:3:65). The Italian Count Fosco in Wilkie Collins's *The Woman in White* is both repulsive and comic, and John Jasper, the cathedral choir master in *The Mystery of Edwin Drood*, is English, tall, handsome and mellifluous (cf. Dickens 12:103), but also an opium-addicted, brutal and possessive lover and quite possibly a murderer.

Effeminacy, the third deficiency of musical males, is a trait found in most musical foreigners, but also represented by English characters like Julian Westbrook in Charles Aïdé's *The Marstons* (see above 121) or the languid dilettante Frederick Fairlie in *The Woman in White*. In George MacDonald's verse play *Within and Without*, a widowed lord in love with his daughter's married piano teacher is given to "composing at his pianoforte" (3:5, p. 84) or improvising "low, half-melancholy, half-defiant" preludes (3:11, p. 105). Philip Wakem in *The Mill on the Floss*, lame and "half feminine in sensitiveness" (Eliot, 5:3:291), is "cursed with susceptibility in every direction, and effective faculty in none" and interested in all sorts of literature as well as "painting and music" (5:3:287). The same fluttering multiplicity, reminiscent of the tutoring schedules of Regency belles, characterizes the sociable dilettante Blackburn Tuckham in George Meredith's *Beauchamp's Career*, who "betrays [...] his accomplishments one by one":

> He sketched, and was no artist; he planted, and was no gardener; he touched the piano neatly, and was no musician; he sang, and he had no voice. Apparently he tried his hand at anything, for the privilege of speaking decisively upon all things. (28:312-313)

In his courtship, Tuckham, "never intrusive, never pressing", decorously relies on social ritual: "They sketched in company; she played music to him, he read poetry to her, and read it well" (48:549), but that the heroine should marry him instead of the doomed idealist Neville Beauchamp is dismissed as an "incomprehensible espousal" (56:628).

Lastly, it is a lack of maturity or seriousness that may discredit musical masculinity, as it does in the sixteen-year-old boy soprano Henry Arkell in Mrs. Henry Wood's *Mildred Arkell*, or in "little De Lisle", who, after "having weakly admitted that he can play a little dance music", is forced to hammer away at waltzes during a wet afternoon in Rhoda Broughton's *Belinda*. Fulfilling the hope that "some one can play, or even whistle a tune, or set the musical-box tinkling", he turns into a musical toy while the unhappily married heroine is enjoying a giddily exciting dance with another man. De Lisle is only remembered when somebody stumbles over a dog because "the poor boy at the piano" is, like the dog, "getting cross, though he tries not to show it" (2:6:87-89).

The temperamental rather than biological boyishness of Dickensian musicians such as Tom Pinch or Harold Skimpole parallels his child-women. Playfulness also characterizes Thackeray's beefy Captain Ned Strong, who is "very gay with his good humour and ceaseless flow of talk". His "scores of songs, in half-a-dozen languages" performed at the piano "in a rich manly voice" are considered "delightful" by the ladies and ensure the admiration of the effete Sir Francis, who is impressed with Strong's readiness to play "anything, pitch and toss, pianoforty, cwibbage if you like" (*Pendennis* 12:216). Wilkie Collins's *Man and Wife* features an avid pianist of striking virility in Julius Delamayn, but he exists only to serve the anti-athletic message of the novel by exposing beefy English prejudice that sees him as a "degenerate Briton" because he knows nothing about horses and practises "the foreign vice of perfecting himself in the art of playing a musical instrument" (3:16:180).

> Women and the Clergy are upon the same Footing.
> The long-robed Gentry are exempted from the Laws of Honour.
> HENRY FIELDING. *Amelia*

John Ella reckoned that the "encouragement" of music in England depended "chiefly on the female sex and the clergy" (38), and most musical clergymen in Victorian fiction indeed display some of the non-masculine characteristics outlined above. The good-natured, "accommodating" Mr. Larynx in Peacock's *Nightmare Abbey* can "drink Madeira, [...] crack jokes, [...] hand Mrs. Hilary to the piano, take charge of her fan and gloves, and turn over her music with surprising dexterity" (1:361); Mr. Crisparkle in Dickens's *Edwin Drood* is "musical, classical, [...] contented and boy-like" (2:6), Mr. Honeyman in Thackeray's *The Newcomes* repulsively sweet, and Mr. Cartwright in Frances Trollope's *The Vicar of Wrexhill* an out-and-out villain. The eponymous hero of Trollope's *The Warden*, an enthusiastic 'cellist with the nickname "catgut" (4:47) and the trick of miming 'cello-playing gestures during difficult conversations, combines an admirable moral force of renunciation with some minor weaknesses which are also feminine. No wonder that an ambitious young minister in Margaret Oliphant's *Salem Chapel* feels he has to defend his superiority by the assurance that "I don't perform at all [...] not in any way; but I am an exemplary listener. Let me take you to the piano" (1:1:15). Only the Scottish minister in William Black's *Daughter of Heth* escapes depreciation; he is surprised into deep appreciation of music when Coquette, his French-raised orphan niece, tries to make amends for her unwitting musical violation of Sabbath laws by improvising on sacred tunes to the family on the following day. The sternly pious man is overwhelmed by the power of "a dumb instrument to speak such strange things" and amazed "to find that this carnal invention of music had awoke such profound emotion within him" (1:5:64). His strong faith at once safeguards this narrative of musical ravishment and saves him from ridicule.

1.2. The Musical Hero

Within the discourse outlined so far, it is almost impossible to have a musical man good and strong enough to carry the plot of a novel. Two examples who try shall be mentioned here because their precarious negotiations complete the picture of Victorian male musicality in an instructive way: Samuel Butler's autobiographical *The Way of All Flesh* and Charlotte Yonge's *Heir of Redclyffe*. Sir Guy Redclyffe (whose talents are explained by his parentage: a romantic Italian misalliance of his father's) has all the most admirable traits of a Victorian hero*ine*: highly-strung, physically weak but morally hard-fighting, he sacrifices his health and ultimately his life nursing a grudging opponent. His more conventionally masculine cousin Philip Morville thinks Guy should be "ashamed to parade his music" (1:8:121) and his domineering older sister implicitly criticizes Guy's femininity: he is "clever, but superficial; and with his mania for music, he can hardly fail to be merely an accomplished man" (1:14:200). '*Merely* accomplished' is of course an impossible phrase for describing a young woman: for her, accomplishment was all that mattered. But music, unsuitably enough, is far more than an accomplishment for Guy and is therefore allowed full expression only at his death: "All was as usual. Only the piano was closed, and an accumulation of books on the hinge told how long it had been so" (2:18:527).

Unlike the Tractarian Charlotte Yonge, Samuel Butler was writing against convention, and the passion which Ernest Pontifex in *The Way of All Flesh* has for music purposely subverts gender stereotypes. In the holidays, Ernest gets up early to "play the piano before breakfast without disturbing his papa and mamma, or rather, perhaps, without being disturbed by them". Instead, he is listened to by a servant who is dusting and sweeping while he plays, and "ready to make friends with most people" (38:162), the boy strikes up a friendship with her. This musical performance violates both class and gender norms and needs to be hidden from his parents and protected against them. Ernest's father (himself lured into marriage by music, see above 144) worries that music might give the boy "low associates later on if he were to be encouraged in his taste for music" (34:144).

But as with Guy Redclyffe, this taste stays with Ernest for life. On leaving school he has "a farewell practice upon the organ [...] after which he felt more composed and happier; then, tearing himself away from the instrument he loved so well, he hurried to the station" (44:199). When Mary Burgan describes the hardship which the final loss of a piano in financially difficult situations signifies for women in Victorian fiction[73], she does not mention Ernest's despair at the same prospect. But Butler expresses it in far more dramatic terms than any novelist writing about a woman:

> The winter had been a trying one. Ernest had only paid his way by selling his piano. With it he seemed to cut away the last link that connected him with his earlier life, and to sink once for all into the small shopkeeper. It seemed to him that however low he might sink his pain could not last much longer for he would simply die if it did. (76:338)

A hero romantically ready to die for the loss of his piano certainly goes against all Victorian notions of decency. At least Ernest's music-making deviates significantly from female practice in that he rarely performs (except for the little maid); his introversion makes it almost indifferent whether he plays the church organ or the morally more ambiguous piano.

This seems a rather convincing counter-narrative. However, Ernest's passion for music, so much stronger than that allowed to any female character, is allied to deficits in masculinity just as much as that of Guy Redclyffe. Ernest confirms his father's fears of "low associates" by marrying an incurable drunkard, whose convenient death

---

[73] Burgan discusses examples like the poor Quiverful family in Trollope's *Barchester Towers*, Mrs. Nickleby's tearfully detailed "account of the dimensions of a rosewood cabinet piano they had possessed in their days of affluence" (Dickens, *Nickleby* 10:97) and Amelia Osborne's piano in *Vanity Fair* (chapters 17 "How Captain Dobbin Bought A Piano" and 18 "Who played on the piano Captain Dobbin bought?").

eventually frees Ernest for a fulfilling dilettante life once his children
have been farmed off to the country. Peter Coveney calls *The Way of
All Flesh* a novel "with a negative thesis" which fails to define positive virtue (287-288). Convention decrees that positive, manly virtue
is irreconcilable with a passion for music, and it is ironic that the
iconoclast Samuel Butler should respect this convention just as punc-
tiliously as the pious Charlotte Yonge. Charles Hamilton Aïdé was
obviously indulging in wishful thinking when he claimed in 1863 that
"the gloomy days [...] when our grandfathers despised the accomplishment as one unfit for men" were over:

> The quiet firesides of thousands in our middle classes, when, evening after eve-
> ning, husbands, sons or brothers sit down, after the day's work is done, to conquer
> the difficulties of some instrument, to make the stiff fingers pliant [...]: this fact
> alone would sufficiently refute any objectors to the rapid development of a musi-
> cal taste among us. ("Amateur Music" 93)

Aïdé projects the contemporary feminization of music onto the recent
past to bolster an optimistic estimate of the contemporary standing of
music. But his own description expresses the limitations set on male
practice: it must remain inept in order not to threaten masculinity.
Aïdé's fiction corroborates this analysis. In his novel *The Marstons*,
the heroine observes an attractive womanizer she used to admire
playing the French horn at a party. While the ladies present admire the
feminized quality of Julian Westbrook's playing in their whisperings
of "So sweet!", "So very soft!", Olivia Marston is now impatient with
"all those windy spasms of agony" and amazed at her former infatuation and "belief in the player's true and passionate feeling. It was intolerable to her now." (85-86)

1.3. "Men can't help it on a music-stool, poor dears!"

Victorian men never recoil so explicitly from their musical infatua-
tions; the male capacity for erotic conditioning continues to determine
musical accomplishment. Female sensibility is of little account in the
rituals which accompany the transition from 'innocence' (read: sexual
ignorance) to the wifely 'experience' of the Angel in the House.
Courtship, "the little interval between coming into life and settling in
it" (Anon., *Eliza Cook's Journal* 8 [1852] 58-59), leads to what is "in
effect a renunciation of desire" (Belsey, 120) yet necessitates desire.
However much women were defined through their capacity for sexual
reproduction and held in suspicion for their erotic power, they needed

to have "sufficient charms to attract a mate in the first place" (Binstock, 132). Frances Power Cobbe remembers in her *Life* that music was her most important school subject, whereas "the bottom of the scale" was occupied by 'Morals and Religion': "The order of precedence [...] was naively betrayed [in the admonition to a girl] who had been detected in a lie. 'Don't you know, you naughty girl [...] we had *almost* rather find you have a P –' (the mark of Pretty Well) 'in your music, than tell such falsehoods?'" (64) Lady Helen Craven, a passionate music-lover, remembers her resistance to her mother's attempts at making her daughters accomplished:

> [With] my sisters she succeeded well enough. Clelia's [...] piping, [...] Juliet's insipid watercolours and Adelaide's mechanical thumping of "Les Cloches de Corneville" assisted them each and several by leaps and bounds into the sacred sphere of matrimony. (4)[74]

Young Helen despises these machinations: "The music I cared for [wasn't for these purposes ...]. I took no earthly interest in any subject that might have been discussed *tête-à-tête* behind the piano". (4)

In Victorian fiction, '*tête-à-têtes* behind the piano' continue because the marriage plot remains a "dominant form of literary fiction [...], concerned both with the expression of sexual desire and with its limitation within comfortable, familiar social boundaries" (Dever, 157). The piano was such an ideal locus for the representation of these mechanisms that many scenes indicate a near-automatic association of piano and courtship. Disraeli's *Lothair* proposes two days after observing a girl in the family circle at needlework "while two fair sisters more remote occasionally burst into melody, as they tried the passage of a new air" (1:1). Rosamond Vincy and the ambitious young doctor Tertius Lydgate in *Middlemarch* are considered engaged "without the aid of formal announcement" because Rosamond has been observed to be "spinning industriously at the mutual web [...] in the corner of the drawing-room where the piano stood" (Eliot, 4:36:338). A comic poem spells this inevitable progression out as a recipe from "Cupid's Cookery Book": the young and tender lad, at table, should be well soaked with wine and plied with hints about 'Miss'. When red "in the gills", he should be sat

---

[74] David Copperfield's first unhappy marriage with Dora Spenlow originates in a flash, which does not even give David the time to hear and watch Dora play ("All was over in a moment") – but siginifiantly, 'Phiz' put a piano in the foreground of the illustration for this scene, "A fall into captivity" (Dickens, *Copperfield* 4:27:333).

> by the lady, though shy he may be,
> And sop them both equally well with green tea –
> Lead them to the piano – the handiest of things –
> And blow up the flame till the young lady sings – (Moncrieff, ll. 13-18).

After careful simmering in a quiet corner and two or three repetitions of the whole procedure the pair should be "ready for marriage whenever you want" (28).

This sounds like a flippant Regency text, but the poem actually dates from 1850. What gives it away as Victorian is the warning that follows: "But the first sigh you hear the young gentleman puff, / Take them off, for they then will be warm enough" (ll. 17-18). Whether the ambiguous sigh denotes love or satiety with the music which has fuelled love, it typically has to be *contained*.

In more serious narratives, piano music is allowed to lead to true lovers' confidence only unintentionally. Olivia Marston, the retiring, but powerfully moral and determined protagonist of Charles Aïdé's *The Marstons*, declines to play at social gatherings, explaining that "her musical capacity was small, and only fit for home consumption", for her father and herself. Her neighbour, the painter Thompson, only discovers her talents when she is playing to her father and letting her thoughts wander in reminiscences of her mother. She does not hear his knock.

> The fire-light [...] just trembled fitfully, no more, upon the profile of the girl at the piano. [...] [u]nconscious of his presence, [she] kept dreamily repeating that old air. Presently, the music, of a sudden, stopped: one hand hung listlessly on the keys; she bowed her head forward upon the music-desk, and low sob broke from her. She rarely gave way thus. [...] A hand was laid gently upon the hand which had fallen on the keys: its touch thrilled her. A shiver, but not of fear (for she felt whose hand it was), ran through her. She raised her head – so quickly that the painter's beard, as he leant across the piano, brushed her forehead before he had time to draw back. (10-11)

The heroine's musicality is here allowed to generate romance only because she is "portrayed as unconscious of the emotional impact of her musical performance on her listener" (Da Sousa Correa, 80). Music can never *not* be represented, but even in its most bourgeois, most socially contained and approved form, at the drawing-room piano, sounding for who will turn out to be 'Mr. Right', its ambiguous potential has to be restrained.

Some writers warn their readers of the traps of musical courtship by pointing out incongruities between musical metaphor and reality. This may happen through the voice of a particularly perceptive character. Maggie Tulliver in *The Mill on the Floss* – who also refuses to read "more books where the blond-haired women carry away all the happiness" – declines to be called the tenth Muse because carrying a harp around "in this climate" would necessitate "a green baize cover" (Eliot, 5:4:353). Molly Gibson in Mrs. Gaskell's *Wives and Daughters* is similarly sober about an admirer's poem which compared her step-mother's heart "to a harpstring, vibrating to the slightest breeze": "I thought harpstrings required a pretty strong finger to make them sound" (2:12:119)[75]. Men, on the other hand, are denounced or pitied for the way in which metaphors cloud their judgment. The imbalance of their education makes them more susceptible to musical clichés than to real music, and the consequences can be terrible. Tertius Lydgate in *Middlemarch* falls for Rosamond Vincy – decidedly the wrong woman – because he perceives her "to produce the effect of exquisite music" and "to have the true melodic charm" (Eliot, 1:11:92). He sees, or rather constructs, Rosamond as

> an accomplished creature who venerated his high musings and momentous la-bours and would never interfere with them; who would create order in the home [...] with still magic, yet kept her fingers ready to touch the lute and transform life into romance at any moment. (4:36:344)

Like any second-rate poet, Lydgate clumsily conflates metaphorical lute and actual piano[76]; the piled-up musical clichés indicate his blind-ness to Rosamond's reality and the outcome is, predictably, a desper-ately unhappy marriage.

Charles Reade gets more broadly comic mileage out of the topic. In his novel *Hard Cash* – a programmatically non-metaphorical title – a mother contemplates the "living radiance and incarnate melody" of her daughter's singing "in a sort of stupor; it seemed hardly possible to her that a provincial banker could refuse an alliance with a creature so peerless as that" (1:5:167). The most soberly sarcastic observer of linguistic and social abuses is, as always, William Thackeray. In *The Newcomes* he bridges the gap between imagery and reality with un-

---

[75]   Cf. Benedick wondering about the fact that "sheep's guts should hale a man's soul out of his body" (Shakespeare, *Much Ado* 2:3:58-61).

[76]   Winthrop Praed's historicizing poem "Lidian's Love" ironizes youthful dreams of "Houris of the heart's creation", romantically unreal figures not in thrall to fashion, who "never thrummed upon the virginals, / Nor tripped by rule, nor fortunately fainted, / Nor practised paying compliments and calls, / Looking satirical, or looking sainted." (8:56-60)

matchable elegance in the story of Miss Billing's musical campaign for an eligible colonel. As he is "a practitioner on the flute, she hoped to make all life one harmonious duet with him; but she played her most brilliant sonatas and variations in vain". Marriage becomes possible only when the piano is recognized as a seductively expensive piece of *furniture* rather than an embodiment of metaphorical harmony. Once Miss Billing's playing has had its effect, she carries "her grand piano to Lieutenant and Adjutant Hogdkin's house, whose name she now bears" (5:55).

Commercial metaphors for the marriage transaction are usually bitter. Thackeray makes the motif of a 'Mahometan' education into an Oriental vignette:

> If there's a beauty in a well-regulated [...] family, they fatten her; they feed her with the best *Racahout des Arabes*. They give her silk robes and perfumed baths; have her taught to play on the dulcimer, and dance and sing; and when she is quite perfect, send her down to Constantinople for the Sultan's inspection. (*Newcomes* 43:453)

Like Reade's stance, this irony owes a lot to the Regency discourse. Dickens's use of the market metaphor, on the other hand, is very Victorian in its melodramatic weight. Edith Dombey in Dickens's *Dombey and Son* is a 'fattened beauty' as described by Thackeray, trained to perform mechanically: after playing the harp, she gets up and "receiving Mr. Dombey's thanks and compliments in exactly the same [indifferently polite] manner as before, went with scarcely any pause, to the piano, and began there" (21:210). Edith later laments:

> [From childhood I have been] offered and rejected, put up and appraised, until my very soul has sickened. I have not had an accomplishment or a grace that might have been a resource to me, but it has been paraded and vended to enhance my value, as if the common crier had called it through the streets. (54:541)

This kind of explicitly accusatory outburst is rare, and particularly so because it is not voiced by the narrator but by an extravagant and embittered character. This turns the description of her predicament into an individual drama rather than a critique of society – the typical Victorian move of blaming abuses on individual musical practitioners rather than social norms.

When social uses *are* mentioned, it is with far more reticence than in the 1790s or 1810s. It may be admitted that the "allurement which served its purpose" (Aïdé, "Amateur Music" 96) is generally given up after marriage, but when Robert Burton is once again echoed, 231 years on (see above 18) in a Victorian ladies' magazine, the tone is more careful:

> No mother – no woman, who has passed over the first few years of life, sings, or dances, or draws, or plays musical instruments. These are merely means for displaying the grace and vivacity of youth, which every woman gives up as she gives up the dress and the manners of eighteen. (Anon., *Eliza Cook's Journal* 8 [1852] 59)

Courtship is not mentioned here, only implied in the juxtaposition mother/woman, and the disappearance of music is made into a natural phenomenon connected merely with advancing age.

2. Practice and Prescription at Home

> It is well that all girls should play to a certain extent;
> and this will no doubt involve
> some unpleasantness to themselves and others.
> THE REV. HUGH REGINALD HAWEIS. *Ideals for Girls*

To complement the denial of the erotic agenda of music, conduct literature adduces additional domestic purposes for the piano, as if to distract further from the sexual and mercenary implications of performance in courtship. The purpose of learning to play well and the moral and intellectual disadvantages of an excessive musical training are now outweighed by newly-discovered beneficial side-effects of *practising*. Merely practising the piano turns out to have disciplinary and even 'hygienic' benefits which can outweigh the potential dangers of virtuosity and seduction; it becomes a purpose in itself which need not even lead to suspicious levels of competence. A modest skill was enough to provide a private balance for the emotional demands made on girls and to refresh male relatives. Erna Olafson Hellerstein's distinction between a 'positional' and a 'personal' view of family duties is useful here. The former asks women to function in a static position in society (daughter, sister or wife), whereas the latter focuses on the emotional capacities which are necessary to be fill those roles properly as a submissive daughter, sympathetic wife, and loving mother. This through-going antithetical impulse determines women's musical experience: musical skills enhanced the positional duties of a daughter and wife, but could also provide personal support for the emotional requirements of those duties and necessary self-awareness of a girl as a sensitive individual. Both functions of music are insistently recommended in conduct literature, but are, interestingly enough, only very rarely described in fiction. Although music in the family reached its theoretical apogee in the mid-Victorian period, the eighteenth-century tradition of *representing* it positively in fiction was suspended.

2.1. For Fathers, Brothers and Husbands

According to conduct literature, music serves "to soothe the weary spirit of a father when he returns home from the office or the counting-house, where he has been toiling for her maintenance; to beguile a mother of her cares; or to charm a suffering sister into forgetfulness of her pain" (Ellis, 104). For brothers, such musical ministering had a particular importance: "So many temptations beset young men, [...] that it is of the utmost importance, that your brothers' evenings should be happily passed at home" (Arthur, 97). Conduct books even resort to emotional blackmail ("If they have played and sung to attract the lover [...] why not sometimes play and sing to gratify the husband?" [Mrs. Roe, *A Woman's Thoughts*, quoted in Da Sousa Correa, 68]) or narrative insets:

> "This has been a tiring day," says the hard-worked, often perplexed father; "come, Annie, let me have a little music to rest me. I am so glad you have not gone out this evening. We are getting selfish about you, I am afraid; but I don't know how to spare you, even for an evening". (Farningham, 12-13)

The pianist Francesco Berger remembers a girl mutilating her exam pieces in order to sweeten her father's rest: "Pa can't bear the *minor*; so I always leave out *those* bits in order not to distress him when he's tired" (213).

'Literary' representations of the warmly recommended musical ministering within the family are rare and usually describe less than ideal relationships[77]. Charlotte Yonge's *Hopes and Fears* endorses the recommendations of simple music and accordingly characterizes a whole family by their reactions to the limpid, non-virtuosic playing of their daughter and sister Phoebe. Her tired brother asks her to play and is touched by some old airs unsuitable for the drawing-room, asking,

---

[77] Not surprisingly, Charles Dickens provides the counterexample in *David Copperfield*'s first love and eventual second wife, who is also a devoted daughter: "Agnes set [out] glasses for her father, and a decanter of port wine. I thought he would have missed its usual flavor, if it had been put there for him by any other hands. There he sat, taking his wine, and taking a good deal of it, for two hours; while Agnes played on the piano, worked, and talked to him and me." (5:15:192)

"his face softer than usual": "'Where did you get that, Phoebe? [...] play it again; I have not heard it for years.' [...] He was shading his face with his hand, but he hardly spoke again all the rest of the evening." Phoebe's music also charms her retarded sister Maria (who sits "entranced, with her mouth open") and wakes her vacuous mother from a doze: "Was that Phoebe? [...] You have a clear, good touch, my dear, as they used to say when I was at school at Bath. Play another of your pieces, my dear." This incites Phoebe's nasty, accomplished elder sisters to play a duet for their mother, after all, but characteristically "Maria's face became vacant again, for Juliana's music awoke no echoes within her". Yet another sister seems to be "studying 'coming-out' life as she watched her sisters surrounded by the gentlemen who presently herded round the piano" (2:3:35). The hapless conditioned males do not respond to Phoebe's purer musicality, but to the playing of her sisters who are clearly signalling the purpose of their performance: captivation. In Mrs. Gaskell's 'industrial' novel *Mary Barton*, music in the family attracts bitter criticism. John Barton reviles a "do-nothing" lady who worries "shopmen all morning, and screeching at her pianny all afternoon [without doing] a good turn to any one of God's creatures but herself" (1:1:10). A burnt-down mill means dire poverty for the unemployed workers – and pleasant leisure for the owners who have time, while waiting for the insurance payments, "for becoming acquainted with agreeable and accomplished daughters, on whose education no money had been spared, but whose fathers [...] had so seldom had leisure to enjoy their daughters' talents" (1:6:58).

Music for fictional husbands is similarly double-edged. None of the extended scenes of marital life in *Middlemarch* – certainly co-responsible for Virginia Woolf's estimate that George Eliot's masterpiece is "one of the few English novels written for grown-up people" (quoted in Carroll, 28) – feature happy music-making of the recommended kind. Dorothea Brook, who despises conventional accomplishments, is "very glad" that her first husband is indifferent to the piano: "She smiled and looked up at her betrothed with grateful eyes. If he had always been asking her to play the 'Last Rose of Summer,' she would have required much resignation." (1:7:64) The ambitious young doctor Tertius Lydgate is meditating on a scientific problem while enjoying the sounds of his wife's "quiet music which was as helpful to his meditation as the plash of an oar on the evening lake". He has blissfully forgotten everything "except the construction of a new controlling experiment" when Rosamond, who has left the piano to watch him, shocks him out of his reverie with a galling reminder of their financial difficulties (7:64:643-644). Finally, the eponymous heroine of George Eliot's verse narrative *Armgart* is aghast at the suggestion that she should neglect her professional work as an opera star in order to "Sing in the chimney corner to inspire / My husband reading news" (2:137-138, p. 129).

2.2. "A good cry upstairs"

> A good play on the piano
> has not infrequently taken the place of a good cry upstairs.
> Society, whilst it limits woman's sphere of action,
> frequently calls upon her to repress her feelings.
> THE REV. HUGH REGINALD HAWEIS. *Music and Morals*

Like family duties, the private musical relief which music could provide is recommended in conduct literature and debunked in fiction. Conduct manuals mention personal comfort as a well-deserved but accidental side-effect of the effort of learning to make music for the family: "All accomplishments have the great merit of giving a lady something to do; something to preserve her from *ennui*; to console her in seclusion; to arouse her in grief; to compose her to occupation in joy." (Aster, 237) The prolific Reverend Hugh Reginald Haweis uses an almost shocking metaphor, comparing the limited activities offered to women's capacities to "setting the steam-hammer to knock pins into a board": "Some outlet is wanted. [...] The steam-hammer, as it contemplates the everlasting pin's head, cannot help feeling that if some day, when the steam was on, it might give one good smashing blow, it would feel all the better for it". However, there will be no smashing of *pianos*: Haweis concludes tamely that music offers "a gentle grace of ministration little short of supernatural" (*Morals* 526).

While women's diaries and letters confirm that music did fulfil such therapeutic functions in women's lives (cf. Solie), textual strategies in fiction consistently belittle women's practice of mustering and mastering their own emotions through music[78]. As Richard Leppert

---

[78]   As so often, exceptions come from non-realistic genres such as poetry or a historical verse drama such as Edwin Arnold's *Griselda*, where the dutiful wife offers her depressed husband to "fetch the virginals" and console him with music that her own experience has taught her to use, "a measure that I love to play / When I am sad" (3:3, p. 106).

comments, a woman's music was to be "a positive reflection, not on her, but on her husband" and so she had "to restrain any acknowledgement of musical devotion (her attachment to music for her own sake)" (70). Consequently, music is trivialized into a mere anodyne relief from boredom or tension, a noisier alternative to needlework. The recently married Lady Isabel in Mrs. Henry Wood's bestseller *East Lynne* finds it hard to describe her day: "Trying the new piano, and looking at my watch, wishing the time might go quicker, that you might come home" (1:240). When Phoebe Fulmort in Charlotte Yonge's *Hopes and Fears* deafens herself to family tensions early in the morning, subtlety is destroyed and music silenced to become a mere screening noise: "Aware that nothing pleasant was passing, and that, be it what it might, she could do no good, she was glad to stop her ears with music, until eight o'clock brought a pause in the shape of breakfast" (1:2:134).

Music may also simply fail as a solace. Rosamond Lydgate, depressed with her husband's financial difficulties, cannot even muster the energy to play:

> [S]he arranged all objects around her with the same nicety as ever, only with more slowness – or sat down to the piano, meaning to play, and then desisting, yet lingering on the music stool with her white fingers suspended on the wooden front, and looking before her in dreamy ennui. (Eliot, *Middlemarch* 8:77:760)

The blind heroine of Wilkie Collins's *Poor Miss Finch* tries to get a new acquaintance out of her mind by listening and playing to herself pieces from "Beethoven to Schubert. From Schubert to Chopin [...] with all the will in the world to be pleased", the distraction fails: "No! [...] His voice was still in her ears – the only music which could possess itself of her attention that night. [...] 'I can't help thinking of him!'" (1:5:26) When she celebrates the futile hopes she invests in an eye operation by improvising and adapting melodies to the refrain "I shall see him! I shall see him!" "with hands that seemed mad for joy – hands that threatened every moment to snap the chords of the instrument" (2:33:229-230), the piano is threatened by her exuberance and transgressively unsophisticated performance, and she seems to be punished for this: her emotions are not stilled by music and her sight is restored only for a very short time.

Lucilla Finch's disappointed hopes are an example of the third way in which women's private playing is restrained: Wilkie Collin's sensation novels recurrently use such repressive plot turns. Magdalen Vanstone in Collins's *No Name* daydreams about a man who turns out to be too weak and selfish for a satisfactory husband: like Miss Finch, she appropriates music, combining pieces such as "the Songs of Mendelssohn, the Mazurkas of Chopin, the Operas of Verdi, and the Sonatas of Mozart" to produce "one immortal work, entitled 'Frank'", then retiring to her room to dream away the hours in luxurious – and illusory – visions of her married future (10:100). At the beginning of *The Moonstone*, Rachel Verinder and her fiancé Franklin Blake sing and play duets contentedly, "in a manner most wonderful and pleasant to hear through the open window, on the terrace at night" (1:7:81). When Rachel begins to suspect Franklin of theft, she uses the piano to vent her worries and ward off explanatory conversations.

> I heard a few plaintive chords on the piano in the room within. She had often idled over the instrument in this way [...]. After the lapse of a minute, I roused my manhood, and opened the door. [...] At the moment when I showed myself in the doorway, Rachel rose from the piano. I closed the door behind me. We confronted each other in silence, with the full length of the room between us. (2:3:6 and 7:390)

This erotic tension, set up – though not accompanied – by music, is detestable to the sanctimonious Miss Clack, who criticizes Rachel's selection "of the most scandalously profane sort [of music], associated with performances on the stage which it curdles one's blood to think of" (2:1:7:295). Miss Clack is a caricature, but her narrative co-constitutes Collins's novel, and here provides some fun but also a reassuring framework for Rachel's disquieting femininity.

> BEETHOVEN – keeps me company.
> WILKIE COLLINS. *Armadale*

For better pianists, stronger containment is needed: the two best players in nineteenth-century English literature are ultimately restrained by death, punished for their powerful personalities which unite superlative musicianship with bigamy and murder. From girlhood through to her bigamous second marriage, the heroine of Mary Elizabeth Braddon's *Lady Audley* represents that perfect surface ideal of musical womanhood which is, paradoxically, never represented as genuine. In her childhood, her "singing, her playing, her dancing, her beautiful smile, and sunshiny ringlets" (1:3:32) were perfect, although her former employer at a girls' school qualifies her as "only ornamental; a person to be shown off to visitors, and to play fantasias on the drawing-room piano" (2:8:235). For her second, rich husband she plays "dreamy melodies by Beethoven and Mendelssohn till [he] fell asleep in his easy chair" (1:1:10) – a textbook scenario, marred only by marks on her wrists which witness the recent struggle to push her first husband down a well (cf. 2:11). Once this secret threatens to come out, Lady Audley can no longer enjoy the womanly refinement and artistic perfection of her room: "My lady's piano was open, covered with scattered sheets of music and exquisitely-bound collections of scenas and fantasias which no master need have disdained to study" – but she is so wretched that "the pleasure we take in art and loveliness being an innocent pleasure had passed beyond her reach" (1:11:170).

Lydia Gwilt in Wilkie Collins's *Armadale* has not become as famous as Lady Audley but is far more interesting[79]. This murderess enjoys music as long as she can make it, and her intelligence and sardonic wit make it hard to imagine her soothing any lord and master. Her unusual and impressive wickedness – which includes a touch of integrity in her remorse and suicide after saving her husband from her own murderous plot – corresponds to a highly individual attitude to music. Miss Gwilt never plays in company and despises average performers: "Half the musical girls in England ought to have their fingers chopped off, in the interests of society" (2:6:344). Music is for her own comfort and she vigorously defends her right to practise against her husband's needs: "I can't go out – it's raining. If I open the piano, I shall disturb the industrious journalist who is scribbling in the next room. [...] Shall I read? No; books don't interest me; I hate the whole tribe of authors." (4:1:662) Lydia Gwilt's music does not aim at the 'gentle relief' recommended by the Reverend Haweis: "I must go and forget myself at my piano. There is the 'Moonlight Sonata' open, and tempting me, on the music-stand. Have I nerve enough to play it, I wonder? Or will it set me shuddering with the mystery and terror of it, as it did the other day?" (3:10:515) Violating further codes of feminine performance, she professes indifference to men in general and puts a musical demi-god to her exclusive personal use: "I am very comfortable in this lodging. [...] I have hired a reasonably good piano. The only man I care two straws about – don't be alarmed; he was laid in his grave many a long year ago, under the name of BEETHOVEN – keeps me company." (3:1:193)

Beethoven is a highly significant choice. For the mid-Victorians, he meant intellectual rigour; the pianist and composer John Francis Barnett remembers being told as a young man that "it was a pity my

---

[79] I am grateful to Alison Samuels for bringing this character to my attention.

playing was thrown away on such dry music" (2). In Mary Elizabeth Braddon's *Aurora Floyd*, the handsome Captain Bulstrode, conducting a conventional courtship with chess, duets and advice about watercolours, classically "lean[s] over Lucy [Floyd]'s piano or drawing-board". However, he is becoming more and more fascinated with Lucy's cousin Aurora, as can be seen from the fact that he frequently "forgot to turn over the leaf in the Beethoven sonatas [...] and gave her wandering, random answers when she spoke to him" (1:5:100-101). The pious poet and hymn-writer Frances Havergal, who mapped the "Moonlight Sonata" bar by bar onto a spiritual itinerary in her poem of the same name, yet describes a young piano pupil's dismay at being told to practice the piece:

> Oh, such a music-task as this
> Was never hers before!
> So long and hard, so strange and stern, –
> A piece she thinks she cannot learn,
> Though practised o'er and o'er.

> It is not beautiful to her, –
> She cannot grasp the whole:
> The Master's thought was great and deep, –
> A mighty storm, to seize and sweep
> The wind-harp of the soul. ("Moonlight Sonata" ll. 26-35)

Wilkie Collins does not aim such preaching at Lydia Gwilt's transgressively self-determined music, which is extinguished together with her independence only in death, but fascinating as she is, the narrative cannot ultimately condone her crimes or the riotous intellectual autonomy with which she plays Beethoven.

The idea that truly accomplished playing for personal pleasure can only belong to a highly suspect character is not just extrapolated from the sensation genre which *Armadale* represents. It is also implicit in the notable degree to which the notion of passivity, an essential desideratum of Victorian womanhood, determines texts about women playing for themselves. At the opening of the first women's college in London (which did have music on its curriculum), Frederick Denison Maurice opined that women should "view music more simply, and therefore more profoundly, to care less for its displays and results, and therefore to have their hearts and understandings more open to the reception" (8). A girl "whose performance is quite unfit for society in these days of artist-like perfection"[80] will find solace in playing for herself because, while drawing or intellectual pursuits require energy for preparation, the piano is always ready and will itself wake up a languid performer: " [A]t first, perhaps the hand will wander listlessly over the notes, but the chords of some favourite air are struck almost unconsciously, and then gradually the languor is dispersed, the interest roused, and a whole new train of associations excited" (Grey and Shirreff, 2:228-229). Passive grammatical constructions take over defensively as soon as the woman is activated by her own incipient music.

The two most lovable heroines in George Eliot's mature work, which habitually uses musicality as "an index to the individual's potential for growth" (Binstock, 229), have a passive, receptive musicality completely unassociated with performance. Dorothea Brooke in *Middlemarch* disagrees with her uncle's idea that "up to a certain point, women should", and the narrator considers that Dorothea's "slight regard for domestic music and feminine fine art must be forgiven her" (1:7:64), but proves her *receptive* musicality by, for example, her liking for "the grander forms of music": "When we were coming home from Lausanne my uncle took us to hear the great organ at Freiberg, and it made me sob" (1:7:54). Maggie Tulliver in *The Mill on the Floss* is no performer either, but deeply susceptible to music and – symbolic perhaps of her fundamental isolation – poignantly her own listener:

> The mere concord of octaves was a delight to Maggie, and she would often take up a book of studies rather than any melody, that she might taste more keenly by abstraction the more primitive sensation of intervals. Not that her enjoyment of music was of the kind that indicates a great specific talent; it was rather that her sensibility to the supreme excitement of music was only one form of that passionate sensibility which [...] made her faults and virtues all merge in each other. (6:6:426)

What such images of passivity and receptive sensibility obliterate is the fact that both Maggie's etudes and the chords of the favourite air which steal their way back into a girl's passive fingers must earlier

---

[80] Mrs. Frances Hullah is the only source I have found to claim that "ten times more musical power" would be necessary for a solitary player "to make the pianoforte an agreeable companion", while in company "it is not so much music, as something to break silence and dissipate dulness, that is wanted" (23).

have been deciphered and assiduously practised to become so readily available in moments of dreamy reminiscence.

2.3. Practising: 'Music and Morals'

> The piano makes a girl sit up and pay attention to details.
> THE REV. HUGH REGINALD HAWEIS. *Music and Morals*

As the discursive frankness of the decades before Victoria's accession disappeared, courtship was no longer freely available as a justification of long practice hours. A wide array of substitute prescriptions came into play, which reasserted the English tradition of valuing the social *effects* of music over the *quality* of performance in way which amounts to a perverse hidden agenda of mediocrity. *Music and Morals* is the title of a popular book of the period, but that relationship is more complex than the simple "and" suggests. Musical industry is demanded from every girl, but the virtuosity which it might foster is cautioned against rather than admired. However, the recommendations to limit practising are no longer motivated by a concern about stunted moral and intellectual development but by worries about neglected familial duties. In turn, such duties could include practising the piano, which was problematic also because, as Ros Ballaster puts it, "man's domestic pleasure depended on the illusion that home was maintained without any work other than his". The home, and that includes the piano, is "both the site of woman's work *and* of the denial of that work" (89). This cycle of contradictions necessitates convoluted arguments which fight the threats of female empowerment and musical rapture on many fronts at once. The central aim of enforcing and containing music in a way that makes non-threatening social uses possible becomes particularly visible through an analysis of regulations and representations of practising.

A new argument in favour is that the *expense* for instrument and tutoring is "a clear indication of the duty of the child to strive after proficiency". A daughter who refuses her family's musical wishes but plays anything they like to guests and strangers is a "painful spectacle": "What must the parents of such a daughter feel, if they recollect the fact that it was at their expense their child acquired this pleasing art, by which she appears anxious to charm any one but them?" (Ellis, 106) Such duty does not cease with adulthood and the removal of the "constraints of authoritative education" but turns her skill into "an element to be taken into account in regulating her future avocations,

and in estimating the duties of that state of life to which it has pleased
God to call her" ("Agnes" 405). On the other hand, music "is abused,
when it is made so important as to engross much time and money;
[...] and when the gratification is sought in public assemblies, in
which the company, the display, and the expense are all objection-
able" (*British Mothers' Magazine* quoted in Da Sousa Correa, 67). It
is the family, rather than "company" that must be serviced by the
piano, but expense remains ambigouos.

This service ethic also determines musical choices: "[N]ever does a
daughter appear to more advantage than when she cheerfully lays
aside a fashionable air, and strums over, for more than the hundredth
time, some old ditty which her father loves." The conclusion is chilling: "To her ear it is possible it may be altogether divested of the
slightest charm. But of what importance is that?" (Ellis, 104) Indeed,
practising that becomes a passionate pursuit is mere "abuse", as when
a woman "neglects her children's education for the sake of practising
four hours a day" or when a man "fancies himself a Mario [i. e. a rival
for the famous operatic tenor Giovanni Matteo Mario], and is a nuisance to all his friends" (Aïdé, "Amateur Music" 93). Matilda Pullan
considers that where accomplishments are "the *best* part of a girl's
education, they lose half even of their beauty, and almost all of their
value" (72). Mediocre playing suffices for most purposes and is morally safer than great skill, which is a "temptation to pride and vanity"
("Agnes" 407) and can be made "to minister to sin and to foster the
natural evil of the heart" (406).

Fiction follows suit. Anne Brontë's Agnes Grey, a governess, criticizes over-application in a vivacious teenage pupil: "[T]he love of
display had roused her faculties, and induced her to apply herself, but
only to the more showy accomplishments [...]. To music, indeed, she
devoted too much of her time: as, governess though I was, I frequently
told her" (*Agnes Grey* 7:67). Charles Reade's *Hard Cash* makes these
conventions explicit: music is a pious duty but leads to vanity. Young
Jane is asked to play to cover an embarrassing moment at a party and
worries:

> "I have forsworn these vanities. I have not opened my piano these two years. [...]
> I don't go so far as to call music wicked: but music in society is such a snare. At
> least I found it so; my playing was highly praised; and that stirred up vanity: and
> so did my singing, with which I had even more reason to be satisfied. Snares!
> snares!" (1:5:162)

The consideration that finally makes Jane relent and play is the idea that her mother is "not to be disobeyed upon a doubt" (1:5:162) – parental will being the ultimate authority.

Since technical excellence is so dubious, the question arises: why practice? To abandon music as an element in girls' education was simply inconceivable and so other reasons for the activity had to be found. Hugh Reginald Haweis famously state that Latin strengthens the memory (of boys) while "the piano makes a girl sit up and pay attention to details" (*Morals* 515). Piano practice is useful because the

> cultivation of *any* power or talent [...] demands in some degree, industry and perseverance; and may be employed as an instrument for gaining the mastery over that indolence and self-indulgence which are among the great hinderances [sic] to spiritual life, and to usefulness in the world. ("Agnes" 405)

Practice is no longer aimed at mastery of the instrument but becomes an instrument for mastering the self. In her evangelical youth, at nineteen, George Eliot was the best pianist at her school but doubted the pureness of musical pleasure because it "involves the devotion of all the time and powers of an immortal being to the acquirement of an expertness in so useless [...] an accomplishment" (*Letters* 1:13). Thirty years later, for all her love and understanding of music, which had even led her to visit Franz Liszt in Weimar, she still contemplated non-musical rationales for what was not supposed to be striving for 'expertness': "I think it will be good for me hygienically [!] as well as on other grounds, to be roused into practising." (4:478)

It was William Thackeray, ever the sharpest observer, to denounce these obsessions with hygiene and perseverance for what they really meant. He calls music "prison-work" for women, done because they have "no other exercising ground for their poor little thoughts and fingers; and hence these wonderful pincushions are executed, these counterpanes woven, these sonatas learned" ("Ravenswing" 411). The association of pincushions with sonatas would seem correct in "few times and places apart from Victorian England" (Smith, "Music" 521) but is no mere joke here. There really were pianos that incorporated sewing tables and work boxes or could be turned into couches[81]; all symptomatic of the Victorian project of turning threatening musical femaleness into domesticated femininity. The disciplinary effect of practising could be enhanced by 'industrial' methods: scales and exercises were no longer regulated just by the speed-keeping metronome,

---

[81] Cf. Closson, 140-141, Harding, 435-436, and Burgess, 14.

but also by gymnastic machines and straps, which reinforced the piano's potential for controlling the body. Beginning with the 1814 Chi-
roplast, there were Patent Elastic Bracelets, Bohrer's Automatic Hand
Guide, Improved Hand Guide, Wrist Strengthener, Ostrovsky's Musician's Hand Development Apparatus, Musical Gloves and many others (cf. the advertisements quoted in Scholes, 331-334) that trapped
hands to the keyboard, immobilized wrists and weighted down single
fingers to enhance the independent action of others.

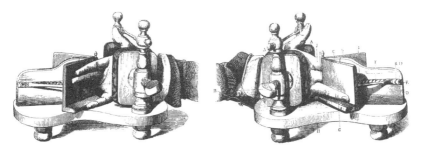

*Figure 3: Nineteenth-century device for controlling a pianist's hand position (Gaines,
29).*

Small wonder that Thackeray's "too susceptible heart" bled at the
sight of "kind innocent fresh-cheeked young women go[ing] to a piano" and that he scolded: "what evidences of slavery, in a word, are
there!" ("Ravenswing" 411)

   Ultimately, the aim of practising is not mastery, but slavery. This is
underlined by the recurrent remarks that those efforts are doomed to
failure in any case. Piano apparatuses contributed to placing technical
mastery out of reach in a realm of mechanical perfection. Without extraordinary talent and application, "an enormous proportion of the
time required for general education" may go into piano practice yet "it
is not to be expected that she will rise above mediocrity" (Baker,
"Early Education" 245, quoted in Binstock, 111). Hours and hours of
practice were forced on hopeless players, as Frances Power Cobbe
remembers in her memoir:

> One day I said [...] "My dear Fraulein, I mean to practise this piece of Beet-
> hoven's till I conquer it." "My dear" responded the honest Fraulein, "you do
> practise that piece for seex hours a day, and you do live till you are seexty, at the
> end you will not play it!" Yet so hopeless a pupil was compelled to learn for
> years, not only the piano, but the harp and singing! (64-65)

Most teachers were not as honest as this German lady: as a rule, untalented pupils were encouraged to persevere with the promise that they might master the piano *eventually* – "and what is of more consequence, [acquire] habits of perseverance, industry, method and good humour" (Hullah, *Words* 49). Nobody "would wish a wife or a daughter, moving in private society, to have attained such excellence in music as involves a life's devotion to it" (Pullan, 82), but devoted practice still had to happen.

A manual on *The Habits of Good Society* describes – without the slightest irony – mediocre musical performance as an outright necessity because the English are not "a nation of talkers" ("naturally, our talent is for silence") and therefore need substitutes for conversation. To that end, there is nothing like music, "carefully played" and "without that great execution which *compels* listening", serving as a "slight and agreeable interruption" from which conversation "flows the more easily" (Aster, 230-231). As Arthur Sullivan said: "We do indeed love music, but it is with an inferior affection to that [for] other objects in life. We have not yet ceased to talk while music is being performed" (271). Although the cultivation of "second and third class faculties" is "the bane of the musical world" and "never worth while spending much time, money and trouble upon" (Haweis, *Ideals* 24), "the benefits of being able to play even a little" were "substantial", adding as they did "to a girl's social utility" (40).

If talent *was* undeniable, it was just conceived as saving time because a talented girls could easily attain the wherewithal to accompany simple songs "for the recreation of the domestic circle [...] without involving a sacrifice of the time required for other pursuits". If superior achievement was unquestionable, it could yet be ridiculed as mechanical. What is achieved "by perseverance" (the perseverance which is itself a moral goal of practising!) "is not real excellence, and cannot be regarded as worth the time and labour expended upon it" (Baker, "Early Education" 245, quoted in Binstock, 111). Unlike the violin, the piano can be mastered to some degree by "a certain mechanical process, similar to that by which she acquires dexterity in [...] crochet-knitting". Such "fruitless waste of time and application" may yield "the habit of touching the right keys, but all which constitutes the soul of music must be wanting" (Ellis, 101). "Two-thirds of the young ladies who can rattle through a host of polkas and waltzes with a brilliant finger, would be completely posed when they attempted Beethoven or Mendelssohn" (Hullah, *Words* 4-5).

The piano pest is tyrannical and absurd.
ANON. *Eliza Cook's Journal*

Such enforced, mechanical piano practising is of course a tremendous nuisance. In the home of "some Country Snobs" as described by Thackeray, "strumming begins at six o'clock in the morning" and never stops except for "a minute's intermission, when the instrument changes hands, and MISS EMILY practises in place of her sister, MISS MARIA", to be followed by the governess who "hammers away [...] and keeps her magnificent fingers in exercise" ("Snobs" 16:392)[82]. The head of the family feels compelled to apologize: "My girls, you know, practise four hours a-day, you know – must do it, you know – absolutely necessary." In fact, clubs are the only refuge from "the interminable discords and shrieks which are elicited from the miserable piano during the above necessary operation" (27:435). A poem jocularly incites girls to annoying musical frenzy:

> Play, play, your sonatas in A,
> Heedless of what your next neighbour may say! [...]
> Sing, play – if your neighbours inveigh
> Feebly against you, they're lunatics, eh? [...]
> Rattle the 'bones,' hit a tinbottom'd tray
> Hard with the fireshovel, hammer away! (Calverley, 22-33)

It was too much. Even Shakespeare was called to repent of his advice to distrust "a man that hath no music in himself" (*Merchant of Venice* 5:1:83): "If you could but contemplate the evils [this] has occasioned! [...] In families the piano has extinguished conversation and the love of books [...], and it is difficult to pass between two houses without having a sonata thrown at you from one of them." (H. C. M., 7) The annoyance with practising spills over on to performances, focussing on their ridiculously mechanical aspects or an inferior repertoire: "For once that you hear any real music from a piano, do you not five hundred times hear mere artistic somersaults, distorted jingling, and the hapless pretence of music?" (Thomas Carlyle, quoted in Young, *Concert* 34-35) With such saturation, even page-turning lost its once-effective charms (see above 84). Arthur Hugh Clough's Oxford undergraduates on holiday in Scotland exalt the unspoilt local girls who do not demand "dull farces of escort" such as "going shopping together, and hearing [girls] singing, / Dangling beside them, and turning the leaves on the dreary piano" ("Bothie" 2:56-57, p. 51).

---

[82]   Piano skills were vital for obtaining and keeping governess jobs.

Such complaints about the dreariness of mediocre playing make it even more striking that fiction does not allow for admirable female virtuosity in the service of great music. As conduct literature continues to insist on both the necessity of practice and the undesirability of proficiency, admirable effort and admirable achievement are both elided from fiction. Extraordinary talent in a positive character is only allowed when death and piety circumscribe it. Camilla Toulmin's *Hildred* features a girl with "the double gift of a rich voice and a rare genius for music" (169) – but that prodigy is only seven years old, incredibly pious and the daughter of a terminally ill seamstress. An offer of free tuition leaves her speechless – she can only reply to her mother's remonstrances: "I was thanking God first." (152)

There was worse. An Oxford sermon from the 1860s fights Darwinist ideas with reference to music: "When I have listened to those inspiring words 'I know that my Redeemer liveth' sung to Handel's divine music, I have felt that it is indeed a long way from that to the squealing of some hideous ape in a primeval forest" (quoted in Weatherly, 59). Just as only words could make music impure (see above 112), it is the biblical words set to music by a near-sainted composer (the sermon omits to mention that the aria from *The Messiah* is set for soprano, a female voice) that make music fit to be instrumentalized for a Creationist argument. The opposite potential was always lurking very close beneath the surface. A nasty little newspaper item about a monkey "educated [...] to become a good pianist" reports in 1886 that after "only forty-eight lessons [...] the monkey, Tabitha, who is a real ornament to her sex, could play scales with surprising dexterity" (*Musical Times* September 1886, 528). The wordlessness and stupidity of the piano repertoire makes the humanity of its practitioners irrelevant, reducing them to a gendered placeholder. When she sits at the piano, the monkey is not heard to produce 'hideous squeals' and it becomes glorisouly obvious that practising scales is more essential to femininity than being *homo sapiens*[83].

This is one extreme of the social and literary constraints on performance that are turning into a straitjacket in the mid-nineteenth

---

[83]   An early example is Thomas Love Peacock's civilized ape Sir Oran Haut-Ton. He superficially conforms to male stereotyping because he plays the flute and the French horn, but is more significantly feminine because he is mute and cannot read music, but performs by ear "with great exactness and brilliancy of execution" (*Melincourt* 130-131).

century. The piano becomes a victim of its own indispensability: mediocrity is demanded; musical enjoyment must be disparaged; musical achievement must be denied. Any number of imaginable options for plot and nuances of characterization that were open to earlier and later writers are excluded in these attempts to define and weigh down what Richard Leppert calls the "unstable locus of music in Victorian society" (186). In *Hildred*, too, the containment of music is overdetermined: a strikingly repressive narrative combines piety, silence, immaturity, and death to still its disquieting potentials.

3. Strategies of Representation: 'Handel with Care'

> Sex [as is music] is not a thing which stubbornly shows itself,
> but one which always hides, the insidious presence
> that speaks in a voice so muted, and often disguised
> that one risks remaining deaf to it.
> MICHEL FOUCAULT. *The History of Sexuality*

Repressive narrative techniques like those in *Hildred* – although usually less spectacular – determine virtually all accounts of women's music in fiction. A more systematic analysis of the narrative strategies which contain and repress music throughout the canon will therefore end this chapter. Some of them, such as disapproval and specularity, continue time-honoured topoi with a new intensity, while the distancing effects of religious 'sanitizing' and the deflection which exempts positive female figures completely from keyboard proficiency are more particular to the Victorian discourse.

3.1. Disapproval (Deprecate and Denounce)

Denunciation is the most immediately striking of the Victorian containment strategies because it is based on the standard plot elements of adultery and artful husband-trapping. The stratagems of Becky Sharp in *Vanity Fair* or the likes of Annabella Wilmot in Anne Brontë's *Tenant of Wildfell Hall*, who stings the eponymous heroine into jealousy of a despicable husband by singing and playing to him (cf. 2:8:233), have become proverbial. The stereotype is so strong that even the saintly Dorothea Brooke feels "some wonder, that Will Ladislaw was passing his time with Mrs. Lydgate in her husband's absence" (Eliot, *Middlemarch* 5:43:426) when she overhears them at music. She feels the need to extrapolate a "sad, excusing vision" of pleasurable companionship between Will and "that fair creature, who most likely shared his other tastes as she evidently did his delight in music" (8:77:760). Dr. Lydgate, who finds no such excuses, is simply annoyed:

> When he opened the door the two singers went on towards the key-note, raising their eyes and looking at him indeed, but not regarding his entrance as an interruption. To a man galled with his harness as poor Lydgate was, it is not soothing to see two people warbling at him, as he comes in [...] The singers feeling themselves excused by the fact that they had had only three bars to sing, now turned round. (6:58:577)

The greetings are curt; Will, "too quick to need more", leaves immediately. Although Rosamond does not technically betray her husband, her alienation is unmistakeably coded in this short scene.

Musical intimacy between partners that are not or will not be married to each other is a recognized pattern of transgression[84] which is inevitably punished within the paradigm that adultery must never come to fictional good. Even non-adulterous musical scheming regularly results in the failure to make the desired match or in the unhappiness of the ensuing marriage. Victorian fiction knows no successful marriage that begins with musical infatuation: in order to contain the subversive, disturbing potential of music, texts must first of all suppress also its positive results.

One topic of denunciation harks back to such Regency frights as Mrs. Falconer (see above 87): blaming marital misery on musically scheming mothers. The shallow, spoilt, "eternally strumming" Rosey Mackenzie in Thackeray's *The Newcomes* has her mamma at her "with prodigious vehemence of language, and sometimes with a slap on poor Rosey's back" (23:226). Rosey herself has no opinions, preferring to have her ideas "dealt out to her like her frocks, bonnets, handkerchiefs, her shoes and gloves". She "trusts for all supplies corporeal and spiritual to her mother" and is, for herself, "pleased with

---

[84] In George Meredith's *Ordeal of Richard Feverel*, seduction begins with dinner and drinks for two and is then intensified by music. Secure of young Richard's sentimental attachment ("O Bella! Let me save you", 38:454), the experienced Bella Mount pulls the musical stop: "'You don't know all my accomplishments yet, Richard. [...] You saw the piano – why didn't you ask me to sing before? I can sing Italian. I had a master – who made love to me.' [...] He was in the mood when imagination intensely vivifies everything. Mere suggestions of music sufficed", and no "word of love" is necessary (38:455)."Was ever hero in this fashion won?" (38:458)

everything in nature. Does she love music? O, yes. Bellini and Donizetti? O, yes." (24:248) Thackeray's descriptions of her performances obliquely preclude admiration: "To her mother's excellent accompaniment Rosey sang her favourite songs (by the way her stock was very small – five, I think, was the number)" (23:231). Nevertheless, the sensitive, thoughtful artist Clive Newcome is trapped, with depressingly predictable results. Two years into a hellish marriage, Rosey has given up playing "the most magnificent piano" (63:658) in her fine new house, and even after her death in childbirth, the narrator can imagine Clive's marriage to his true love Ethel only in a remote "Fable-land".

Mrs. Gaskell describes the comeuppance of a "piano mother" with a less tragic relish in her magazine story "Uncle Peter". Parading her daughter to a rich relative, Mrs. Howard overreaches herself: "A moment, my dear; you have not asked your dear uncle what he would like. What style of music do you prefer, sir? my daughter sings all – French, German, Italian, Scotch, Irish, or English; which shall it be?" Uncle Peter, not to be manipulated, chooses German and forces the mother to ask her demurring daughter "with the slightest approach to acrimony in her benignant tones" for 'all' her German songs. Julia has just one and is asked to play "whatever you have, then, my dear". The performance, "throughout a semitone too low" (443-444) drives Uncle Peter from the room, his musical discernment functioning as a positive quality in order to thwart Mrs. Howard.

The Way of All Flesh (see above 119) contains a report (probably based on childhood memories) on the courtship stratagems of the numerous and desperate Allaby sisters who play at cards for the right to ensnare Theobald, their father's latest curate. The winner is Christina, "the second unmarried daughter, then just twenty-seven years old and therefore four years older than Theobald" (Butler, 11:43). Theobald is an easy victim: "He told a college friend that he knew he was in love now; he really was, for he liked Miss Allaby's society much better than that of his sisters" (11:45). Butler's description of Christina's actual strategies gains an extra edge from his unusually precise technical knowledge of music. She uses "what was supposed to be a very beautiful contralto voice", making up what it "wanted in range and power" by "the feeling with which she sang" and some technical adjustments:

> She had transposed "Angels ever bright and fair" into a lower key, so as to make
> it suit her voice, thus proving, as her mamma said, that she had a thorough knowl-

> edge of the laws of harmony; not only did she do this, but at every pause added an embellishment of arpeggios from one end to the other of the keyboard [...]; she thus added life and interest to an air which everyone – so she said – "must feel to be rather heavy in the form in which Handel left it". (11:45)

Butler's personal admiration for Handel's (no longer very fashionable) music adds a particular bitterness to the satire of this passage. Butler notes that he made his *alter ego* Ernest, the son of Theobald and Christina, play the music of modern virtuoso composers such as Beethoven and Mendelssohn "simply *ad captandum* [... but] as a matter of fact he played none but early Italian, old English music and Handel – but Handel most of all" (*Notebooks* 110). This observation confirms the disdain for Christina's success with 'embellished' Handel. To make sure that the reader keeps a distance from the helplessly fascinated male, the narrator adds: "Nevertheless, it was some time before Theobald could bring his courage to the sticking point of actually proposing." (*Way of All Flesh* 11:45) Theobald's claim, years later, that he has "always disliked" (34:144) music, rounds off the depreciation.

Even the blazons that outline a girl's marketability use not subversive irony but open disdain for their subjects (usually secondary characters). Catherine Sinclair, whose anti-accomplishment agenda had been obvious since her 1837 *Modern Accomplishments* (see above 78), has a later heroine disparage her sisters' skills as "mere Palais Royal jewellery, of no intrinsic worth" and requiring "no mind or exertion":

> Elizabeth was a brilliant musician of the new school. Singing the most astonishing bravuras, and performing long [piano] pieces full of chromatic difficulties and wonderful effects, with frequent changes in the key. [...] To the generality of visitors, such frantic pieces were an unknown tongue. (*Jane Bouverie* 7:77-78)

This is fairly transparent campaigning, but novels with a less palpable educational agenda also contain perceptibly soured descriptions, as the one introducing Trollope's Lizzie Greystock, whose narrator does not pretend that 'we' truly admire her:

> Lizzie's eyes were not tender, – neither were they true. But they were surmounted by the most wonderfully pencilled eyebrows [...] We must add that she had in truth studied much. She spoke French, understood Italian, and read German. She played well on the harp, and moderately well on the piano. She sang, at least in good taste and in tune. [...] She forgot nothing, listened to everything, understood quickly, and was desirous to shine not only as a beauty but as a wit. (*Eustace Diamonds* 1:2:18)

Mention of the showy harp adds to the disapproval by which such narratives avoid readerly identification with the listeners.

The implicit suspicion of an art which is supposedly incapable of expressing an "impure thought" parallels the contradictory myth of the pure woman which Isobel Armstrong has described:

> [A]n impossible female docility can only be given ultimate credence when it is seen as the product of artfulness or duplicity. Hence […] the pure woman is contemplated with an odd mixture of adulation and anger [because …] a coercive model of womanhood as pure and weak leads to an equally coercive notion of woman as cunning and artful. ("Browning" 270-271)

This combination is perfectly expressed by a musical rebus, "MATERNAL ADVICE Addressed to a young English lady on her début into fashionable life" (Ella, 28):

Figure 4: Musical Rebus *(Ella, 28).*

The implicit injunction is "See [i. e. look] natural, be sharp" – to hide intelligence or cleverness under an innocent appearance. The fact that C natural and B sharp are actually the same pitch makes this succinct summary of (musical) tactics that are denounced in fiction even more telling: Purity *equals* weakness and cunning, but also necessitates and therefore excuses or masks them. This corresponds exactly to a second set of literary strategies: those of belittling the influence of women's music while praising it – often literally – to the skies.

3.2. Disinfection

> Only in England,
> musicianship has been really seriously hampered
> by the unmusical seekers after edification.
> ERNEST WALKER. *A History of Music in England*

Victorian texts rob powerful, potentially exciting musicianship of its impact in two ways. On the one hand, music is exalted to celestial status, to an unreachable height and away from concrete, threatening performances; on the other hand, the strong emotions which it provokes are dampened by a chastening context which often involves religion and/or death[85]. In a prayer for brides on the eve of the wedding that is suggested in H. R. Haweis's *Ideals for Girls*, the young woman is advised to preserve her "childlike" mind "Till at the last you set yourself to move / Like perfect music unto noble words" (140). "[At] the last" hints at consummated, matured marriage, but is also a formula for death – presumably the woman's; and she is once again an abstract inarticulate commodity – "thou, my music" –, subordinate to the masculine word. Her virtue is defined negatively as 'all that not harms distinctive womanhood' (140) or as childlikeness; the sanctification of music and de-eroticisation of musical emotion clearly derogate both music and fully adult womanhood.

Dickens was particularly good at this. The "perfect rapture" (*Oliver Twist* 2:32:211) which Rose Maylie's playing provides for the convalescent Oliver Twist on balmy summer evenings is subdued by his bad health and soon further 'disinfected' by hers: Rose turns out to be Oliver's aunt, which excludes romantic attraction, and her next performance is the prelude to a serious illness. Playing a low and solemn air, she is heard to sob "as if she were weeping" and stops: "'I don't know what it is; I can't describe it; but I feel –' [...] The young lady, making an effort to recover her cheerfulness, strove to play some livelier tune; her fingers dropped powerless on the keys: and covering her face with her hands, she sank upon a sofa" (2:32:212-213). Time and again, narratives intervene before powerful music can overcome the man or rob the woman player of her strength or voice ("I can't describe"). In Thackeray's *The Newcomes*, ageing spinsterhood hedges the powerful musical experiences which nurture Clive Newcome's budding artistry. Haydn, Handel and even *Don Giovanni* inspire Clive through the "beautiful sounds and thoughts which Miss Cann conveys to him out of her charmed piano"; but the piano is "[o]ld and weazened" and her voice "feeble and cracked" (11:122).

Even when music is at work within long-established marriages or families, distancing gestures are unmistakeable. Death, silence and limited skill contain Amelia Osborne's music when she is mourning her husband and "touching, to the best of her simple art, melancholy harmonies on the keys, and weeping over them in silence" (Thackeray, *Vanity Fair* 59:582). The old air which prompts Florence Dombey's

---

[85] In elegiac poems, this often takes the form of the actual death of the woman pianist who is then merely remembered, often by a lover sitting at her instrument (cf. Hohl Trillini, "The Dear Dead Past").

memories of her little brother Paul is "so softly played and sung, that it was more like the mournful recollection [...] than the reality repeated" (Dickens, *Dombey* 18:175). Minutes before Mr. Vanstone in Wilkie Collins's *No Name* dies in a railway crash, his wife, at home, is moved to find that he has kept her old music-book among his things. She starts reminiscing happily about "the golden days when his hand turned the pages for her, when his voice had whispered the words which no woman's memory ever forgets" (10:103).

Strong pre-marital attachments such as the pupil-teacher relationship in a didactic tale from the Reverend Haweis's *Ideals for Girls* require even stronger safeguards. The dedicatedly musical Emily has lessons from a great musician, but only when this genius dies of consumption, Emily is explicitly happy to "*have had* [my emphasis] such a master, and caught from such a gifted and pure genius her earliest musical aspiration". The narratorial approval of her careful tending of the master's grave – "You are quite right, my dear, I honour you for it; for you owe to him who lies beneath the deepest art impulses of your life" (43) – betrays a palpable sense of thankfulness that a further development of these "impulses" should have been so neatly curtailed. In *The Autobiography of Mark Rutherford*, a young woman refuses the hero's suit, pleading duties to her ageing father, only to die shortly after him. Rutherford discovers his love when she is singing: "Mary pleaded that as they had no piano, Mr Rutherford would not care for her poor voice without accompaniment. But I, too, protested that she should, and she got out the 'Messiah'" (White, 6:114). Mary's voice, perfectly feminine, "was not powerful, but it was pure" and in "He was despisèd" it "wound itself into the very centre of my existence" (6:115-117). Such powerful emotion can only be expressed here because the musician and the relationship are doomed, because the piano is avoided and because the choice of music is eminently chastening: the text of the contralto aria is a description of the suffering Redeemer taken from Isaiah 53 and opens the narrative of the passion in Handel's oratorio.

Coventry Patmore's verse narrative "The Angel in the House", a celebration of a perfect Victorian courtship and marriage, could be expected to offer a respectable space to the piano. When the prospective lover and husband is approaching the house where the "little Honoria" he used to know has grown nubile in the six years since his last visit, the instrument could come triumphantly into its (or her) own. But there is merely an open window revealing that "some one in the Study play'd / The Wedding-March of Mendelssohn" (1:1:2:19-20, p. 8). This is all. The bride-to-be and her piano remain invisible and instead of a bewitching drawing-room piece, the epitome of musical respectability firmly establishes the goal of the whole poem. Before the partners even meet, musical courtship is sketched in and got out of the way: none of the later encounters between the pair feature a piano.

3.3. Specularity

> This is quite the place for you,
> where you can hear all the music, and see all the young ladies.
> MARGARET OLIPHANT. *Salem Chapel*

When Oscar Wilde (not a great music-lover) announced his engagement, he described Constance as "a grave, slight, violet-eyed little Artemis, with great coils of heavy brown hair which make her flower-like head droop like a flower, and wonderful ivory hands which draw music from the piano so sweet that the birds stop singing to listen to her" (*Letters* 224). It is the birds that listen while the fiancé is concentrating on his lady's visual appearance! Wilde was obviously hamming up a very popular stereotype: "with the exception of such gentlemen as approach the piano for the sake of admiring the young ladies' fair hands and rounded arms, no-one pays the smallest attention to [their] performance" (Hullah, *Words* 21). The visual attraction of music even outweighed that of art; Frances Power Cobbe remembers that drawing commended no great respect in her boarding-school days because it was not considered "a sufficiently *voyant* [!] accomplishment" (65-66) in comparison to *music*! The "*raison d'être* of each acquirement" was not the art or craft achieved but the display of the girls, treated "like ornamental volumes for the drawing-room, to amuse an idle hour, by their external decorations of beauty and accomplishments" (Sinclair, *Jane Bouverie* 4:45). In other words: a girl had to *be* an "Ornament of Society" rather than to create ornaments.

Virtually every piano scene in fiction alludes at least in passing to the spectacle offered: "I remember your graceful figure seated at the piano in the long drawing-room, with the sunshine on your hair" (Braddon, *Aurora Floyd* 2:19:286). In Thomas Hardy's early effort *A*

Pair of Blue Eyes, Elfride Swancourt and her socially inferior admirer Stephen Smith first meet at the piano:

> Every woman who makes a permanent impression on a man is afterwards recalled to his mind's eye as she appeared in one particular scene [...]. Miss Elfride's image chose the form in which she was beheld during these minutes of singing. (1:3:38)

This image, including the lighting effects of the piano candles, is described at length. Finally, Stephen positions to "gaze [...] wistfully up into Elfride's face. So long and so earnestly gazed he, that her cheek deepened to a more and more crimson tint as each line was added to her song." (1:3:39) Continuing her song, Elfride is unable to react articulately to this extremely intrusive 'gaze of the listener'; just a flush of embarrassment 'speaks' her unease, only to render her even more attractive.

While Hardy at least records Elfride's embarrassment, other texts use the inherently belittling visual perception to criticize female figures by making them appear complicit in the visual consumption they are subjected to. Thackeray sums one heroine up: "Most persons [...] were pleased with the pretty little Rosey. She sang charmingly now, and looked so while singing" (*Newcomes* 56:589), and the troubled, immature Gwendolen Harleth is described as having "the rare advantage of looking almost prettier when she was singing than at other times" (Eliot, *Deronda* 1:5:41-42). The spectacle of Georgina Beauclerc's fairly ordinary playing in Mrs. Henry Wood's *Mildred Arkell* manages to seduce even the musical prodigy Henry Arkell. She alternately torments or upstages him: "You are stupid, Henry. Play a little louder. How I wished I played with half your taste. [...] Do you think I'd have Fred St. John? No, not though he were worth his weight in gold. [...] Henry! how exquisitely you play!" (274) Having offered to sing a song which he has forgotten, she is "found" unable to do so "and after two or three attempts, she began a waltz instead". The waltz is not described, since Henry is not listening but watching:

> Georgina wore an evening dress of white spotted muslin, a broad blue sash round her waist, and a bit of narrow blue velvet suspending a cross on her neck. She had taken off her bracelets to play, and her pretty white arms were bare. [...] What she really said [...] will never be wholly known: certain it is, that she led him on, until he resigned himself wholly to the fascination. (281-282)

Here it is quite obvious where the blame lies.

Charles Dickens has more sympathy for the troubled Edith Dombey, whose first performance is for a future husband who has "little taste for music, and no knowledge of the strain she played". He does not listen but "*saw* [my emphasis] her bending over it" and fantasizes: "perhaps he heard among the sounding strings some distant music of his own" (*Dombey* 21:210). But the passage that illustrates the suppressing effect of visuality most strikingly is one where no blame whatsoever can rest on either party – and still the music is not allowed to sound to full effect. *The Woman in White* silences the pianist even as she is playing[86]. All the sensations which Walter Hartright describes on his first evening near Laura Fairlie at the piano are visual, from Laura's profile "just delicately defined against the faintly-deepening background" to "the dawning mystery of moonlight", and the passage ends: "We all sat silent in the places we had chosen – Mrs. Vesey still sleeping, Miss Fairlie still playing, Miss Halcombe still reading – till the light failed us." (Collins, 1:8:45-46) The word 'silent' implies that nobody is speaking – but Laura Fairlie's 'playing' seems to be meant as well. Similarly, the scene does not end with the end of the (already silenced) music but with the failing of the light. Music is silenced by visual perception and silences the woman player; her wordless voice cannot keep the attention of the audience.

> As women, then, the first thing of importance is
> to be content to be inferior to men.
> SARAH STICKNEY ELLIS. *The Daughters of England*

Piano playing stops the pianist from speaking, and if her playing is not listened to, she loses her 'voice' doubly. In a poem about his fiancée Marie Vulliamy, George Meredith opposes talk and music as the culmination of a series of male-female antitheses: "She can talk the talk of men, / And touch with thrilling fingers" ("Marian" ll. 7-8). The truly womanly woman leaves talk to men, and submits to their gaze. Miss Vulilamy offered far less of an intellectual challenge than Meredith's first wife, who had left him for another; in his own words, she was "intensely emotional, but without expression for it, save in music. [...] But when she is at the piano, she is not dumb. She has a divine touch on the notes" (*Letters* 1:265). She perfectly satisfied Meredith's statement that "[t]here's something right in one – a woman – who knows her capabilities to be not brilliant, sitting down to do her duty at the piano to pass the evening properly" (1:106).

---

[86] Musical scenes in *The Woman in White* have been studied extensively, see Vorachek and Losseff.

In Arthur Hugh Clough's "Amours de Voyage", the beloved's
"rare gift" of "rational" talk about "matters of mind and of thinking" is
praised but immediately aligned with inarticulate music: "Though she
talk, it is music; her fingers desert not the keys; 'tis / Song, though you
hear in the song the articulate vocables sounded, / Syllabled singly and
sweetly the words of melodious meaning." (2:10:260-262, p. 111) So
even if a woman does talk, her listener turns her utterance into sweet
and unmeaning metaphorical music; women are watched rather than
listened to whether they speak or play. John Ruskin accordingly ex-
horts girls to renounce speech when giving directions for musical performance:

> [T]hink only of accuracy; never of effect or expression: [...] most likely there are
> very few feelings in you, at present, needing any particular expression; and the
> one thing you have to do is to make a clear-voiced little instrument of yourself,
> which other people can entirely depend on for the note wanted. (*Sesame* 38)

Woman should *be* an instrument rather than raise her own voice.

George Bernard Shaw debunks this whole complex in one unfor-
gettable paragraph. Countering Ruskin's exhortation to "consider all
[...] accomplishments as means of assistance to others", he proffers
his own "earnest" advice "to cultivate music solely for the love and
need of it" because on others it will "most likely inflict[...] all-but-
unbearable annoyance":

> Some day, perhaps, when it is like a page out of *Wilhelm Meister* or *Sesame and
> Lilies*, when the piano is dead and our maidens go up into the mountains to prac-
> tise their first exercises on the harp, Mr Ruskin's exhortations [...] may gain some
> sort of plausibility. At present they will not wash. [...] The greatest assistance the
> average young lady musician can render to others is to stop. (*Musical Criticism*
> 3:197)

Shaw denounces the conflation of the inevitably quotidian piano and a
symbolic instrument as indicative of musical vagueness and of a conservative attitude to women. He realizes that only when the piano has
died and become a harp, only when the players are ready to "go up",
in the biblical phrase, to some mountain in the guise of impossibly
pastoral sylphs; musical girls may become truly 'clear-voiced instruments' instead of living performers when they are dead, shielded from
the contaminations of both praise and blame. As long as the piano is
alive and well, such metaphors signal a repressive ideal, the silence of
the ornamental girl who is practising music as a *voyant* accomplishment.

In Frederick Locker-Lampson's "Castle in the Air", the musical woman becomes a "[f]orm from some pure region sent" (though sitting next to work-box and embroidery frame):

> Her mouth had all the rose-bud's hue –
> A most delicious rose-bud too.
> Her auburn tresses lustrous shone,
> In massy clusters, like your own;
> And as her fingers pressed the keys,
> How strangely they resembled these! (59-64, p. 115)

Silently rose-lipped, tactilely delicious and only perfunctorily celestial, this pianist is last of all a maker of music. The concluding lines, on the surface a compliment to the ivory whiteness of her skin, turn her into an instrument: fingers become keys. Even when praised in erotic terms, the woman is not so much a living creature as the instrument which Ruskin wanted her to be, not a performer but symbolically contained as "thou, my music". Lovely to behold and muted by her own playing, with a kissable mouth and fingers caressing the keys who are compared to a living thing, Shakespeare's Dark Lady would have been supremely attractive specimen to a Victorian listener.

3.4. Deflection: Tall, Dark, Handsome – and Strangers to the Piano

There *are* female characters in Victorian fiction who are neither villainesses nor country bumpkins and yet do not conform to the exploitative ideal of beautiful silence. A large number of positive, strong women speak out for themselves, sometimes even carve out an independent existence – and are all unmusical. While Victorian conduct literature sketches edifying prescriptive fictions of that familial bliss and individual solace which fiction proper ignores in its turn, the musical performances of these female characters are not ridiculed, but neither are they praised. That would be impossible. Instead, strong women simply do not play. This subversive trope is prefigured in the seventeenth- and eighteenth-century technique of the subverted blazon, emerges more distinctly in Jane Austen's work and becomes pervasive by the mid-nineteenth century.

Exempting positive figures from the ritual of piano playing is the most telling indictment of the humiliating aspect of musical performance, but is so deceptively unobtrusive as to have (to my knowledge) escaped scholarly attention so far. From Mary Burgan's early article "Heroines at the Piano" to the most recent studies, research has been focussing on representations of musical activity. This disregards the strong, intelligent and morally superior female figures[87] who are regularly described as unmusical or reticent to perform liberated them from commodification and able to preserve their 'gravitie' (see above 15), which would be impaired by playing the 'dreary piano' or practising scales to rival those of an exotic pet[88].

The strength of the piano convention becomes evident from the mitigating explanations which fictional narratives regularly offer for the unmusicality of a heroine. Margaret Hale in Elizabeth Gaskell's *North and South* enlists filial obedience as an unanswerable defence for her inability: "I am fond of hearing good music; I cannot play well myself; and papa and mamma don't care much about it." (1:12:97) The fact that Margaret declares her alleged lack of talent herself enables her limited skills to signify also commendable modesty, especially when it is coupled with industriousness and an intelligent appreciation of music. For Molly Gibson in Gaskell's *Wives and Daughters* playing is a "martyrdom", but we are assured that she has an "excellent ear [...] and both from inclination and conscientious perseverance of disposition, she would go over an incorrect passage for twenty times". With such guarantees of virtue and industry, Molly's musicality can afford to be compromised: "But she was very shy of playing in company; and when forced to do it, she went through her performance heavily, and hated her handiwork more than anyone" (1:24:273), Molly refuses the flirting aid of page-turning and wishes to be covered in conversation: "Please go away! [...] I can quite well fit for myself. And oh! if you would but talk!" (1:24:275) While she plays she overhears an engrossing conversation that ensues between Roger Hamley (whom she loves) and her flirtatious stepsister Cynthia, who is, unsurprisingly, a showy pianist.

Mrs. Gaskell's notes indicate that she intended Molly and Roger to marry, but the last (penultimate) finished chapter sees Roger leaving

---

[87]   The too-perfect heroines as satirized by George Eliot in "Silly Novels by Lady Novelists" have perfect morals, dancing skills and dress-sense in addition to an ability to read the Bible in the original tongues and "a superb contralto and a superb intellect" (302). However, they have no piano skills; brilliant variations on "Home, Sweet Home" would be out of tune with Greek and Hebrew.

[88]   The conservative flip side of this coin is that this abstinence also saves novels from the powerful and potentially unsettling effects which the fully realized talent of energetic, intelligent *and* virtuous performers might have.

for an African expedition without having proposed. Molly suffers the typical trial of non-musical characters, whose marital happiness is often delayed and occasionally denied. In a poem by James Smith, one Gertrude quotes John Locke and takes "to wisdom" before she is twelve, whereas her sister Emma on "all such topics is dumb", but conventionally accomplished: "The grand piano Emma greets / With fingers light and plastic / But never like her sister beats / The drum ecclesiastic." ("Two Sisters" ll. 25-28) And inevitably "Emma, light Emma, blooms a bride, / And Gertrude fades a virgin!" (ll. 39-40) Rhoda Broughton's brilliant, lively Kate Chester who loves "not wisely, but too well", wilts alone after having been tempted and abandoned by a cad. She won't even go to hear Arabella Goddard[89] play: "The bump of music on my head is represented by a hollow. [...] Saint Cecilia has neither part nor lot in me." (*Not Wisely* 26:236) The most striking case is probably Marian Halcombe in *The Woman in White*, half-sister of the angelically insipid Laura Fairlie, who of course plays delightfully. Marian is tall, dark, ugly, moustachioed and a wonderfully resourceful woman of the highest integrity, who claims not to "know one note of music from the other" (Collins, 1:6:27). The only man ever to fall in love with her is the perverted, effeminate Italian Count Fosco, and so her 'happiness ever after' consists in going to live with Laura and her husband Walter Hartright.

> I'm determined to read no more books
> where the blond-haired women carry away all the happiness.
> GEORGE ELIOT. *The Mill on the Floss*

Marian and Laura represent yet another musical stereotype that indicates the predominance of visual elements in the perception of female musicians: non-performers tend to be visually unsatisfactory. If they are not downright plain, their charms – like Marian Halcombe's – are of the mannish 'tall, dark and handsome' kind, while the conventionally efficient players around them are weaker, pretty and usually blond. Such figures are often paired as sisters, friends or rivals, providing a complete projection surface for the two contradictory main roles of an ideal woman, erotic object and virtuous soul-mate. These pairs act out the contradiction between an established canon of female duties and the simultaneous critique of its actual uses. Rosa Bud and

---

[89]   The highly respected Arabella Goddard (1836-1922) is the only historical concert pianist I have come across in nineteenth-century English fiction.

Helena Landless in Dickens's *Mystery of Edwin Drood* are the physically most emblematic couple, the musical Rosa being everything her name promises, and the orphaned, neglected Helena, "unacquainted with all accomplishment" (7:52), is "an unusually handsome lithe girl [...] very dark, and very rich in colour [...] of almost the gipsy type" (6:44).

The musical differentiation within such pairs is sometimes very lightly sketched, as between the half-sinister, half-ridiculous Blanche Amory and the hero's modest and virtuous cousin and wife-to-be Laura in Thackeray's *Pendennis*: "Laura had a sweet contralto voice, and sang with Blanche, who had had the best continental instruction and was charmed to be her friend's mistress" (23:216). Displaying rosebud lips and "the sweetest little pearly teeth ever seen" in her singing, Blanche practically flirts with Laura, playing "her some of her waltzes, with a rapid and brilliant finger". When Laura is so charmed as to forget "even jealousy in her admiration", Blanche "smiled, looked in the glass [...] sat down to the piano, and shook out a little song" (23:214-215). Magdalen Vanstone, the precarious heroine of Wilkie Collins's *No Name*, habitually spends "the morning at the piano", while her sister Norah, virtuous throughout, has "a fondness for reading" that has "passed into a family proverb" (1:22). Disraeli's extremely high-minded Sybil, who first appears as "A Religious" and only sings, reluctantly, Spanish hymns, represents a sanctified rather than intelligent and practical version of the non-musical heroine. At the beginning of the novel, the hero Egremont is still fascinated by a more conventional lady:

> Soon the dear little Poinsett was singing, much gratified by being invited to the instrument by Mr. Egremont, who for a few minutes hung over her, and then, evidently under the influence of her tones, walked up and down the room, and only speaking to beg that she would continue her charming performances. (*Sybil* 2:6:77)

It is completely unimaginable that Sybil would be diminished and as a background noise in this way.

Margaret Hale, the protagonist of Mrs. Gaskell's *North and South*, has a "tall, finely-made figure" which "set off the long, beautiful folds of the gorgeous shawls that would have half-smothered Edith" (1:1:9) – Edith being her pretty cousin, "a soft ball of muslin and ribbons and silken curls" (1:1:5). Margaret is also contrasted with a girl who first appears "practising up a morceau de salon" and later dismisses Margaret because "she's not accomplished [...] she can't play" (1:28:142). To

Margaret she wonders "how you can exist without [a piano]. It almost seems to me a necessary of life" (1:12:97). Her mental range is clearly defined by this insistence, as is that of Edith when we hear how she worries about

> her future life at Corfu, where [her fiancé's] regiment was stationed; and the difficulty of keeping a piano in good tune (a difficulty which Edith seemed to consider as one of the most formidable that could befall her in her married life). (1:1:5)

In a significant drawing-room scene, a man who later turns out to be not quite worthy of Margaret leaves her side for Edith's company: "'Now I must go. Edith is sitting down to play, and I just know enough of music to turn over the leaves for her; and besides, Aunt Shaw won't like us to talk.' Edith played brilliantly." (1:1:13)

For all her riling of silly novels, even George Eliot was not quite above such stereotyping: her non-performer heroines, Maggie Tulliver and Dorothea Brooke, are both contrasted with fluffy friends or rivals. Dorothea has not only Rosamond Vincy as a musically accomplished counterpart, but also her own younger sister Celia, who is playing an "air, with variations [...] a small kind of tinkling which symbolised the æsthetic part of the young ladies' education" (*Middlemarch* 1:5:44) at the very moment when Dorothea decides to accept the offer of marriage of the elderly scholar Edward Casaubon. The faint praise which damns Celia's musicality implicitly criticizes the commodification of musical accomplishment. This was promptly taken up by an anonymous contemporary review, whose author fears that young female readers of *Middlemarch* would imitate Dorothea and "regulate their own conduct on the system of a general disapproval of the state of things into which they are born" (quoted in Carroll, 315). On the other hand, the accomplished Celia (who happily and suitably marries the conventional baronet whom Dorothea refused) is held up as a positive example of a girl "who not feeling it her duty to subvert the world [...] can take her place in it naturally" (326) – on the music stool.

In Trollope's *Framley Parsonage*, the modest parson's sister Lucy Robarts wins her man over a statuesquely blond, bloodless and mindless heiress thanks to her integrity, courage and biting wit. Lucy "neither played nor sang" whereas Griselda Grantly's playing shows "that neither her own labour nor her father's money had been spared in her instruction". Lucy gets fed up with this: "She had turned her back to the music, for she was sick of seeing Lord Lufton watch the artistic motion of Miss Grantly's fingers, and was sitting at a small table as far away from the piano as the long room would permit." Lord Lufton approaches Lucy to wonder: "Perhaps you don't like music?" and is rebuffed: "I do like it, – sometimes very much" (11:139-140). This pert girl is, no surprise, "thoroughly a brunette" (10:118).

The eponymous hero of Charles Kingsley's *Alton Locke* is smitten with a pretty pianist at his first evening in society: "I found Lillian singing at the piano. I had no idea that music was capable of expressing and conveying emotions so intense." (1:14:162) But this conventionally charming girl – "all April smiles and tears, golden curls, snowy rosebuds, and hovering clouds of lace" (2:2:216) – turns out to be unworthy of the earnest young man. He belongs with Eleanor Staunton, "a strong-minded woman" (1:16:169) with glorious black-brown hair – "the true 'purple locks' which Homer so often talks of – [and] a tall and rounded figure" (2:2:216). Their serious exchanges culminate in an almost mystical union, effecting Alton's conversion and departure as a missionary. It is inconceivable that music should be part of such a woman's attractions. In the case of Clara Talboys, the virtuous counterpart of the blond-ringletted villainous Lady Audley (see above 131), music is made serious to match her "purely classical" face "sublimated by sorrow" and her dress, which, "puritan in its gray simplicity, became her beauty better than a more beautiful dress would have become a less beautiful woman" (Braddon, *Secret* 2:5:201). Clara plays – the organ.

Music is further deprecated in the many unhappy matches it engenders: when music is involved, Cupid's darts "ofttimes fly of merit wide" (Smith, "Two Sisters" 37). If two contrasting women are rivals for a man and he marries the musical one, misery is guaranteed. Rosamond Vincy and Tertius Lydgate have been mentioned before (see above 124): the superficiality of Rosamond's attractiveness is further reinforced by the little historicizing tag that describes her as "the irresistible woman for the doomed man *of that date* [my emphasis]" (Eliot, *Middlemarch* 3:27:262). In Dickens's *Little Dorrit*, the wrong match is only narrowly avoided: the aptly nicknamed "Pet" Meagles is blond and dressed in white when Arthur Clennam sees her for the first time and decides, to no avail, not to fall in love: "In the evening they played an old-fashioned rubber; and Pet sat looking over her father's hand, or singing to herself by fits and starts at the piano. She was a spoilt child; but how could she be otherwise?" (1:16:192) Little Dorrit herself, the "Child of the Marshalsea", who eventually becomes Arthur's wife, has never had the slightest chance of acquiring ornamental accomplishments; she earns her family's living as a seamstress. For once, the non-pianist in the couple is not imposingly tall; Little Dorrit's superior dignity is constituted by the fact that her childhood in the debtors' prison has moulded her moral stature although it has stunted her physical growth. Plain Olive Rothesay in Dinah Mulock Craik's *Bildungsroman* is born slightly deformed and "scarcely would have been called a clever child; was neither talkative nor musical" (1:11:142). Her father comments predictably: "Of course, she will never marry." (1:10:139) Olive "listened to Sara's performance for hours, with patience, if not with delight" (2:12:157). Sara is Olive's ruthless blonde charmer of a cousin, who will betray her first lover and make her husband (who much later marries Olive) unhappy.

In *Mildred Arkell*, the flashy Charlotte Travice is Mildred's direct rival for the love of her cousin William. Mildred, "a quiet, sensible, lady-like girl" who knows Latin and mathematics, has "no great pretension to beauty; not half as much as Charlotte; but William had found it enough before" (Wood, 51). She has also not been taught "a single accomplishment" (8). With the arrival of clever, fashionable Miss Travice, this becomes a problem. She is "all smiles and sweetness" and shy glances, "and before that tea-drinking was over, they were all ready to fall in love with her". She then goes to the piano, "unasked, and played a short, striking piece from memory. They asked her if she could sing; she answered by breaking into [...] 'Robin Adair', [...] one of William Arkell's favourites, and he stood by enraptured" (23). This corresponds exactly to the advice in a manual called *Habits of Good Society*, which recommends a "short, perhaps brilliant, thoroughly well-learned air by some good master [... as] the best response" to requests for piano music:

> The loud, thumping style should be avoided; if possible, the piece should not be quite common and hackneyed; not what 'every one' plays. It should not be too mournful, nor too rapid. [...] Be ready also to quit the instrument [... for] it is bad policy to wear your audience out. (Aster, 233-234)

Charlotte Travice in fact cleverly refreshes her audience by suggesting to William that they play together. He takes his flute out and the evening passes "insensibly" (Wood, 23) with duets.

Mildred is left to wish passionately that people could see Charlotte "as she really is! [...] false and false!" (25), but educational convention is on the side of Miss Travice:

> "How is it you never learnt music, Miss Arkell?" [Miss Travice] was pleased to
> inquire one day, as she finished a brilliant piece, and gave herself a whirl round on
> the music-stool [...]. "[Your parents] must have been rather neglectful of you." "I
> suppose they thought I should do as well without [...]," was the composed an-
> swer. [...] "But everybody is accomplished now – at least, ladies are. [...] I won-
> der they did not have you taught music, if only to play with [William]." Mildred's
> cheek burnt. (25)

Mildred so far has only *listened* to William's playing and mentions
defensively that this has seemed enough so far. But William's passion
for music cannot withstand this more intense enjoyment: cue an unhappy marriage with Charlotte Travice. Mildred goes away because
she cannot bear to see him suffer and eventually makes good some of
the damage wrought by Charlotte's music when her savings enable
William's son to marry his perfect soul-mate.

> Woman as I am, I will dare all things – endure all things!
> Let me be an artist!
> DINAH MULOCK CRAIK. *Olive*

Some unmusical characters are credited with a talent for the visual
arts. There are no professional female pianists in mid-Victorian fiction, but heroines are allowed to earn money by painting – as indeed
they may *need* to do to compensate their want of conventional feminine char and, consequently, of a husband. Olive Rothesay is not a
performer, not interested in attracting: "Her yearning was always *to
love* rather than *to be loved*" (Craik, 1:12:163); hers is a creative, "ar-
dent, almost masculine genius" (2:5:115), and after reading Shelley
and Byron, she becomes a painter: "Woman as I am, I will dare all
things – endure all things! Let me be an artist!" (1:12:157) Helen
Huntingdon, Anne Brontë's 'Tenant of Wildfell Hall', keeps herself
and her little son by painting after having left her dissipated adulterous
husband. She is "most painfully, bitterly" jealous of a rival's music
because she herself is unable "to awaken similar fervour. I can amuse
and please him with my simple songs, but not delight him thus"
(2:7:230). This imbalance is possibly exacerbated by the fact that she
– uniquely – uses music to improve her profligate husband: "As he is
so fond of music, I often try to persuade him to learn the piano, but he
is far too idle for such an undertaking; he has no more idea of exerting
himself to overcome obstacles than he has of restraining his natural
appetites." (2:6:227) Her husband's ambiguous compliment confirms
the opposition of music and virtue: "She is a daughter of earth; you
are an angel of Heaven [...] and remember that I am a poor, fallible

mortal." (2:7:237) In this dense cluster of clichés, the religio-musical metaphors of marital harmony are deconstructed even as they are applied: music is only erotically attractive during courtship (be it legitimate or adulterous). Once the player has become the 'Angel in the House', music becomes ineffective, to be replaced by a visual art when the marriage fails.

> You play a *little*, I see.
> CHARLOTTE BRONTË. *Jane Eyre*

In *Jane Eyre*, the roles of visuality and music are integrated into a romantic counter-narrative[90]. Jane's playing is a part of the conventional procedure when Edward Rochester interviews her for the post of his ward's governess. However, he unconventionally listens to her from a different room, purposely making himself unable to *watch* her performance. He finds it wanting with the same disregard for trifles which he has for her lack of beauty (and she for his): "You play a *little*, I see: like any other English schoolgirl; perhaps rather better than some, but not well." (1:13:151) Jane does not care. Only when Rochester voices a suspicion that somebody helped her with her sketches and paintings does she defend her achievements. They go on to analyze Jane's unusual artistic efforts in careful and sensitive detail and later, she indulges her fantasies by dreamily sketching his face. Despite this interest, she does not realize at first that Rochester shares her unconventional preference for art over music and so becomes wildly jealous when she hears that her apparent rival Blanche Ingram is reported to have been "greatly admired [...] not only for her beauty, but for her accomplishments" and for singing a duet with Rochester. Jane does not understand that Rochester calling Blanche's execution "remarkably good" (2:1:200) is a patronizing insult rather than the usual signal of conditioned infatuation. Chastened out of the excitement which his apparent interest for her art has provoked, she tries to scold herself out of her dreams and back into maidenly independence of mind.

Characteristically, Jane Eyre uses a painting metaphor to force herself into a salutary confrontation with the beauty[91] of her rival: "Draw in chalk you own picture, faithfully" and then "take a piece of smooth

---

[90] Cf. Da Sousa Correa, 95-96, and Binstock, 119-120.

[91] Another unconventional detail is that the worldly Blanche Ingram is an accomplished flirt and musician but also a statuesque and *dark* beauty.

ivory [...] mix your freshest, finest, clearest tints" (2:1:200-201). Jane fears defeat in direct sexual competition. Although she has not yet interpreted Rochester's reactions to music correctly, she does not start to practise the piano more assiduously to compete with Blanche, but retires to an observer's position, rendering and commenting instead of being 'consumed' on display at the piano. In this way she avoids the humiliation of being watched and instead establishes – literally – her own point of view. Painting is her defence, and she does not mention it in her famous denunciation of female accomplishments:

> Women [...] need exercise for their faculties, and a field for their efforts as much as their brothers do; [...] it is narrow-minded in their privileged fellow-creatures to say that they ought to confine themselves to making puddings and knitting stockings, to playing the piano and embroidering bags. (1:12:133)

Both the activity and the metaphor of painting subvert the usual visual focus of male listeners; Rochester's indifference about Jane Eyre's plainness parallels his lack of interest in her pianistic accomplishments, sidestepping both visual commodification and the double-bind of imposed yet repressed playing. And of course Jane is not punished for her lack of musicality[92], but can finally announce: "Reader, I married him."

Rochester's indifference to Jane's looks protects her from the gaze of the listener but also from any blame for her lack of musical skill. This, too, is unusual. More frequently, disdain of mediocre musicianship is used to reinforce moral comments with subtle gradations of disapproval and ridicule; an almost incredible discursive twist, given the standard denials of practise and virtuosity. Such characterizations range from the slightly flawed, but essentially likeable young lady whose performance is graceful, but incorrect ("but she herself was so charming, that it was only fanatics for music who cared for false chords and omitted notes"; Gaskell, *Wives and Daughters* 1:24:273) to the "plump" and "pink" provincial girl whose musicality is dismissed as a "thin superficial lacker" (Oliphant, 2:10). In the case of Christina Allaby and her 'improvements' on Handel (see above 144) the double-

---

[92] Also in *Villette,* a plain and unmusical woman carries away the prize: Ginevra Fanshawe, dressed in deep crimson, has "the advantage in material charms" while Paulina's attractions are "more subtle and spiritual" and her attire "in texture clear and white". Of course it is Ginevra who, after dinner, when the "gentlemen were heard to move [...] flew to the piano, and dashed at it with spirit", attracting the attention of Dr. John Graham Bretton (27:397-399), who, however, marries Pauline.

bind is particularly visible: her moderate but undeniable keyboard skills are not acknowledged but ridiculed because she uses them to cover up her vocal limitations – which in turn are made to tell against her. If a woman plays so well that such satire cannot work, her achievement is put into second place by other mean: "[T]he sensitive touch of a female pianist [is] often found to invest a pathetic, slow melody, with an indescribable charm 'beyond the reach of art'." (Carl Czerny quoted in Ella, 40)

The phrase 'beyond the reach of art' puts it in a nutshell: woman's performance is beyond, that is, celestially and metaphorically above, but also excluded from, real achievement. A narrow and easily-missed middle path of milk-and-watery piano-playing is the only musical activity that can be counted upon not to be in some way punished by narratives under a powerful, unwritten literary law which all Victorian fiction obeys. Nobody plays really well happily or with ultimate success; musical performance is always a precarious or contaminating event. In the devious textual proceedings by which Victorian novels handle domestic piano-playing, a patriarchal society's ambiguous attitudes to women, and English fears and longings about music come to a head. And yet in the exemption from music which is granted to strong woman characters, the end of the piano is prefigured; in the decades after 1880, even musical women ultimately move 'beyond the reach' of an art whose social uses were finally recognized as crippling.

V. Triumph and Oblivion
The Piano after 1880

The cost of my music lessons
would have paid for nearly a year at Oxford.
VERA BRITTAIN. *Testament of Youth*

In the decades leading up to the Great War, accomplishment persisted as a social practice but the piano was more and more perceived as an exasperating, outmoded domestic fixture. In 1914, Vera Brittain needed a scholarship to go to university because her parents refused to spend money on her academic education, "though the cost of my music lessons, and of the expensive piano which was ungrudgingly bought for me to practise on, would have paid for nearly a year at Oxford" (Brittain, 53). In the same year, E. M. Forster describes a perfectly Victorian bride (ignorant of sex on her wedding night) as "accomplished but delightful", the representative of a species that "every year England grew less inclined to pay" (*Maurice* 34:153-154). The 'but' speaks volumes: here is the prospect that the piano might cease to be compulsory. The moralistic paralysis is lifting, and a wide range of literary and social possibilities comes into play. There is exasperation with a tyrannous ritual; there is triumph as the joys of music-making become available to representation, and soon, there is oblivion as emancipation from accomplishment is reaching a point of no return. Several aspects of this brief but colourful phase, such as representations of professional musicians or male music lovers in homoerotic contexts, have been objects of scholarly research and will be pointed to in the following chapter. But attitudes grow more varied also within the focused topic of women's domestic music-making. For a few decades, traditional accomplishment coexists in fiction with the triumph of outstanding musicians as well as their complete opposite (the mode that was to last): the possibility of liberation from the piano itself.

Before freedom for the piano could turn into liberation *from* it, it had to be fought for. After half a century of trivialization and pious downplaying, denunciations of the emotional manipulations implicit in musical courtship rituals became again explicit, picking up where the scathing criticism of the Regency years had left off. The novelist May Sinclair uses terms reminiscent of Mary Wollstonecraft and her

indictment of the 'seraglio' mentality, to blame the "extreme shaki-
ness" of male sexual morality on "the debilitating, the disastrous influence of the Early and Mid-Victorian woman" with her "wilful ignorance, her sentimentalism, her sex-servility", which could produce
nothing but "viciousness in the unhappy males exposed to it" (quoted
in Raitt, 44). Katherine Mansfield's anger at Virginia Woolf's *Night
and Day* includes the males. Young William Rodney (himself just
able to pick out opera tunes), ponders the fact that the woman he will
leave for her cousin, has "no particular liking for music", whereas the
more pliable girl he has chosen instead has "a very fine taste in music,
and he had charming recollections of her in a light fantastic attitude,
playing the flute [...] The enthusiasms of a young girl of distinguished
upbringing appealed to William" (22:267). These are the passages
which made Mansfield call Woolf's novel "a lie in the soul", which
implies, with an "*utter coldness* & indifference [which] positively
frightens me", that the war "never has been" (Mansfield, 204-205).
Rodney's musings on the "womanly side[s] of the feminine nature"
(*Night and Day* 26:328-329) are taken as evidence of a refusal to rec-
ognize that musical accomplishments are trifles, but damaging.

However, just as the twilight of the 'Household God' was thus announced, piano scenes of unprecedented diversity were flourishing.
The composer Hubert Parry found that piano music displays "a wider
range of characteristics [...] than [...] any other branch of the art" and
"puts a wide range of musical expression into the hands of one performer" (322), and this also goes for performers in fiction. 'Odd
Women', 'New Women', aesthetes and empire-builders, aspiring professionals and rebellious young ladies with an impressive repertoire
now join the 'accomplished' girl at the instrument. Moreover, texts
begin to reveal those players' states of mind. It is this perspective that
distinguishes a Sherlock Holmes story from a Victorian scene: a
young lady client suspects that her employer "takes a great deal of
interest in me. We are thrown rather together. I play his accompaniments in the evening. He has never said anything. He is a perfect gentleman. But *a girl always knows*". (Doyle, 529, my emphasis) More
and more fictional women and men now 'know' about music and its
effects and can either communicate their knowledge or refuse communication intentionally, even explicitly. For a brief historical moment, a prescribed social activity that was represented in shifting yet
usually standardized ways is taking part in truly individualized literary
characterizations. Excellent playing no longer guarantees just erotic

leverage and aspersion, but also personal empowerment and the expression of a rebellious individuality which even non-fictional discourses begin to represent as desirable.

1. Victorian Transmutations

1.1. Exasperation

> The piano is too much with us.
> ANON. "The Piano as a Cause of Neuroses"

So many different people played also because the piano had become more affordable than ever: with one instrument for every ten to 20 inhabitants of Britain in 1910 (cf. Ehrlich, 7), it was virtually ubiquitous – too much so for some unwilling listeners. A magazine article suggested a parliamentary "Act for the protection of minors from this form of cruelty" because

> the torture of professional performance, the ineffective strumming of the amateur, and the damnable iteration of the learner, [have] sundered ancient friendships [...] driven studious men from their books to the bottle [...] and stimulated peaceful citizens to the commission of violent assaults (Anon., "Cause of Neuroses" 988).

Even fairly competent piano performances were getting obnoxiously thick on the ground, witness George Bernard Shaw and Ezra Pound, who both worked as music critics in London. Shaw reckoned that "[d]eath is better than eighteen [piano] recitals per week" (*Musical Criticism* 2:93-94) and Pound reasoned:

> The pye-ano, Ge-entlemen, the PYE-ano is the largest musical instrument known to man [...]; [but it] may, with four fat men and considerable difficulty, be moved from on spot to another (Mr. Kipling notwithstanding[93]); all of which is no reason for pye-ano recitals outnumbering all other concerts three to one, or seven to one, or seventeen to one in the damp season. (Quoted in Schafer, 203)

Abusing the piano became a literary fad. John Gray's poem "Sound" calls upon a long list of quaint or exotic instruments such as oboes, dulcimers, gongs, and bugles to "Beat! Blow! – Insult the tiresome Piano" (30). James Kenneth Stephen mischievously lists a series of

---

[93] Pound is referring to Kipling's poem "Song of the Banjo" which derides immobile instruments: "You couldn't pack a Broadwood half a mile – / You mustn't leave a fiddle in the damp – / You couldn't raft an organ up the Nile, / And play it in an Equatorial swamp." (1-4)

"sounds to rejoice in", which include "[t]he whistle of the railway guard despatching the train to the inevitable collision, / The maiden's monosyllabic reply to a polysyllabic proposal, / The fundamental note of the last trump, which is presumably F natural" ("Of W. W." ll. 2-4). And what is better even than a train wreck, a refused marriage or the end of the (pious, middle-class) world – and in a way includes them all – is "the absolutely last chord of the apparently inexhaustible pianoforte player"! (6).

More explicit criticism of the instrument describes it as a deceptive screen just as did Regency educators (see above 89), but with a crucial difference: Edwardian criticism is not levelled at a ruling fashion craze but at something that is increasingly perceived as old-fashioned. If *Night and Day* is not as progressive as Katherine Mansfield expected, it does identify the piano with an older generation. Mrs. Hilbery's identity as the daughter of an 'eminent Victorian' is obvious in her comment on William Rodney's approaching marriage to her niece Cassandra rather than to her daughter Katherine: "I own I was a little grudging at first, but, after all, [Cassandra] plays the piano so beautifully" (Woolf, 33:462). The fact that Katharine is unmusical, intelligent and single is another Victorian throwback, but also identified as such when she doubts the family legends of "chandeliers, and the green silk of the piano": "The house [...] and the sweet-voiced piano [...] and other properties of size and romance – had they any existence?" (7:101-102) In George Egerton's short story "Virgin Soil", a young woman berates her mother for sending her unprepared into a degrading marriage, characteristically in a room where the piano is "open with a hymn-book on the stand" (149). The rare wives who still "affect a liking for music, and duly endeavour to soothe their lords of an evening by trips up and down the key-board" (Anon., "Women and the Piano" 37) are now objects of ironic scorn, but so are the truly "commonplace wives [...] who drop / Their friends and their French and pianos, and put to the Past a full stop" (2:15-16, p. 159) in the view of young Hilda in Walter Chalmers Smith's "Hilda and the Broken Gods". Hilda also despises unmarried school friends who are still "strumming pianos [...] for catching the youthful fools" (2:857-858, p. 176), as she herself once did:

> Oh, the old-maiden morals we had,
> So scrupulous, prim, and demure!
> What the decalogue never forbade
> Our consciences could not endure. [...]

> And the scales that we practised for hours,
> Till we hated the sight of the keys! (2:139-142 and 163-164, p. 182)

This woman is certainly not going to replicate domestic music-making in her daughters' lives.

An even more striking (though indirect) indictment of Victorian musical mores are the increasingly frequent and disturbing death metaphors. Ezra Pound reviewed a song recital as reminiscent of Madame Tussaud's, and compared the piano to "a hearse covered with bouquets" (Schafer, ed. 75). Austin Dobson telescopes the ultimate destination of a piano-fuelled flirtation into the story of two young people sharing a train carriage who start chattering about books, singers and the relative difficulty of Chopin and Spohr.

> And oh! the odd things that she quoted,
> With the prettiest possible look,
> While her talk like a musical rillet
> Flashed on with the hours that flew. ("Incognita" 40-43, p. 384)

The emphasis on the look of the girl and the musical metaphor prepare the reader for the following disaster: in a dream the speaker sails over a sunny sea with "Incognita": "And we split on a rock labelled Marriage, / And I woke, – as cold as a stone" (79-80, p. 385). Musical courtship is clearly doomed.

The most admirably economical example is the 'Intended' of Mr. Kurtz in Joseph Conrad's novel *Heart of Darkness*. This petrified 'Angel in the House', in mourning more than a year after the death of her fiancé, looks "as though she would remember and mourn forever" (126), which is of course what she has been trained to do. Her grand piano stands "massively in a corner; with dark gleams on the flat surfaces like a sombre and polished sarcophagus" (125). The funereally empty instrument, devoid of the usual embroidered covers, vases and framed photographs, is closed because the player's life is over, but also suggests a whole dying epoch with its lethal entrapment of women.

1.2. Fears and Fascination: Old and New

> Fingers of roseate tint, that dazzle the ravish'd beholders
> Watching them over the keys moving adroitly a-row.
> JONES BROWN. "The Heroine"

The terms in which Mark Gurdon, later the husband of a scandalous 'New Woman', remembers first falling in love with a model of Victo-

rian womanhood contain overtones of a dead and fading past in his
description of Margaret at her old piano as "a picture, an etching of
the type – a silver-point" (Dowie, 17:110); but he also still enjoys her
in a very traditionally visual way.

> He had sat in the little Hammersmith drawing-room and *watched* Margaret's fine
> *flower-like* hands moving over the *yellow* keyboard of the *old sweet* Broadwood,
> and his cold nature had warmed and warmed as he *looked*. [...] Or he had *seen* her
> singing. Margaret singing was a *picture for the gods*. (13:87, my emphases)

This is the classic Victorian 'man looking on', but a new sensuality
now colours – and superficially softens – sexist stereotypes. Many
texts remodel "received images and patterns [...] to accommodate female sexuality" (Stubbs, 59), but continue to privilege the male gaze
on the desirable woman to provide, if anything, for more explicit
erotic fantasizing. The woman musician is still often wordlessly on
visual display (although with more initiative in the process) or becomes a played-upon instrument. The domestic attractions which are
no longer interesting are substituted by self-consciously luscious detail:

> Ah, we all know very well that a heroine ought to be charming;
> She whom the hero loves ought to be dainty and fair [...]
> Chiefly, whoever she be, she is bound to have beautiful shoulders,
> Beautiful hands and arms, white as the virginal snow;
> Fingers of roseate tint, that dazzle the ravish'd beholders
> Watching them over the keys moving adroitly a-row. (Brown, 1-2 and 9-12)

Although the heroine's beauty is also revealed as a literary cliché, the
spectacle remains enjoyable and the woman objectified.

The enigmatic Irene in John Galsworthy's *Forsyte Saga* is another
instance of the new old sexism. To her estranged and traditionally
unmusical husband, her subjectivity remains as elusive as that of an
Elizabethan temptress, but her silence has overtones of unavailability,
a conscious and powerful refusal to share or explain emotions: rather
than make her shy, being looked at disgusts this beautiful woman.
This may seem emancipatory, but the text continues to indulge in conventional visual fantasies. Her husband remembers his first night out
during their marriage:

> With what eagerness he had hurried back; and, entering softly as a cat, had heard
> her playing. Opening the drawing-room, he had stood watching the expression on
> her face, different from any he knew, so much more open, so much more confid-
> ing, as though to her music she was giving a heart he had never seen. And he re-
> membered how she stopped and looked round, how her face changed back to that
> which he did know, and what an icy shiver had gone through him. (2:1:4:378)

This scene is re-enacted years later when Soames finally goes to ask
Irene for a divorce. His materialist eye notices that her new piano is
made of satinwood, but his wife remains bafflingly opaque to him.

> She had risen and stood recoiled against it; her hand, placed on the keys as if
> groping for support, had struck a sudden discord, held for a moment, and released.
> [...] 'Yes, it's a queer visit. I hope you're well.' 'Thank you. Will you sit down?'
> She had moved away from the piano, and gone over to a window-seat. [...] Soames
> moved towards the piano and back to the hearth, to and fro, as he had been wont
> in the old days in their drawing-room when his feelings were too much for him.
> (2:1:9:419)

In 1926, Elizabeth Drew commented with annoyance on such "typical
Galsworthy women", who are wonderfully dressed even when alone
and spend "perfumed passionate existences playing the piano, till the
lover appears, bringing some fate which can never be possibly settled
by a straightforward divorce, and plunging them both forthwith into
death or despair or disappearance" (167-168). The magic of Irene's
music works – pointlessly and miserably – even on her son, who is in
love with Soames's daughter: "He gazed at his mother while she
played, but he saw Fleur [...] – in his mother's hands, slim and white
on the keys, in the profile of her face and her powdery hair; and down
the long room in the open window where the May night walked outside." (Galsworthy, 3:1:10:689) Exasperating indeed.

The re-emergence of the Elizabethan trope of the feminine – or effeminate[94] – soul being touched and vibrating like a chord or string
(see above 25) is similarly double-edged. The popular metaphor is
now used to represent a woman's subjectivity (her active imagination)
through her voice but also perfectly conserves a Victorian ideal of female passivity. Virginia Woolf uses it to describe her reaction as a
child when her mother "liked something I had written! Never shall I
forget my extremity of pleasure – it was like being a violin and being
played upon" ("A Sketch of the Past" 95)[95]. The image is taken up in
the title of George Egerton's bestselling short story collection *Dis-*

---

[94] Lord Henry Wotton describes Dorian Gray as "an exquisite violin" answering "to
every touch and thrill of the bow" (Wilde, *Dorian* 3:33) and Dorian himself feels that
"some secret chord that had never been touched before [...] was now vibrating and
throbbing" (2:28). Numerous poems using this metaphor are discussed in Sutton, "The
Music Spoke for Us".

[95] I am indebted to Werner Wolf for drawing my attention to this passage.

cords[96], from which the following passage is taken. "No man ever played on me. I am like a harp that has lain away until the strings are frayed, and no one ever called out its deepest music" (171). The metaphor of harmonic vibration also dominates a highly charged exchange between a pair who never speak except in improvised musical dialogues and echoes.

> One night he played to me – ah! how can I tell you of it? – music such as I had heard in dreams, or in mad hours when he restless spirit worked in me [...]. I walked up and down the garden in my white gown; he could see me from his window, and he drew my soul with his bow as one wind silk out of a cocoon, and he bent it across the strings of his violin. (78)

When the man finally sings, the woman is silenced by overwhelming passion and can only throw him a rose: "[T]he fingers of fate were clutching my throat, choking down the sound [...] though I groaned his name with all my being." (78-79)

It was the 1890s genre of the 'New Woman' novel which first attempted to break this mould, making women's subjectivity active and denouncing music's part in their dependence. Grant Allen's 'Woman Who Did', the tall dark Girton student Herminia, explicitly refuses the vibration stereotype when her lover addresses her as "O my child" and asks her not to play "too hard on those fiercest chords in my nature": "It isn't those chords I want to play upon. I want to convince your brain, your intellect, your reason" (5:55). Herminia's "strange ideas" ruin the attraction of the conventional musical blonde for him: "How could he listen with becoming show to Ethel Waterton's aspirations on the piano after a gypsy girl – oh, a gypsy life for her! – when, in point of fact, she was a most insipid blonde from the cover of a chocolate-box?" (4:47)

The musical-unmusical pair of girls is another motif that lives on in variously modified forms, now often weighted more explicitly in favour of the unmusical one. In *The Mayor of Casterbridge*, Hardy presents a version which makes him truly seem 'the last Victorian'. It is the coquettish Lucetta Templeman (to die of a miscarriage) who owns an instrument and calls a new-fangled agricultural implement "a sort

---

[96] Another volume was called *Keynotes*, and its success inspired the publisher John Lane to a whole 'Keynotes Series', the volumes of which were designed by Aubrey Beardsley and featured, among others, Stanley Makower's *The Mirror of Music* and Grant Allen's *The Woman Who Did* as well as Victoria Crosse's rebuttal *The Woman Who Didn't*.

of agricultural piano" (24:166) while Elizabeth-Jane Henchard muses: "[i]f they only knew [...] that I can't show any of the accomplishments they learn at boarding-schools, how they would all despise me!" (15:100). The eponymous heroine of Ménie Muriel Dowie's shocker *Gallia* is never seen playing and her friend Gertrude, a "shining example of the modern girl [... who doesn't] play a note, doesn't paint a stroke". Contrarily, Margaret Essex, the first flame of the man whom Gallia will marry for eugenic reasons, is a perfect specimen of Victorian womanhood enabling old-fashioned romance-based marriage, with accomplishments "ever and ever so far above the amateur average" (17:110). Of the two sisters in Douglas Sladen's verse narrative about *A Summer Christmas* in Australia, the "pretty", "soft", "dainty", "tender" and "graceful" Lil lacks "the robust and keen / Brain of the other" (302-303, p. 10-11). And tastefully the keys she played, / Whether for Lied of Mendelssohn / Or new waltz she was called upon" (288-290, p. 10). The unmusical sister Kit is predictably older and of "noble, queenly loveliness", brainy and with "rough sports and manner" based on "manly canons of good taste" (271-272, p. 9-10). This is not the denunciation of a virago it would have had to be thirty years earlier; more intimations of masculinity in unmusical women need not preclude or even delay marriage. The title of Arnold Bennett's *These Twain* foregrounds the marital happiness of the unfeminine yet highly likeable Hilda Lessways, who does not play (although she enjoys organizing musical evenings) but works in her husband's printing press: "immature, graceless, harsh, inelegant, dowdy [...], in the midst of all that hard masculine mess, – and a part of it" (1:7:77).

Typing provides an instructive parallel. It was often described in similar terms as the piano as a decorous female occupation which is "sedentary in character [and] does not take very long to learn" (quoted in Mitchell, *New Girl* 36). Both piano and type-writer can be seen as "badges of slavery" (Barrie, "Twelve-Pound Look" 228) and a "fair typist['s] [...] fingers dancing quickly over the tiny ivory keys" (quoted in Mitchell, *New Girl* 36) are described with exactly the scopic orientation that musicians are exposed to. Typing and uninteresting piano performances could be used to derogate each other, as when Shaw admires a "swift, accurate, steely-fingered" concert pianist "as I admire the clever people who write a hundred and eighty words a minute with a typewriter" (*Musical Criticism* 1:764), or when Wilfred Owen wonders why certain people "buy pianos at all, when a good typewriter is so much cheaper, and makes almost the same noise" (541). Arthur Conan Doyle is more conservative: Sherlock Holmes, examining a client's trained hands, concludes that she is a musician because he finds "a spirituality about the face, [...] which the typewriter does not generate" (Doyle, "Cyclist" 527). The 'New Woman' Rhoda Nunn in George Gissing's *Odd Women*, on the other hand, finds no such spirituality in music; she maintains that there "should be no such thing as a class of females vulgarized by the necessity of finding daily amusement" (10:99) in playing the piano and promotes office skills to save girls from shop-assistant drudgery. She considers music with a professional pragmatism that would have horrified pious Victorian educationalists, regretting her own lack of piano skills only because they might have improved her typing: "The fingers have to be light and supple and quick" (4:36).

> I adore [music], but I am afraid of it.
> OSCAR WILDE. *The Picture of Dorian Gray*

As earlier moral fears of music relaxed, several bestsellers profited from a certain morbid fascination that substituted them and is recognizable even in Oscar Wilde's flippancy: "I adore [music], but I am afraid of it. It makes me too romantic. I have simply worshipped pianists – two at a time, sometimes [...]. I don't know what it is about them. Perhaps it is that they are foreigners. They all are, aren't they?" (*Dorian Gray* 4:40-41) No mid-Victorian musical villain could approach the demonic intensity of the musical master Svengali in Gerald Du Maurier's *Trilby*, and as Henry James' little Miles and Flora envelop their worried governess "in a cloud of music and love and success and private theatricals. [...] The schoolroom piano broke into all gruesome fancies" ("Turn of the Screw" 9:57), an even more seriously ambiguous evil is associated with music. Miles uses the piano to distract the governess and provide yet another opportunity for his sister to meet the evil ghosts that may or may not be lurking around the house. "He had never [...] been such a little gentleman as when [...] he came round to me and asked if I shouldn't like him for half an hour to play to me. David playing to Saul could not have shown a finer sense of the occasion." (18:92) When the governess recognizes that she has been tricked, the old concept of the double moral identity of music is evoked: "'He found the most divine little plan to keep me quiet while she went off.' 'Divine?' Mrs. Grose bewilderedly echoed. 'Infernal, then!' I almost cheerfully rejoined." (18:94) The (pseudo?-)

religious terms 'infernal' and 'divine' would never have been used so bluntly in mid-nineteenth-century literature, which worried about sensuality rather than demons.

Madness is another newly-apprehended danger. In Stanley Makower's *Mirror of Music*, a cursed heredity kills a girl composer at 24, after a hugely successful performance of her "opera" scored for wordless choir and orchestra. Her father's diary notes relate how *his* mother died in a fit of musical insanity. Sleepwalking and playing "exquisitely" on moonlit nights "whilst her eyes stared in a dull senseless way", she sang along to her own playing of Schumann's piece "Aveu" from the *Carnaval* cycle, but suddenly "burst into loud hysterical laughter, and then fainted away" (99). Soon afterwards she dies, leaving only a crumpled note saying simply "Aveu". The grand-daughter is deeply impressed by this account and her own diary from then on chronicles a parallel decline: "Perhaps I am mad already. No rest all night. I was haunted by the thing that I had read. I can see the figure at the piano in the moonlight" (ibid.). Anxieties about music are now not so much moralistic or religious as psychological, as in Ernest Newman's assertion in 1879 that the "musical temperament probably borders more closely than any other on some form of dementia" (150). Shaw's mockery of "the Religion of the Pianoforte" is typical for the new pagan-sounding contrast of 'divine' versus 'demonic' which replaces squarely biblical dichotomy of 'godly' versus 'sinful'.

Images of musical women evolve analogously. Judith Rowbotham notes that the term 'Angel in the House' was substituted by 'Home Goddess' after 1880, "being more suited to a later development in the feminine stereotype" (11, note 2). Formidable women of the physical type that used to be unmusical and unlikely to marry are now both musical and attractive[97]. In Austin Dobson's pastoral "Autumn Idyll", students compare their ideals of feminity. Frank imagines a simple girl singing "on a June-lawn, to the water sloping" (43, p. 85), "not too divine to toss you up a salad" (59, p. 86) and with a real identity: "Jack's sister Florence, – now you know her name" (87, p. 87). Lawrence's "gem, – the paragon of girls" is "in the Row, supreme among

---

[97] The statuesque element also surfaces in interior decoration, for instance in the notorious 'Byzantine' grand inlaid which Sir Lawrence Alma-Tadema designed in 1885 for a Roman-Oriental interior. George Bernard Shaw found it "difficult to contemplate it for five minutes without looking about for a heavy woodchopper" (*Musical Criticism* 1:359).

the riders" (39-40, p. 85), dark-haired and statuesque "with splendid
tresses plaited / Back from the brows, imperially curled; / Calm as a
grand, far-looking Caryatid, / Holding the roof that covers in a world"
(45-48, p. 86). She is a "musician" and therefore superior to a mere
singer, for "Best is the song with the music interwoven" (53, p. 86).
This "queenly" (77, p. 87) lady "[t]hrobs to the gathered grieving of
Beethoven, / Sways to the light coquetting of Mozart" (55-56, p. 86)
and is "worshipped" by all, remaining suitably remote, ideal and
nameless.

The heroine of William Barry's *New Antigone* does have a real
name, but is identified as a mythological, non-domestic creature by
the novel's title. She, too, to is tall, with "dark and full" eyes, "hair as
black as night" and "intelligence in the forehead" (1:2:2:25). At first
her future husband Glanville, who dislikes learned women as "unfeminine, the most beautiful thing in the world spoilt" (1:1:2:23), finds her
knowledge of church history unsympathetic. When it turns out that her
intelligent remarks were attempts to please her father, he is relieved to
think that she is not a "dictionary after all; she is only an affectionate
daughter" (1:1:2:27) and they proceed to converse about music at a
moonlit window.

> "Oh," said Lady May, looking pleased, "have you those feelings when you hear
> music? Do you translate it into figures of people moving, scenery, a sense that you
> are journeying on and on into unknown lands? I am constantly doing so." "And I,
> too." (1:1:2:29)

When they have agreed to liken the weather to a Chopin piece, he asks
her to play and she complies with Victorian good manners and the
simplicity of a true soul-mate: "Yes, I play [...] and there are many of
Chopin's works in the drawing-room." But then Lady May turns a
Chopin nocturne into a threateningly impressive improvisation, singing along in a foreign tongue, "now proudly defiant, now self-accus-
ing and full of regret, now fainting to utter weariness" (1:1:2:30-31).
The listener, quite forgotten, wonders: "What sort of temperament was
it that broke loose in such perilous fashion? A Medea! [...] he could
not tell what to think, except that in this high-born, delicately-nurtured
lady there were unknown possibilities of good and evil" (1:1:2:32).
On returning to the company minutes later, Glanville observes with
"an eerie feeling" how Lady May turns back into a dutiful daughter,
"as if he had seen her in the form of panther or tigress vanishing in the
twilight" (1:1:2:34).

That a work by Chopin, that "classical signifier of femininity"[98],
performed by "only an affectionate daughter", could call up such violent associations is typical of the incomplete way in which traditional
gender norms are overcome in the Edwardian period. Sophocles' rebellious Antigone is doomed, the impressive weight of her performance, though sufficient to counterbalance her unwomanly intellect, is
not enough to save Lady May from dwindling into a wife. Twenty
years earlier, her emotional abandon would have made death as narrative closure inevitable. Now the demonic or liberating forces of music
are made explicit and serve for romantic titillation, but they are still
worrying.

1.3. Old Effeminacy, New Men

In 1854, Sir Frederick Ouseley was told by his Dean that it would be
"utterly derogatory for a man in his social position" to consider acquiring a Mus. Bac. Degree. Edmund Fellowes comments in his
memoirs: "Times have changed. I have heard a Vice-Chancellor and
an ex-Vice-Chancellor, both of them Heads of Houses, perform a duet
for two pianofortes at a meeting of the Oxford University Music club
[...] early in 1914" (9). From 1875, classified ads in the *Musical
Times* offered musical jobs to men, invariably specifying that what
was wanted was "A Gentleman" (*Musical Times* 1 April 1876, 443) or
an "efficient performer, and one of gentlemanly manners and address". Music and gentlemen, music and masculinity are no longer
completely mutually exclusive. Norman Gale's 1912 poem "The Old
Piano" is a plea to save an instrument from the attic that has served the
misery of schoolchildren, the fantasizing of girls and young brides and
the lullabies of the next generation; but also the "Lad of twenty made
the tramp / Of regiments pass along the keys" (ll. 17-18). The piano is
now of all ages and of all genders.

However, as has been shown, musical gender norms were shifting
but slowly; overtones of effeminacy and immaturity clung to male
music lovers for a long time. *The Boy's Own Paper* derides a musically inclined student as "the greenest fresher of the year" in 1893
(quoted in Gillett, *Musical Women* 228). Wilfrid Owen considered
music as a profession ("If only I dare say Yes!"), which is very un-
Victorian, but he also planned "to conceal the passion, for fear it be

---

98   See also Asbee and Cooper, 126.

thought weakness" (255). What is new about the effeminacy trope in Edwardian fiction is that it is not associated with evil; heterosexual men that love music need not be sinister foreigners but may be English and are then described as, at worst, ridiculous or ineffective. A variety of musical gender roles becomes available to positive figures, from playful inversion of Victorian clichés to new scenarios that include loveable amateur and homoerotic seduction. At the truly progressive end of the continuum, there are some professional musicians (who are not the subject of this book) and some 'real men' who enjoy music and play the piano without the slightest slur on their masculinity.

> Yes, he was such a dear little man Oh!
> And he sang them the properest songs.
> FREDERICK WILLIAM ORDE WARD. "Robin Redbreast"

A rather awful magazine short story from 1890 takes Victorian effeminacy to Edwardian emotional limits. Roselin Tudor, a young consumptive, faints at the execution of the murderer of an actress he loved from afar. He takes care of her little golden-ringletted girl, who however dies soon, too. As she lies on her deathbed, a musical score is open on the piano "as if the player had suddenly been interrupted in his playing". The narrator recognizes the music on the piano as "a waltz of Chopin, a posthumous work, one of the saddest and most touching expressions of a broken heart. Innocent and tender in its utterance as this child's life", the music "invariably steals into [his] ear" (Field, 236-237) when he visits the grave of Roselin (who did not survive long, either). His name is about as emblematic as can be for a male Victorian pianist: the surname putting him in the realm of a decorative past, the sweetly flowery first name as feminized (and diminutive) as he is through his instrument, his foster-parenthood and his early death. The impossibly beautiful Duke in Max Beerbohm's *Zuleika Dobson* also sports a feminized list of accomplishments that includes "all modern languages" and "a very real talent in water-colour", and he "was accounted, by those who had had the privilege of hearing him, the best amateur pianist on this side of the Tweed" (2:30). The trance-like passivity with which he follows his intuition on the evening before his suicide is another feminine trait: "He had not considered what he would play to-night. Nor, maybe, was he conscious now of choosing. His fingers caressed the keyboard vaguely." (9:147) Little Billee in *Trilby* does not die, but his femininity is completely overdetermined by his physique, his nickname and his passivity: he is "made to sit down to the piano and sing" and complies "very nicely with his pleasant little throaty English baritone" at the piano which has been ordered by his friends at great expense to give him "opportunities of practising this graceful *accomplishment* of his" (Du Maurier, 42-43, my emphasis).

Men who seduce women with their music represent the Victorian trope of disapproval in gender reverse: Lord Henry Wotton mentions that the man "with whom my wife ran away played Chopin to her", and Mr. Bevis in Gissing's *The Odd Women* uses his skill to seduce a disappointed wife: the "gay little piece" of his own composition which he sings at an evening party, seems "one of the most delightful things she had ever heard" to – "at all events" – Monica Widdowson.

> Mr. Bevis came and took a place by her side. "Thank you so very much," she said, "for that charming song. Is it published?" "Oh dear, no!" He laughed and shook his thick hair about. "It's one of two or three that I somehow struck out when I was studying in Germany, ages ago. You play, I hope?" Monica gave a sad negative. (16:170)

Although the invitation to duet playing fails, the relationship continues with an assignation and, soon, "The First Lie". Bevis is able to carry his point by fishing for a compliment:

> "I made this [copy] specially for you, and – if you will forgive me – I have taken the liberty of dedicating it to you. Song-writers do that, you know. Of course it is altogether unworthy of your acceptance." – "No – no – Indeed I am very grateful to you, Mr. Bevis. Do give it me – as you meant to." "You will have it?" he cried delightedly. "Now for a triumphal march!" (20:208)

Monica reads "sadness and longing and the burden of a lonely heart" into Bevis' composition, but the narrator's description of his playing as a "rattle" discredits the lovers musically and morally. (Ibid.)

George Bernard Shaw's one-act "variety turn" *The Music-Cure* also inverts gender clichés in its romance between the "female Paderewski" Strega Thundridge and the "fashionably dressed, rather pretty" Lord Reginald Fitzambey, who is an amateur player and has "absolutely no capacity in any other direction; the day you give up vamping accompaniments and playing the latest ragtimes, you're a lost man socially" (883). Strega wrestles him to the carpet when he insults her by praising her "lovely hands" (887), but then decides to "make a man" (890) of him. He eventually admits: "I am a poor little thing, Strega: but I could make a home for you [...]. I can play quite nicely after dinner. And I shouldn't mind at all being tyrannized over a little; in fact, I like it, it saves me the trouble of having to think what to do." Strega in her turn has been dreaming of "a timid little heart fluttering against mine, of a silky moustache to kiss my weary fingers when I return from a Titanic struggle with Tchaikovsky's Concerto in G major" (892-893). This enjoyable subversion of stereotypes, simultaneously deconstructing and perpetuating normative structures, is typical of the ambiguities of the period.

> A gentleman accustomed to assuage
> His passion at the piano with a song
> While caring little if the notes are wrong.
> THEODORE WRATISLAW. "Going Upstairs"

A similarly ambiguous musical type is the ineffective but unashamed male amateur. The ridicule that clings to such figures is residually Victorian – as is the tacit understanding that his music is an absolutely *private* enjoyment –, but it is a new twist that the ridicule is now directed at pianistic inadequacies rather than musical passion. This implies that musical mastery is basically an admirable thing, although the fact that men's musical shortcomings are not more than ridiculous also means that they are exempted from the work ethic which ruled women's music-making. Consider Phillotson in *Jude the Obscure*:

> [T]he only cumbersome article possessed by the master, in addition to the packing-case of books, was a cottage piano that he had bought at an auction during the year in which he thought of learning instrumental music. But the enthusiasm having waned he had never acquired any skill in playing. (Hardy, 1:1:33)

In Meredith's *One of Our Conquerors*, an amateur flautist playing with a more accomplished pianist is gently mocked:

> [Music] was the saving of poor Dudley. It distinguished him in the group of the noble Evangelical Cantor Family; and it gave him a subject of assured discourse in company; and oddly, it contributed to his comelier air. Flute in hand, his mouth at the blow-stop was relieved of its pained up-draw by the form for puffing; he preserved a gentlemanly high figure in his exercises on the instrument [...] – an Apollo brilliancy in energetic pursuit of the nymph of sweet sound. (8:72-73)

This is the background against which Robert Louis Stevenson, at 36, was making fun about "Himself at the Piano" and "His" modest repertoire: "I am now gay, free and obnoxious. Je ne vis que pour le piano; on the which I labour like an idiot as I am. You should hear me labouring away at Martini's celebrated, beroomed [= berühmt] Gavotte or Boccherini's beroomed famous minuet" (*Collected Letters* 548, note quoting an unpublished letter). Stevenson ironizes these piano transcriptions of eighteenth-century 'hit' tunes in a little poem:

> Where is now the Père Martini?
> Where is Bumptious Boccherini?
> Where are Hertz and Crotch and Batch?
> Safe in bed in Colney Hatch? (1-4)

The painful mispronunciation of Johann Sebastian Bach's name and the old-fashioned repertoire geared towards a player who is not up to modern giants like Beethoven or Chopin speak volumes.

While Robert Louis Stevenson admitted to 'labouring' ineffectually at the piano with generous self-irony, amateurs in fiction are more careful to distance themselves from the practice routines of girls working hard to acquire accomplishments. Zachary Menaida in Sabine Baring-Gould's Devon novel *Roar of the Sea* is a loveable old maid of a man, educated to read law, but precariously maintaining himself as a taxidermist, prone to drink, "not clever" and not even a good pianist. He has only started to practise zealously when "his fingers had stiffened [... and] it was no longer possible for him to acquire even tolerable proficiency" (1:6:70). Menaida blames badly printed sheet music for his errors ("Who, without the miraculous powers of a prophet, could tell that B should be natural?") but also uses the amateur's argument that technically proficient players "can't feel; they only execute. [...]. I give not a thank-you for mere literal music-reading" (1:7:80-81).

This classic excuse is also used by a very different character, the young Algernon Moncrieff, who opens *The Importance of Being Earnest* by asking his servant "Did you hear what I was playing, Lane?". When Lane gets the first laugh in the play by answering "I didn't think it polite to listen, sir", Algernon retorts: "I don't play accurately – anyone can play accurately – but I play with wonderful expression. As far as the piano is concerned, sentiment is my forte." (Wilde, 1:1:1, p. 253[99]) This anticipates the auto-erotic, largely tactile pleasure of the twentieth-century amateur musician who can dispense with acoustically adequate performance thanks to readily available sound recordings. In the chapter "Pianist Envy" of his book *Beethoven's Kiss*, Kevin Kopelson discusses this type with reference to several texts by Roland Barthes and also cites the *Journal* of André Gide, another amateur who preferred playing by himself: "He loved to 'satisfy himself' at the keyboard." (13)

---

[99]   Algernon's speech continues with the tag "I keep science for Life", which rounds the musical comment into a Wildean epigram but is really irrelevant.

Music as a code for homoeroticism in texts by Oscar Wilde and others is discussed in articles on *fin-de-siècle* poetry and sensation novels, for example[100]; I'll just point to E. M. Forster's *Maurice*, in which the emotional development of the protagonist as he matures towards recognition of his sexual identity is partly encoded by music. Maurice relives happy moments at the piano when he is a houseguest with his university friend Clive Durham: "Except for meals we need never be in the other part of the house [...]. Jolly, eh? I've a piano" (16:79). Memories of this harmony haunt a distressing visit which Maurice later pays to the newly married Clive. On a dismal evening, rain starts dripping on the piano through a leak in the ceiling, but then Alec Scudder, the gamekeeper (later Maurice's lover), is ordered in to help moving the piano (cf. 38:181). As Forster himself comments, Alec develops from a "croucher beside the piano and the rejecter of a tip and the haunter of shrubberies [...] into the sharer who gives and takes love" ("Terminal Note" quoted in the appendix to *Maurice* 238). Educated companionship *at* the piano, within conventional society, has failed Maurice at Cambridge; the unconventional love he comes to share with Alec emerges from under the piano, which is now gender equivocal, but continues to signify middle-class status and conventional sexual mores, as it does also in *Howards End*.

> For an educated man to seat himself at the pianoforte
> is no longer thought effeminate.
> ALGERNON ROSE. *Greater Britain, Musically Considered*

A quarter of a century after Charles Aïdé announced the "rapid development of a musical taste among us" (see above 121), prejudice against male musicianship began to soften enough to admit conventional masculinity to the keyboard. Even a tough servant of the Empire could now be comforted by a piano in a colonial outpost:

> In the wearisome monotony of bush life, such a solace cannot easily be dispensed with nowadays. For an educated man to seat himself at the pianoforte is no longer thought effeminate, and a musical instrument renders life in lonely regions less insupportable than it otherwise would be. (Rose, 15)

---

[100] Cf. Sutton, "The Music Spoke for Us", and Law, "The 'Perniciously Homosexual Art'".

In that prototype of the modern detective novel, *Trent's Last Case*, the handsome and effective detective[101] stumbles into declaring his love for the widowed Mrs. Manderson when moved by the masterly "perfection of execution and feeling" of her playing. "'You are a musician born,' he said quietly when she had finished, and the last tremor of the music had passed away. 'I knew that before I first heard you. [...] I think I knew it the first time I saw you'." (Bentley, 13:251-252) This is no longer conditioned seduction by accomplishment because the man knows too much about music. He is finally an adequate listener for a competent and willing female performer who does not need to resort to coyness: "[W]hen he asked if she would delight him again [...] she consented at once." (13:261)

Tertius Ingpen in Arnold Bennett's *These Twain*, a keen amateur musician on several instruments, fascinates the more stolid Edwin and Hilda Lessways with his eccentricities – which are, however, not of the boyish or effeminate sort. He is, solidly, District Factory Inspector in the Five Towns, but has lived in London, prides himself on his (pleasant) outspokenness, rides a bicycle on which he brings interesting scores along to social evenings and remembers only after an evening of duet playing that he has eaten nothing all day. He proposes sight-reading "Mozart fiddle sonatas" with a proficient lady pianist, admits unapologetically: "I thoroughly enjoy playing the clarinet in a bad orchestra whenever I get the chance" (1:5:62) and courageously and enthusiastically plays piano duets with many wrong notes. Edwin Lessways, having learnt to have "a vague idea 'where a player was' on a page" (1:5:61), turns the pages and the performers are pleasantly excited by their success. The upshot is that regular musical evenings are planned and "a new and promising friendship was in the making" (1:5:64) – and nobody is 'punished' for enjoying music. This neutrally presented variety of musical experience is typical of the openness of the Edwardian music discourse; Bennett's world is so saturated with detail as to be almost ideologically opaque, without the palpable narratorial agenda of disapproval that would have been compulsory thirty years earlier.

---

[101] Trent's artistic temperament is a typical feature of nineteenth-century detectives but also points forward to suavely attractive figures like Dorothy L. Sayers' Lord Peter Wimsey and Paul Gallico's Alexander Hero in *Too Many Ghosts* and *The Hand of Mary Constable*.

May Sinclair's *The Helpmate* conventionally avoids musical inter-action between spouses, but shows husband and wife reacting differ-ently to a mutual friend's playing. The Majendies' marriage is in dan-ger because Anne Majendie has been refusing herself to her husband after his honeymoon confession of a pre-marital affair; likeable young Charlie Gorst is in love with Walter Majendie's invalid sister Edie. Eventually, Anne's unsympathetically drawn righteousness drive both Walter and Charlie from the house and into the arms of 'fallen' women. The reactions to Charlie's playing for Edie as he "joyously" dusts the instrument to play Chopin's "Grande Polonaise"[102] sharply define the three listeners' characters.

> He let himself loose with it, with a rush, a vehemence, a diabolic brilliance and clamour. The quiet room shook with the sound he wrenched out of the little hum-ble piano in the corner. And as Edith lay and listened, her spirit, too, triumphed, and was free, it rode gloriously on the storm of sound. [...] This was the miracle that he alone could accomplish for her. (15:128)

To Anne downstairs it seems "the most immoral music, the music of defiance and revolt", while her husband's face lights up "responsive to the delight and challenge of the opening chord". Anne meantime re-solves "that Mr. Gorst's music was never to be heard again in this house" (15:128) and the continuing music provides an ironical com-ment to their arguing. When she threatens to go out for his dinner vis-its, Mr. Gorst upstairs bursts into a "hilarious" dance piece; "'As long as Edie will go on seeing him, he'll think it's all right.' Overhead Mr. Gorst's gay tune proclaimed that indeed he thought so" (15:132). The end of Gorst's performance signals time for Edie to retire for the night. The denunciation of Victorian gender norms includes contempt for a too-conservative wife, but also a shared experience of music between a group of people who are differentiated by their reactions to music but never mocked for liking it.

---

[102] Chopin's *Grande Polonaise* op. 22 is preceded by a quiet "Andante spianato". Possibly the Polonaise op. 53 in A flat is meant, an impressively fiery work which does open with a series of loud chords with 'rushes' of semiquavers in between.

2. Triumph: Passion and Professionalism

2.1. A New Perspective on the Drawing Room

As musical expertise was becoming acceptable and even fashionable, the voices of professionals emerge to underscore the increasing value of musical quality in Edwardian literature. Musicians' memoirs were very popular and their accounts of eager female students afford interesting material for the study "of that curious disease, pianomania" (Shaw, *Musical Criticism* 2:207). Musical aspirations were still hampered, as in the anecdote about Anton Rubinstein quietly advising a young hopeful: "My dear young lady, get married" (quoted in Kuhe, 220). The Victorian argument for music as service could still backfire on young pianists, as in this magazine editor's answer to a letter in *Our Mothers and Daughters* of 1892:

> Your work and your mission are [at home]. God can accept no service which is self-imposed while positive duties are neglected. I am sorry your father's tastes and yours do not agree about music; but you owe the cultivation of your talent to his money and should certainly humour his fancies. (Quoted in Gorham, 183)

Even the composer Sterndale Bennett encouraged a woman student: "though you are not a public player, yet remember that I tell you you have not for all that missed your vocation" (quoted in Walker, *Experiences* 39). Artistic reasons are adduced to bolster this line of argument: "There is [...] one training which the amateur does not get – that of public opinion – and yet to this the artist is at times compelled to sacrifice his convictions" (25). The familiar unfair bargain (though on a much higher technical level) now demanded true proficiency but still forbade professionalism. Frederick James Crowest observes that the socially imposed role of "great Listener" had been reversed into "sole performer": every "educated girl [has] to shine musically in the drawing-room [while] those who would have her ambitious there, decline to countenance anything approaching what they term a 'public' [...] appearance" (282-289).

Analogously, fictional narratives now pit professional musical ambition against marriage. Musician novels (cf. Binstock, *Study*, Fuller, "Cribb'd", and Weliver, "Music") continue to be plagued by technical blunders, but they are becoming more plausible as representations of both musicians' experiences and general attitudes to music. In George Gissing's *The Whirlpool*, a fatal neglect of wifely and motherly duties is the inevitable collateral of a woman violinist's ambition, while

Frank Frankfort Moore's *The Food of Love* ends with the marriage of 'cellist Maurice Neverne to a soprano who does retire immediately after marriage, but only because her mother does not have the time to help out with domestic duties (cf. 29:318-319). The couple's German mentor even prophesies: "You will come back, both of you. You cannot help it. You will come back to the lyric platform", and the novel concludes: "Well, perhaps they will." (29:319)

As the experience of professionals and advanced amateurs becomes (re-)presentable, ridicule for the inept emerges also in musicians' memoirs. Francesco Berger reports a milkman's boasts about his daughter being "a *completitioner* at the 'Universal Palace' for the Piano-prize": "There's three minutes allowed for each player to get through [the set piece], but my S'lina she can do it in two, that's why I know she'll get the prize" (187). Wilhelm Kuhe, fed up with working hard for nothing at musical 'At Homes'[103], one evening played the same piece three times over, asked the hostess which she preferred and got a serious answer: "'not that I didn't appreciate the others, only the second one was sweetly melodious.' I told her I thought her discrimination wonderful. And so it was." (367) Although the liberty to speak during music was over with an increased (if token) respect for music, the enforced appreciative comments ring as hollow as ever: "The music stopped with a crash. The hostess cried 'Oh, how delicious! Thank you! And which of the dear old masters was that?' The conversation leaped joyously into freedom." (Bottome, 264)

Fictional listeners, too, are now laughed at for ignorant *pretence* to musicality rather than for loving music. Instead punishing excessively good and obnoxiously bad playing, novels now ridicule gushing or ignorantly patronizing hostesses and inept hopefuls as well as bad taste[104] and fashionably pretentious ignorance. This ironic perspective is often provided by music teachers that give a new lease of life to the Regency topos worked out in *The Wanderer* (see above 69). The young piano teacher Ellen Carstairs, protagonist of Catherine Carswell's *Camomile*, describes how a solo of 'Yankee Doodle' on a comb with left-handed piano accompaniment produces "unconcealed

---

[103] For a description of similar incidents involving Arthur Sullivan, Joseph Joachim and others cf. Gillett, "Ambivalent" (325).

[104] Wilfrid Owen, for example – not a first-rate pianist himself – prayed to be "preserved from [...] the player who in the same chord strikes the bass before the treble" (557, 09/06/1918).

relief in every face! And the applause – what a reflection upon any applause that had gone before!" (Carswell, 166)

Alma, the Story of a Little Music Mistress focuses its disdain on one Mrs. Law who is too mean to pay for an expensive professor ("Dr. Earle was so far out of her reach! And yet, in that social ladder of success up which she longed to see her girls climb, music was such an important factor!"; Marshall, 1:7) and instead hires Alma. At the humiliating interview (where Mrs. Law is mainly intent on lowering fees), she wakes the old piano to new life and holds Mrs. Law's son Herbert spellbound with "the plaintive cry of Beethoven's sonata in E flat".

> "That is music," he thought; [...]. But when Alma ceased, Mrs. Law said in her dry, unsympathetic voice: – "Something a little more lively now, Miss Montgomery; that kind of music is not what takes in a drawing-room. Have you no waltz or air with variations?" Something like an amused smile rippled over Alma's face, but she made no reply, merely striking a few sharp chords, and then playing with quick spirit a set of waltzes which were popular at the time. (2:18)

By avoiding the cheap and tedious delight of an 'air with variations', Alma demonstrates her good taste even when requested to play popular music.

Like Juliet Ellis' worst clients (see above 69), Mrs. Law prolongs her daughter's lessons or sits in on them at Alma's expense, but would never "waste the time by talking" to this musical lackey. She also forces Alma to play dance music at the parties she gives for her three daughters, but intervenes sharply when her son Herbert is so impressed with Alma's playing that he asks her to dance with him: "'Miss Montgomery, will you have the goodness to return to your duties at the piano,' she said, the feathers on her head vibrating with the wearer's repressed emotion." (10:119) When Alma and Herbert nevertheless confess their love on the way home, Alma is dismissed the week after. Through the way in which Mrs. Law punishes what to her is the scandalous misbehaviour of a grasping 'professional person', the novel represents the episode as true love at odds with unjustifiable and occasionally ridiculous snobbery[105]. Alma herself does not make

---

[105] Frank Frankfort Moore's *Künstlerroman Food for Love* contains a delightful passage ridiculing outmoded clichés of gender and nationality: a mother confides her worries about her son's plans to become a professional cellist: "I have never met any of these foreign musicians, but I suspect they are rather dreadful. [...] Whatever he may be, Maurice will never be a foreign musician", and is consoled by a friend: "I am

her moral superiority explicit, but is merely conscious of a professional musical advantage.

Ellen Carstairs in *The Camomile* defends herself with rather more spirit from predatory lady clients. When she is asked to play, regularly and for free, to the unborn child of a society lady while the mother (who hates classical music) is taking a nap, she ends the employment by "executing" two forbidding Bach preludes and fugues: "Executed is just about the right word! I played them with such vigour that sleep was out of the question for her, and I scarcely paused between the end of one and the beginning of another. Strangely enough, I don't think I ever played them better" (168-169). Ellen exits in high spirits and is never asked back.

Such disdain for philistine 'pillars of society' also bolsters the stature of a pianist who never teaches in Mary Patricia Willcock's *Wings of Desire*. The socialite Mrs. Woodruffe wants Sara Bellew's music and her husband's fame to "burn like sacred lamps before the shrine of the Woodruffe gentility" at her parties:

> "Dear Mrs. Bellew, we cannot possibly let you off! Such a cachet! It will be like having Paderewski or Madame Schumann within our portals[106]. Do, do let me entreat you. And if I might suggest before the lovely Brahms you play so exquisitely, just some Beethoven – perhaps the Kreutzer Sonata." (6:98)

Mrs. Woodruffe is "catching wildly at the tail of culture", but recants immediately when reminded of the "aroma" which Tolstoy's 1891 eponymous novella about a murdered adulteress has given to Beethoven's Kreutzer Sonata: "No, no, of course not [...]. Of course one wouldn't wish dear Mrs. Bellew to play it." (6:98-99) However, Sara's desire is in the end allowed to spread its wings unpunished: she leaves her unworthy husband, achieves a perfect partnership with a perfect lover and becomes a successful concert pianist. Married off for convenience by her scheming parasitic father, young Sara had resented compliments about her performance: "What's the good? I never can do anything with it, tied as I am down here. I feel like a rat caught in a trap" (7:128), but finally escapes to study abroad and become a professional. Physically, she is the type of the Victorian non-pianist:

---

glad that you have put down your foot down there; it is well to give him to understand that you know where to draw the line." (1:9)

[106] Mrs. Woodruffe's conventionality is underscored by her reference to foreign rather than British virtuosos.

[...] a tall woman with a square head crowned with the black parted hair above a low broad forehead. Her type is found constantly in Provence. Her hair, buoyant and crisp, encircled her head with the curves first caught by a Roman chisel. A still woman, she moved gracefully. (2:2)

It is significant that such dignity is now afforded to a *performer*.

Sara protects the private space of her music-room by deflecting her husband with dance tunes that make "his pulses [...] sway to the music". When he starts dancing with his sister-in-law, Sara herself laughs happily, "swinging to her music, in the glimmer of the candles on the piano" and then returns to her work with relief, "hot on the mastering of difficulties [... stopping] to analyze, to repeat, rejoicing in her own powers" (12:255-256). Even her husband's confession that he used to *really* love (i. e. was engaged and went to bed with) another woman is framed as an unwelcome intrusion on Sara's practice: "Father Bach died away into silence as Sara looked up from her piano keys to find her husband standing just within the lighted circle that revealed the heavy timbered roof of her music room. 'What is it, Archer?' she exclaimed sharply." (13:279)

He characteristically explains his need to confess as a bid for her attention, telling her "[p]erhaps that you might look at me. You always give me the impression that I'm invisible to you. And I don't like the feeling" (13:283). His guilt is a relief to Sara: "I've never been his wife at all. I'm free. Before he – what they call, married me, he gave his best to another woman" (14:308). So she finally braves scandal to go and live with her new lover and embark on a European concert tour. A friend discussing her having "to go through the mud for all their sakes" concludes: "Never mind. She's above it all now." (16:354) This 'above' is not the celestial heaven of Victorian womanhood, nor the virginity demanded by a spiritual dedication to art, but a moral and artistic Parnassus. Ultimately, it is not conventional decency that determines Sara's artistic blossoming, but emotional truthfulness which is associated with music once the social ritual synonymous with deceit is overcome.

2.2. Finally: Playing Well, Unpunished

Sara Bellew's career reflects the fact that after the eight-hour stints imposed on girls around 1800, amateur players in the 1880s were again reaching near-professional technical standards. John Francis

Barnett remembers a girl who played both of Chopin's extremely virtuosic concerti, learning the F Minor one in three weeks at her ladies' school (cf. 149). The popular phrase 'fond of music' no longer meant "eager to please and play", but dedication to practice of "consuming earnestness" (Huneker, 292-293). Such advanced amateurs were not the antagonists of professionals, but co-existed with them on an extended but acknowledged continuum (cf. Gillett, "Ambivalent"). What they had in common was an earnestness that led individuals to "abstain from musical performance altogether, because their musical standards are higher than their own ability" (Schmitz, 18).

As music-lovers with a more informed taste and likings grew more numerous towards the end of the century, complaints about the enduring awfulness of the popular middlebrow piano repertoire are no longer limited to cranky, eccentric music-lovers such as Thomas Love Peacock. In 1892, an anonymous letter to the editor of the *Musical Opinion* deplores the young lady who

> cherishes a belief that "The Maiden's Prayer" – so called presumably because it leads to profanity in others – is the greatest and most tuneful composition in the whole répertoire of music. [...] In this masterly composition the hands of the executant cross over, I believe, and this prodigious feat of gymnastics is supposed to indicate a very high degree of general culture. ("Women and the Piano" 37)

It is new that music of any kind should indicate "general culture" and that mediocre piece is ridiculed for its supposed part in this aspiration. The success of Tea Badarzewska's bland super-seller, which found over 80 publishers in Europe, Australia and the USA from 1856, is indeed almost ridiculous; it consists of a predictably structured eight-bar tune in E-flat which proceeds over the simplest imaginable harmonic pattern (I, II$_6$, V$_7$, I and V-I V-I) and is repeated five times with banal melodic figurations. Soon as famous (and notorious) as the similarly insipid "Battle of Prague" (see above 64), the piece inspired countless follow-up titles such as "Seconde prière d'une vierge", or "Prière exaucée, ou Réponse à la prière d'une vierge" and reams of predictable jokes at the expense of hopeful (or hopeless) maidens[107] who could now be expected to play more substantial music.

---

[107] In Frank Frankfort Moore's musician novel *The Food of Love*, a virtuoso returning to his suburban home inspires numerous young ladies to intensify their piano lessons from the local teacher, in the fond hope that some hastily drilled-in piece will captivate the famous artist. The only one not to grumble about the extra effort is, predictably, "the plainest and most mature" girl, hopelessly at work on "The Maiden's Prayer" (5:55-56).

While "The Maiden's Prayer" is laughed at, the names of Chopin and Beethoven now carry a weight which makes unjustified pretence to (or hopeless effort at) musicality downright immoral. A woman who basically represents the 'strong-but-unmusical' Victorian type in the *Autobiography of Mark Rutherford* is now characterized by a serious love of music which inspires "a great contempt for bungling, and not being a professional player, she never would try a piece in my presence of which she was not perfectly master" (White, 6:109). E. M. Forster makes a music teacher renounce her profession after Beethoven himself has appeared to her to make her hear his A minor quartet: "I have deceived the pupils and the parents and you. I am not musical, but pretended that I was to make money. What will happen to me now I don't know, but I can pretend no longer." ("Co-ordination" 192)

Arthur Pinero's box-office hit *The Second Mrs. Tanqueray* similarly uses musical ability to distinguish the heroine from conspicuously vulgar figures:

> LADY ORREYED. Oh yes, do play! That's the one thing I envy you for.
> PAULA TANQUERAY. What shall I play?
> LADY ORREYED. What was that heavenly piece you gave us last night, dear?
> PAULA TANQUERAY. A bit of Schubert. Would you like to hear it again?
> LADY ORREYED. You don't know any comic songs, do you?
> PAULA TANQUERAY. I'm afraid not. (3:109-110)

Paula uses cheap melodies only as a kind of desperate musical small talk in embarrassing or emotionally fraught situations. When an old friend visits and asks her to play to him, she tries to avoid a serious conversation: "Good morning. (*Brightly*) We've been breakfasting this side of the house, to get the sun. *She sits at the piano and rattles a gay melody.*" (2:64) An anonymous commercial prose version of Pinero's play hints that this inadequate performance falls below her usual standard.

> [She] rattled through a Schubert impromptu, in schoolgirl fashion. Then she turned round. "Don't moon about after me, Cayley," she said." [...] I wish you wouldn't stare so." [...] Paula played a little longer, mechanically, then slipped away in the middle of a phrase, and went to the window. (2:101-102)

Paula Tanqueray is later driven to suicide by hostile prejudice against her 'redeeming' marriage, and many transgressively gifted women in fiction are still not allowed to flourish the way Sara Bellew does[108]. But the male listener's pleasure no longer dominates either the reader's or the player's mind.

As playing becomes an opportunity for self-expression and independence in both genders, representations of the emotional comfort which Victorian treatises promised as a bonus of musical skill no longer reduce it to desperately unsuccessful, melancholy strumming. In the guise of almost professionally skilled players like Mrs. Manderson in *Trent's Last Case* or Lady May Davenant in *The New Antigone* (see above 176), it becomes impressive and effective. Lady May is waiting for her fiancé to recover from brain fever,

> from day to day, without hope, letting the hours creep on, and finding existence like sand in the mouth. She lived a proud solitary life, making the most of her music as the channel of emotions she must otherwise conceal, and conscious every day that she was walking in a vain shadow (Barry, 3:3:33:201).

This description respects the woman's plight and the relief she seeks in playing, while earlier mid-Victorian texts made playing for solace ineffectual and earlier ones despised it as "nourishment of grief" (see above 107) or useless "reveries" (see above 102). In Louise Creed's *The Music Makers*, a woman flees to the piano, deeply depressed after discovering her husband's infidelity. Over Chopin's "wonderful First Ballade [...] gradually all the storm and stress began to die down. The hatred fled from the atmosphere." (Quoted in Gillett, *Musical Women* 5)

Creed's exact mention of the piece that is being played is typical of an increasing respect for women's music (even though the technically very demanding G minor *Ballade* op. 23 was available in a simplified edition). In Ella Hepworth Dixon's *Story of a Modern Woman*, an older friend of the would-be-artist heroine has done sculpture in Paris, swears in French and has "serious views". Also, "with the best heart in the world, she had a somewhat caustic tongue, could interpret Chopin like an artist[109], and always had her hair exquisitely dressed" (46). The generic obligation to 'play the piano' is forgotten: instead of the earlier hints about 'a composition by Handel' (who never wrote anything

---

[108] Cf. James Bailey's Helena, who enthuses to her lover: "I love this instrument; it speaks; it thinks! nay, I could kiss it. Look! / Jealous? Three things love I, half killingly: / Thee lastly; and this, next; and myself first." (23:16'353-356)

[109] The term 'artist' may be tinged with slight irony here, but certainly does not imply exoticism or depravity.

for the pianoforte), or generic 'concertos' (i. e. showy solo pieces) by
third-raters like Kalkbrenner, a composer is specified (Chopin and
Beethoven are the favourites) and a personal quality of performance is
implied. The time-honoured "Literary Maltreatment of Music" (cf.
Edwards, "Maltreatment") continues even in books by near-profes-
sionals such as Catherine Carswell, but descriptions now tend to relate
recognizably to firsthand experience:

> To keep myself from crying I practised frantically at the Brahms Intermezzo in G
> minor. With what a soaring, generous melody it opens! It set my grieving spirit
> free and gave my soul great pinions. But what a state my hands are in with want
> of practice! To-day they are aching badly after half an hour of Czerny. (Carswell,
> 50)

While Brahms left no G minor *Intermezzo*, his G minor *Rhapsody* op.
79/2 is a 'hit' of moderate difficulty which does open with a 'soaring'
theme and a dramatic flying hand-cross, and the technical exigencies
of Czerny's classical finger training are indeed apt to fatigue untrained
muscles. In such descriptions the piano's capability to console its
(woman) players is finally made flesh.

> She struck chords as if firing shots after him.
> JOSEPH CONRAD. "Freya of the Seven Isles"

As women are represented as playing for themselves, the erotic triangle man-woman-piano (which continues to exist) acquires a new centre of gravity. The keyboard instrument no longer weighs the player
down as it had been doing since Shakespeare's Sonnet 128, but becomes the woman's accomplice, while the male listener no longer
controls the scene. Joseph Conrad's Freya of the Seven Isles, an
eighteen-year-old who lives on a South Sea island with her retired
sailor father and an 'upright grand' from which her scales resound to
passing ships, virtually plays an unwelcome suitor off the island.

> Freya, aware that he had stopped just behind her, went on playing without turning
> her head. She played with spirit, brilliantly, a fierce piece of music, but when his
> voice reached her she went cold all over. [...] "I say, won't you leave off this con-
> founded playing?" [...] She shook her head negatively, and in desperation put on
> the loud pedal, but she could not make the sound of the piano cover his raised
> voice. "You are fit for a prince." Freya did not turn her head. Her face went stiff
> with horror and indignation. [...] It was best to ignore – to ignore. She went on
> playing loudly and correctly, as though she were alone, as if Heemskirk did not
> exist. [...] Standing behind her, he devoured her with his eyes, from the golden
> crown of her rigidly motionless head to the heels of her shoes, the line of her
> shapely shoulders, the curves of her fine figure swaying a little before the key-
> board. (4:194-195)

As ever, the sex appeal is visual and the music a mere annoyance –
but the narratorial voice is now distanced from the gaze of the male
listener and makes him look despicable. Heemskirk is reduced to
grabbing Freya's waist, whereupon she smacks him and takes her revenge when he leaves the next day:

> She was excited, she tingled all over, she had tasted blood! [...] She [...] dashed
> at the piano [...] and made the rosewood monster growl savagely in an irritated
> bass. She struck chords as if firing shots after [him ...] and then she pursued him
> with the same thing she had played the evening before – a modern, fierce piece of
> love music. (4:207)

Freya continues "with triumphant malice" until at the last whistle of
Heemskirk's departing boat she feels "a sudden discontent, a nervous
lassitude, as though she had passed through some exhausting crisis"
(4:207). It must be noted that Victorian 'punishment by plot' kicks in
eventually: Heemskirk's revenge is to ruin Freya's fiancé, which
drives him into madness and Freya to an early death of 'anaemia'. But
the retribution for excessive self-determination is at least delayed
(which allows time for its musical expression), and it is not explicitly
blamed on the girl.

A rather less dramatic but emotionally analogous situation occurs
in Keble Howard's pious family saga *The Smiths of Surbiton*. Enid
Smith is quite an imperious young lady, a pianist of the new dignified
sort, "taller than her husband by some two or three inches, carried herself well, knew both how to buy and how to wear clothes, had studied
the piano at the Royal College of Music, sang a little, and regarded her
mother with a dutiful toleration" (7). When her husband angrily goes
for a walk after their first tiff, Enid employs the same means as Freya,
and is perfectly understood:

> Enid, hearing the front door close, rushed across to the piano and began to play,
> with the loud pedal down, the gayest piece she knew. Ralph, although fully recog-
> nizing the futility of the proceeding, bit savagely on the stem of his pipe. There
> was no door to slam, unfortunately, but he did the best he could with the front
> gates. (25-26)

It is in such scenes that Lucy Green's general claim that female in-
strumentalists (as opposed to singers) are by definition in control of
their activity becomes (partly) true for the first time: "The display
[which an instrumentalist] enacts, rather than that of a playful or alluring singing bird, is that of a more controlled and rational being who
appears capable of using technology to take control over a situation"
(Green, 53). Whether it serves private relief or confident communica-

tion, the emotional effectiveness of music is no longer suppressed by disapproving narrators.

> If she had enjoyed his music,
> had he not a right to enjoy hers?
> MAY SINCLAIR. *The Divine Fire*

The suspension of disapproval for emotional relief through music even extends to romantic couples at the piano that would earlier have been condemned as adulterous. The musical meetings of true soulmates who 'shouldn't really' be married to their lawful but unsuitable spouses are often viewed sympathetically. Jude Fawley stops playing a comforting hymn in the "empty schoolroom" when Sue Bridehead comes up: "I can't strum before you! Play it for me." Sue complies without hesitation, "and her rendering of the piece, though not remarkable, seemed divine as compared with his own. She, like him, was evidently touched –to her own surprise – by the recalled air; and when she had finished, and he moved his hand towards hers, it met his own half-way." Both feel the attraction: "'Sue, I sometimes think you are a flirt' [...]. 'I can't talk to you any longer, Jude! [...] It is getting too dark to stay together like this, after playing morbid Good Friday tunes that make one feel what one shouldn't! [...] We mustn't sit and talk in this way any more.'" (Hardy, *Jude* 4:1:219-221)

Ada Leverson's *The Little Ottleys* offers a lighter version of the same scene. Edith Ottley, married to an unutterably fatuous man, is visited by Aylmer Ross (whom she will eventually marry) when she is "trying over a song, which she was accompanying with one hand" because she "felt in the mood to stop at home and play the piano to-day". When Aylmer asks Edith to play it again, she goes "back to the piano at once, and went on trying over the song that she didn't know, without making any excuse for the faltering notes". The narrator comments: "Nine women out of ten would have refused, saying they knew nothing of music, or that they were out of practice, or that they never played except for their own amusement, or something of the kind." (210) Every Regency or Victorian educationalist would have approved of such simplicity and unaffected compliance – except that they are not used to soothe a brother or edify a father, but to impress a man who will make the player break her marriage vows. The unconventional/unsuitable match between an heiress and a cockney poet of genius in May Sinclair's early novel *Divine Fire* similarly begins with her unaffected readiness to play for him: "Why not? If she had enjoyed his music [i. e. poetry], had he not a right to enjoy hers? [...] When she had stopped playing [the "Appassionata"] he rose and held out his hand to say good-night. 'Thank you. I don't think so badly of my life now. You've given me one perfect moment.'" (155) When Lucia plays at his boarding-house, Keith Rickman forgets everything: "as the stream of music flowed through the half-lit room, it swept away all sense of his surroundings [... and] bore down upon the barriers that stood between him and Lucia. And swept them away, too [...] and high above it all, it was as if his soul made music with her." (392-393) It must be noted that those 'barriers' consist of Keith's vulgar young fiancée; such a music-fuelled breach of promise would not have received any narratorial empathy two decades earlier.

The new insistence on the moral worth of emotions that are communicated or liberated by music goes as far as to make a *moral* failure of a lack of empathy or emotional involvement. In Henry James's short story "The Beast in the Jungle", John Marcher perceives his own emotional and moral blindness to love as "selfishness". He is at pains to make up for it "by inviting his friend to accompany him to the opera. His point was made, he thought, [...] for instance, at such hours, when it befell that, her piano at hand and each of them familiar with it, they went over passages of the opera together" (3:81-82). But John Marcher misses love. The shallow, unlikeable heroine of May Sinclair's first novel, *Audrey Craven*, also fails to communicate her intentions by music, in what is half attempt at seduction, half act of self-defence. Her explorer fiancé (one of three altogether, before her marriage to a nonentity) proposes to take her with him to Canada.

> In order to assert herself against the intolerable fascination [of this suggestion] she rose hastily and crossed the room to where her piano stood open in the corner. She played loud and long, – wild Polish music [by Chopin, in all probability] alive with the beating pulses of love and frenzy and despair. It would have roused another man to sublime enthusiasm or delirious rapture. It sent Hardy to sleep. (22)

Audrey continues to play and the reader is treated to an insight into her aggressive fantasies dreaming "that he stood with her on the midst of the burning prairie, they two on a little ring of charred black earth. [...] As he turned to her she thrust him from her into the sea of fire, crying, 'It's perfectly fair, Vincent, for you dragged me here against my will!'"(23) In reality, he simply wakes up when she stops playing and catches a late train home. Audrey, who has "no inner life", is "doomed to a life of performance, to [...] 'the feminine masquerade'", being a "feminine creature artless in perpetual artifice, for ever revealing herself in a succession of disguises" (Raitt, 70). The lack of artistic and emotional authenticity in both listeners and performers, which is indicated by disguise, is as fatal as moral transgressions were earlier.

3. Beyond the Piano

However impressive Sara Bellew's soaring on the wings of pianistic desire (see above 188), however urgent the newly-admitted emotional intensity of musical experience, the literary future did not lie with passionate amateurs or female concert pianists, but with women's liberation from the piano. In many cases, this happened gradually as the musical work ethic began to give way to the Edwardian 'Gospel of fun' and practice regimes lightened thanks to the pianola and recording technology. A more significant trajectory of emancipation is sketched in (often autobiographical) fictions in which a period of intense involvement with music is followed by the realization that the piano is too riddled with its problematic past to be compatible with female emancipation, and the piano is consequently abandoned.

3.1. Practising

> Without the ennui and slavery of practice,
> she was enchanting herself.
> ARNOLD BENNETT. *These Twain*

George Bernard Shaw looked forward early on to that golden age when affordable reproduction technology would help everybody "to recreate him" without a piano so that "everybody will see at last what an execrable, jangling, banging, mistuned nuisance our domestic music machine is, and the maddening sound of it will thenceforth be no more heard in our streets" (*Musical Criticism* 3:123). The Edwardian emphasis on consumption found its most typical expression in the pianola, but there were also other shortcuts being promised as the association of 'music and morals' was loosening:

> NOTICE! NOTICE! NOTICE! – Challenge to the World. – £ 5 to any Person not blind and in full possession of their faculties who fails to play the Piano, Organ, or Harmonium immediately by my MAGIC PIANOFORTE INSTRUCTOR. (Quoted in the *Musical Times* of November 1, 1879, p. 579)

Similarly, "Roylance's Numerical system" was supposed to teach "a choice selection of forty sacred and secular melodies composed for the use of those who have no time to study music. Thousands are now able to play who did not believe such a thing possible" (*Musical Times* March 1883, quoted in Scholes, 329). The gender of the thousands is no longer an issue, nor is it indicated in the consumer's thank-you letter which Scholes reproduces.

More and more women were unable to play but continued to cherish dreams of performance. When Hilda Lessways in Arnold Bennett's *These Twain* remembers a musical evening at which she has heard Dvořák's *Legends* (op. 59) for piano duet, she idly attempts to trace a melody that has impressed her, with "much labour and many slow hesitations".

> She was now exasperatingly spelling with her finger a fragment of melody […]. Now she had recognizably pieced its phrases together, and as her stiff finger stumbled through it, her ears heard it once more; and she could not repeat it often enough. What she heard was not what she was playing, but something finer – her souvenir of what Tertius Ingpen had played; and something finer than that, something finer than the greatest artist could possibly play – magic! (1:7:73)

This is basically the wish for reproduction, a passive musical experience: "It was in the nature of a miracle to her that she had been able to reproduce the souvenir in physical sound. […] And at the same time she was abject because she 'could not play the piano'." Hilda imagines sacrificing "many happinesses" in order to play at least as well as her little son, and considers how rapturous it would be to be a "world-renowned pianist", such as she has never even heard, "dominating immense audiences in European capitals". But she does not practice, remaining in a daydream: "Meanwhile, without the ennui and slavery of practice, she was enchanting herself." (1:7:74)

> The tea-rose tea-gown
> Supplants the mousseline of Cos,
> The pianola "replaces"
> Sappho's barbitos.
> EZRA POUND. *Hugh Selwyn Mauberley*

A big step towards the perfect realization of such recreational, passive enjoyment was the player piano or pianola which flourished in the first three decades of the twentieth century. These self-playing instruments are steered by perforated paper rolls that determine pitches and rhythm. Some models record and reproduce also the dynamics and pedalling of a given performance, while the 'player piano' proper allows for a personalized rendition through levers which allow some control over volume and tempo. More effectively than miraculous practise-free 'Systems', these are "vastly superior" pieces of furniture – mentioned along with gramophone, motor-car and "a lift to bring the plates from the kitchen into the dining-room" in a 1919 novel (Walpole, 1:6) – accelerated the move from disciplinary practice regimes to the consumer culture which was undermining the piano's domestic position. The speaker in Thomas Hardy's poem "To a Lady Playing and Singing in the Morning" decides to "lurk here listening, / Though nought be done, and nought begun, / And work-hours swift are scurrying" (ll. 2-4). Rather than solace a hard-working *pater familias*, female performance now functions as an incitement to the wasting of work time and is welcomed as such. As "desire began to replace property as the 'symbolic badge of individuality'" (Trotter, 13) in the 1870s, the pianola took the musical experience part of the way to the complete passivity afforded by recording technology.

Not surprisingly, male amateurs, who were less inured to extended practising, left particularly passionate testimonials to the 'player piano'. The designer and art critic Charles Ricketts stresses its artistic possibilities as well as the physical and mental effort which the use of the pedals imposed. "The first day of its arrival I played on it for some five hours, and was prostrate in the evening, in a new shirt – the former one had got wet through – and with sore insteps and back of thighs" (quoted in Kermode, 481). While girls had to "sit upright and pay attention to details" (Haweis, *Morals* 515), the male pianola player works up an honest sweat and immediately considers the pianola an accomplice; Ricketts calls it "a friend – a rather expensive friend, but this probably adds to friendship, affection, love!" (Quoted in Kermode, 481)

Other literary appearances of the pianola accentuate the uncanniness of independent "rattle-trap pianos which never stop" (Marshall, 94). In Joseph Conrad's *The Secret Agent*, a pianola echoes the violent plans of political conspirators in a restaurant with its "aggressive [...] brazen" noise. Its keys, which "rose and sank mysteriously" (4:61), are a sad, emasculated shadow of the Elizabethan leaping jacks (see above 20). When the suicide of one of the protagonists, Winnie Verloc, is announced as an "act of madness or despair" in the newspaper, the pianola in a bar plays "through a valse cheekily, then fell silent all at once, as if gone grumpy" (13:310). In Kurt Vonnegut's dystopian *Player Piano*, a proletarian bar pianola is a symbol of a more human past, a "brassy, dissonant antique" (9:91) in a computer-dominated world, a ghost of the past: "See – see them two go up and down, Doctor! Just the way the feler hit 'em. Look at 'em go! [...] Makes you feel kind of creepy, don't it, Doctor, watching them keys go up and down? You can almost see a ghost sitting there playing his heart out." (3:28)

> I don't want a piano, nor a reading-stand, nor a sofa.
> I simply want a place that I can call my own.
> MAY SINCLAIR. *The Helpmate*

The pianola did not last very long: in 1925, more player pianos than ordinary ones were manufactured in England, but sales collapsed in 1929, and long before that literary texts had begun to dispense with pianos of any kind. The most telling portents of the nearing end is not so much the increasing "hostility towards piano ownership", which grew "as the piano gradually lost its exclusivity as an index of social status" (Da Sousa Correa, 211, note 85), nor the continuing complaints about the medical, moral and intellectual perils of the obnoxious instrument, but all the novels that simply do not feature a piano. Famous examples include H. G. Wells's *Ann Veronica* (1910), Iota's *Yellow Aster*, and Emma Brooke's *A Superfluous Woman* (both 1894). In other novels, piano-free 'New Women' are contrasted with more conventional ladies who still play: when three orphan cousins set up house in London in Ethel Forster Heddle's *Three Girls in a Flat*, the only piano (serving mostly as a stand for bird-cages) is in the flat of their poor saintly neighbour Miss de Bréton Trip. Far from guaranteeing matrimony (it is the three "girls in a flat" that get married eventually), the piano is turning into the spinster's accessory it was to become for many a frustrated lady teacher in twentieth-century fiction[110]. Norman Gale's sugary "Aunt Jan" is at least a happy and child-loving singleton; her visits mean romping happiness for her nieces and nephews and even when she plays, "the piano seems alive, / With all the notes as busy as the bees are in a hive" (ll. 1-2 and 13-14), but in the same author's "The Old Piano" (see above 177) a "lank spinster, full of starch" (l. 13) raps the knuckles of tearful piano-pupils.

---

[110] See short stories such as Thomas Mann's "Das Wunderkind" (1904), Eudora Welty's "June Recital" (1949), and novels like Bernice Rubens's *Madame Sousatzka* (1962), Elfriede Jelinek's *Die Klavierspielerin* (1983), or Patrick Süskind's *Geschichte von Herrn Sommer* (1997).

Non-spinsters want out, escaping from the semi-public display of the piano and the constraints of the drawing-room into a more private and liberated place. Seven years before Virginia Woolf's *A Room of One's Own*, Carswell's heroine Ellen Carstairs formulates that central concern:

> Don't you agree that there must be something radically wrong with a civilisation in which a hard-working, serious young woman like myself cannot obtain, without enormous difficulty, expense or infliction of pain on others, a quiet, clean, pleasant room in which she can work [i. e. teach and practice music], dream her dreams, write out her thoughts, and keep her few treasures in peace? (2:18)

At the moment of speaking, the piano is still included in the furnishing of the 'room of one's own', but a few years later, Ellen gives up music to become a writer.

Just as expressing one's subjectivity at the piano is only an intermediate step, earning one's living as a music teacher confers independence but still smacks of the 'governess-trade' (see above footnote 44) or of Victorian piety. The aspiring teenage composer in *The Mirror of Music* is hampered by her mother's worries: "I tried to do some needle work and my mother was so pleased to see me away from the piano that she tried to show herself grateful by talking about music. She said it was one of God's best gifts." (Makower, 16) In Mrs. Humphry Ward's *Robert Elsmere*, the violinist Rosie is also given her first violin by her father, although he thinks it "wicked to care about anything except religion" (1:2:13:310) and asks her "not to make him sad before God that he had given me that violin" (1:2:3:312-313) when she practises too intently. Only when both dreaming and working can dispense with the piano, and when self-expression by music is substituted by communication through words, emancipation is complete. Just as the pianola was a short episode on the way to the gramophone for the lazy, the piano proper is only an intermediate step on the way away from music for passionately intellectual or artistic characters.

In conclusion, this development will be traced in more detail in three novels about proficient amateur pianists (written in 1898, 1905, and 1919 respectively). For E. M. Forster's Lucy Honeychurch, Sarah Grand's Beth Caldwell, and May Sinclair's Mary Olivier, music is simultaneously a prescribed accomplishment and a battleground for rebellion during childhood[111] and adolescence. Drawing, the decorous alternative for independent-minded Victorian women, is not mentioned in E. M. Forster's *A Room with a View*, "was not to be one of [Beth's] accomplishments" (Grand, 4:32), and never figures in *Mary Olivier* except in seven-year-old Mary's dream to "paint pictures and play the piano" (Sinclair, 2:2:2:69). All three women play with passionate emotional involvement but ultimately confront the inadequacy of music as an emancipatory activity and as a means of communication. Lucy Honeychurch is a very timid revolutionary; she does achieve some degree of a more independent 'view' of the world instead of being merely watched at the piano, but learns to speak rather than play only very gradually. 'Her' novel ends conventionally with her honeymoon, whereas the two more complete *Bildungsromane* (marked as such by their biographical titles, *The Beth Book* and *Mary Olivier: A Life*) extend their narrative span to include both childhood and accounts of adulthood that eschew marriage.

For all three girls, the familiar social routine of piano playing becomes available for scenarios of self-expression that transcend the repressive ritual of accomplishment. The childhood dreams of adulthood and emancipation which come into focus often involve music as a rite of passage, as when an eleven-year-old who is beginning to despise her "youth", becomes "important", goes to Evening Service, has a skirt hanging "a full inch below her knees" and practises "an hour every day of her own accord" (Sinclair, *Arnold Waterlow* 8:73). Such self-determined learning processes, practice routines and repertoire choices could be seen as significant attempts to re-define a crippling ritual in a girl's own favour. But although musical experiences often function as an emotional wake-up call to rebellion against the practice regimes enforced by conservative paradigms of femininity, music of any kind is still very closely associated with middle-class courtship rituals and with the kind of wifeliness which precludes moral adulthood. Memories of the disciplinary aspects of practicing imposed on

---

[111] Young Francie Fitzpatrick in Edith Somerville's *Real Charlotte* is taken back to her childhood when she hears a street organ playing a familiar piece of music, remembering herself "strumming it on Charlotte's piano, while Mr. Hawkins holding the indignant Mrs. Bruff on his lap, forced her unwilling paws to thump a bass. Now the difficult part, in which she always broke down, was being played; he had pretended there that he was her music teacher, and had counted out loud, and rapped her knuckles with a teaspoon, and gone on with all kinds of nonsense." (3:40:121-122)

girls and the humiliating position of governesses and music teachers are too vivid for music to be lastingly viable as a truly passionate leisure pursuit or a fulfilling career.

Given the historical ballast of the piano, bidding goodbye to the piano and the adolescent musical delights which it nurtured (music is still so predominantly associated with patriarchal repression that it offers only a temporary, illusionary escape into daydreams) becomes a gesture symbolic of simultaneously achieving adulthood and overcoming crippling gender norms. Frequently, this involves also the abandonment of marriage (actual or planned), that cornerstone of Victorian social constructions of femininity. The passionately and rebelliously musical protagonists of novels such as Sarah Grand's *Beth Book*, May Sinclair's *Mary Olivier*, and Catherine Carswell's *The Camomile*, all ultimately forsake music to find their own voice not in the pseudo-expressive 'language of music' but in the written word, as unmarried journalists or poets. In the course of true liberation and growing up, Edwardian heroines triumph with music and then leave it behind, mapping in their own lives the larger trajectory of the period.

3.2. "Too much Beethoven"

Lucy Honeychurch's subjectivity is not her own at first: "Lucy never knew her desires so clearly as after music" (Forster, *Room* 4:60): the Reverend Beebe's famous remark "I put it down to too much Beethoven" (3:59) in fact deprecates her unsuitable wish for an unaccompanied tram ride. But she has never "translate[d her vision] into human words, and [her] experiences into human actions" (2:50), the classical predicament of the Victorian girl silenced by the piano. The wordless kingdom of music, where those whom "breeding and intellect and culture have alike rejected" can experience success, is to Lucy "a more solid world" than daily life (2:50), as is evident from the helplessly platitudinous way in which she expresses her condition: "Oh, but your son wants employment. [...] I myself have worries, but I can generally forget them at the piano; and collecting stamps did no end of good for my brother." (2:48) In an earlier version of the novel, the Lucy figure is a submissively co-operative pianist who spends entire afternoons "patiently playing a throbbing accompaniment" (Forster, "Old Lucy" 38), but has decided opinions enough to leave her chaperone in Florence to visit friends in Rome. Forster soon abandoned that narrative, and it is indeed more convincing that Lucy should bewilder a parish hall audience with Beethoven's immensely difficult and not exactly 'pleasant' opus 111 yet be pliable enough away from the piano to let herself be dragged away from Florence by her prim spinster cousin.

That Lucy Honeychurch should be able to play Beethoven's last piano sonata somewhat strains realism, but the fact that the work finally found its way into a novel 80 years after its creation is significant. Beethoven had become *the* undisputed musical God towards the end of the century, the epitome of music as Shakespeare was that of drama, but nevertheless dangerous as a reputed rebel, as when a young theologian is told: "Beethoven [...] encourages a luxurious revelling in the incomprehensible and indefinably sublime. He is not good for you." (White, 6:109) This Victorian perspective is, however, no longer shared by the narrator of *A Room with a View*, who is sympathetic to Lucy's longings: "Like every true performer, she was intoxicated by the mere feel of the notes: they were fingers caressing her own; and by touch, not by sound alone did she come to her desire." (Forster, 3:51) The caresses between keys and fingers are no longer, as in Shakespeare's Sonnet 128, the fantasy of an infatuated listener, but the sensation of the pianist herself. Lucy is not playing for an audience: she is discovering and enjoying herself through music: "Once I said that I liked my own playing better than anyone's. My mother has never got over it. Of course, I didn't mean that I played well." (3:52)

This almost auto-erotic phase in Lucy's awakening is short and gives way as Lucy's 'view' broadens and her playing starts to communicate – if almost against her will – something of the emotions she is learning to perceive. During her engagement to the priggish Cecil Vyse, she is asked to play, botches it and then refuses to oblige any further:

> She had seen Gluck's *Armide* that year, and played from memory the music of the enchanted garden [but] such music is not for the piano, and her audience began to get restive, and Cecil, sharing the discontent, called out: "Now play us the other garden – the one in *Parsifal*." She closed the instrument. (15:173)

On discovering that George Emerson (who had kissed her wordlessly in Florence) is listening, too, Lucy exclaims incoherently, gets "very red" and opens the piano again "to escape further conversation. Cecil should have the *Parsifal*, and anything else that he liked. 'Our performer has changed her mind,' said Miss Bartlett. Lucy did not know what to do, nor even what she wanted to do. She played a few bars of the Flower Maiden's song very badly, and then she stopped." (15:174)

Lucy Honeychurch enacts no conscious defiance in the manner of Conrad's Freya Nelson (see above 193); instead narrator and reader share a truth about Lucy that she herself is not yet able to articulate. She is telling herself that she consents to oblige Cecil, while it is obviously the presence of George, to whom she really 'connects', that makes her play. As soon as her difficulty (having refused to play for her fiancé, she finds herself obliging her 'lover') is put into words by another, she stops, because her playing is no longer a secret code. Nor does it ever become an open means of communication; salvation through love only comes when Lucy is finally able to stop the emotional "Lying" to everybody which dominates the final chapters of the book and learns to use words rather than music in order to "come to her desire" (3:51). Lucy has truly had "too much Beethoven" since music has overlaid her personal life: her musically inspired gropings for emancipation are a false start which cannot represent a final revolt. Lucy does make a romantic, 'unsuitably' unconventional choice of partner, but it is rewarded by a conventional happy ending. Forster's tongue-in-cheek addendum, "A View Without a Room" (written in 1958), shows Lucy still married and living in suburban Highgate during World War II. In an attempt "to keep things together", she teaches piano and broadcasts "some Beethoven, who was quite all right this time" (Appendix to *Room* 232): musical rebellion is subsumed in the war effort and the musician is again wordless, without really overcoming Victorian constraints on women's language.

3.3. "If I had not struck the piano, I should have struck you"

Elizabeth Caldwell Maclure, the heroine of Sarah Grand's *Beth Book*, suffers more intensely than Lucy Honeychurch and experiences a less conventional closure which transcends music. From the beginning, music is a solace and a personal challenge, but also part of a disciplinary order which she fights continuously. Beth's first childish steps towards her own music: prompted by the charm of overheard music, she learns to play by herself *in spite* of her environment before the onset of the 'proper' lessons that are part of the Victorian disciplinary regime, and continues to resist them throughout. The unglamorous setting of her first musical experiences already establishes this theme of non-propriety:

> It was down in that empty kitchen that Beth first felt the enchantment of music. Some one suddenly played the piano overhead and Beth listened spell-bound. Again and again, the player played, and always the same thing, practising it. Beth knew every note. Long afterward she was trying some waltzes of Chopin's, and came upon one with which she was quite familiar […] but could not think when or where [she had studied it]. Presently, however, as she played it, she perceived a smell of black-beetles, and instantly she was back in that disused kitchen […], listening to the practising overhead. (2:17)

The narrative voice of the *Beth Book* is not completely in control of Beth's rebellion, possibly because of a lack of technical knowledge. Metaphors such as "the poorest instrument would lay hold of her, and set high chords of emotion vibrating, beyond the reach of words" belong to the worst sensualist kind of discourse, while the disclaimer that Beth's "ear was defective; she rarely knew if anyone sang flat" (17:149) discredits such sensitivity. This may be intended to exempt the girl from stereotypes of silly musicality in the Victorian fashion[112], but it is at odds with the way Beth is supposed to have taught herself music. When given a piano primer "one wet day to keep her quiet", she learns to read notes in one afternoon and "began at once to apply them practically at the piano. She soon knew all the early exercises and little tunes, and was only too eager to do more". This surreptitious use of music promptly meets its Victorian nemesis in Beth's mother (her official teacher), who cannot manage the girl: "[H]er mother hated the music-lesson more than any of the others, and was so harsh that Beth became nervous, and only ventured on the simplest things for fear of the consequences. When her mother went out, however, she tried what she liked." Beth tries to lengthen her fingers to manage a piece she likes ("my head will play it"), peruses music which her sister brings back from a holiday, "and in a few weeks knew all that it had taken Mildred six months to learn" (18:159).

When Beth implores her mother to teach her a difficult passage, she needs to insist: "'But I do so want to learn it,' […] 'Oh, very well […] But I warn you!'" In fact, Beth is soon beaten for not understanding a sign that has never been explained to her. Beth is "a piteous little figure, crouched on the piano-stool, her back bent beneath her mother's blows" (18:159), but by the next lesson, she is ready for confrontation:

---

[112] Like Maggie Tulliver, Beth hates the conventionally faultless and beautiful heroines and refuses to write such a character, "especially if she has golden hair yards long, a faultless complexion, and eyes of extraordinary dimensions" (Grand, 43:396).

on tiptoe, with slight creakings and rustlings [...]. Somebody was saying "how beautifully she plays." Life and warmth flowed into her. Exquisite, tingling life and warmth. "Go on. Go on." Mr. Sutcliffe's voice sounded miles away beyond the music. [...] She could see their hushed faces leaning nearer. You could make them happy by playing to them. They loved you because you made them happy. (4:2:5:216)

Even if it still continues the bargaining for love that her mother habitually enforced, this is one of Mary's happiest musical moments and – an unprecedented literary homage to the power of musical art.

Such musical triumph cannot last, of course; the Victorian constraints embodied by Mary's mother check her 'modern' longings again and again. Mary's supreme moment of progressive command, the Appassionata's concluding presto movement flowing "smoothly under her fingers, at an incredible pace, with an incredible certainty", is brutally curtailed by her father's fatal stroke that forces her back into a filial role. At first she does not realize what is going on: "Something seemed to be happening over there, outside the place where she heard the music. [...] She thought: 'Papa again.' But she was too happy to care. Nothing mattered so long as she could listen to herself playing the Moonlight Sonata." (4:2:5:217) But Mary can ward the interruption off only for a few seconds. Her father dies shortly after and the piano becomes a guilty thing again: "When he was in the fit she had been playing [...], conceited and happy, not caring. [...] She hated the conceited self that hadn't cared. The piano, gleaming sombrely in the hushed light, reminded her of it. She hated the piano." (4:2:11:222) Mrs Olivier is quick to suggest that making music constitutes a sinful refusal of mourning:

Under the [piano] lid the keys were stiffening with the damp. The hammers were swelling, sticking together. She tried not to think of the piano. [...] She turned and looked again at the piano. She went to it. She opened the lid and sat down before it. Her fingers crept along the keyboard; they flickered over the notes of the Sonata Appassionata: a ghostly, furtive playing, without pressure, without sound. And she was ashamed as if the piano were tempting her to some cruel, abominable sin. (4:2:14:229-230)

Now in her early twenties, Mary keeps house and nurses her invalid brother Roddy in increasing desperation: "So the first year passed. And the second. And the third year. She was five and twenty." The day after Roddy's death, "she got up and dressed and dusted the drawing-room. She dusted everything very carefully, especially the piano. She would never want to play on it again." (4:7:11:312)

But Mary does not abandon the instrument forever before encountering its full sensual and sentimental promise. This coincides with the flowering of her last 'romantic' relationship. Mary deduces that her intelligence has found its mate in her brother's friend Lindley Vickers because he reacts so sensitively to her musical language:

> You had only to play and he would come to you. [...] When you played the soft Schubert Impromptu he would sit near you, very quiet; when you played the Appassionata he would get up and stand close beside you. When you played the loud, joyful Polonaise he would walk up and down; up and down the room. (4:7:6:322)

A wordless world of conveniently veiled but effective communication seems finally possible.

However, the language of music is deceptive as ever: Vickers seems to announce his eventual defection through the lyrics of an old German folksong, but Mary does not choose to read this as a personal message:

> "Es ist bestimmt in Gottes Rath / Dass man vom liebsten was man hat / Muss scheiden." [...] She pounded out the accompaniment louder. "We won't, will we?" He jumped up suddenly."Play the *Appassionata*." She played and he talked. "I can't play if you talk." "Yes, you can. I wish I hadn't got to go tomorrow." (4:8:6:322-323)

Lindley Vickers returns to the village hotel after his visit to Dan has officially ended and the pair continue to communicate against Mamma's threatening presence. "Es ist bestimmt" becomes a call to the desired man, always threatening to spill their secret:

> Her fingers pressed and crept over the keys, in guilty, shamed silence; it would be awful if he heard you playing, if Dan heard you or Mamma. You had only to play and you could make him come. Supposing you played the Schubert Impromptu – She found herself playing it. He didn't come. He wasn't coming. [...] Her hands dropped from the keys. It wasn't possible. [...] Mary began to play the Sonata Appassionata. She thought: "I don't care if he doesn't come. I want to play it, and I shall." He came. He stood close beside her and listened. (4:8:7:324-325)

Vickers's ready concern with her playing for its own, for her sake, makes Mary feel that she is really being taken seriously. He compliments her with adroit indirections: "'There's no reason why you shouldn't have played magnificently.' 'Only I don't. I never have.' 'No, you never have.'" The serious conversation grows into a sensual encounter; Mary tries to go back to talking, but the man's desire obscures the exchange:

> He came closer; she didn't know whether he drew her to him or whether he came closer. A queer, delicious feeling, a new feeling, thrilled through her body to her mouth, to her finger-tips. Her head swam slightly. She kept her eyes open by an

effort. He gave her back her hands. She remembered. They had been talking about her playing. "I knew," she said, "it was bad in places." "I don't care whether it's bad or good. It's you. The only part of you that can get out. You're very bad in places, but you do something to me all the same." "What do I do?" "You know what you do." "I don't. I don't really, Tell me." "If you don't know, I can't tell you – dear –" He said it so thickly that she was not sure at the time whether he had really said it. She remembered afterwards. (4:8:7:325-326)

A few days later Mary observes him kissing a farm girl and the deceptiveness of romantic musical 'communication' is exposed.

Finally all the new vistas that music seemed to open on at the end of the nineteenth century have been shown and discarded in the novel: self-expression, great art and the communion of soul-mates. When Dan, the last brother left alive after Mark's death, emigrates to Canada, Mary is left in sole charge of the mother whose will has dominated her life. The piano, significantly, has no part in her finding a true soul-mate in the poet Richard Nicholson, and when her mother's death frees her completely, she discards the instrument, abandoning all Victorian ties along with it to sublimate all her restless energy into the writing of poetry. Her old nanny perceptively considers it "unfaithful not to have kept the piano when Mamma had played on it" (5:5:3:429). The instrument that had lent its voice to so many silenced women becomes a poignant symbol of a passing epoch. One dreary evening scene set in 1897 encapsulates the approaching end of Mary's dependence on her mother and the sunset of a three-hundred-year-old tradition as the old woman is playing her old favourite on the now decrepit instrument[114]:

> The knocking of loose hammers on dead wires, the light, hacking clang of chords rolling like dead drum taps: Droom – Droom, Droom-era-room. Alone in the dusk, Mamma was playing the Hungarian March, bowing and swaying as she played. When the door opened, she started up, turning her back on the piano, frightened, like a child caught in a play it is ashamed of. The piano looked mournful and self-conscious. Then suddenly, all by itself, it shot out a cry like an arrow, a pinging, stinging, violently vibrating cry. "I'm afraid," mamma said, "something's happened to the piano." (4:11:3:371)

---

[114] The piece which corresponds best to this onomatopoeic approximation is the Rakoczy March, first made popular by Franz Liszt's arrangement (1844) and the version which Hector Berlioz included in *La Damnation de Faust* (1846).

Conclusion

The little pianos are closed, and a clock strikes.
WYSTAN HUGH AUDEN. "To a Writer on His Birthday"

From the Tudor period to the Great War, the 'piano' was a constant presence in the lives of young women of the British middle classes. For those three centuries and a half, performance on keyboard instruments was imagined as even more exclusively feminine than musical performance in general, with corresponding reservations about men's music-making that were particularly strict about keyboards. This imbalance was essential to the use of music for courtship rituals but was rarely acknowledged as such. Emphases and explicitly given reasons for women's playing and men's abstinence shift over time, but invariably complement each other: the less-researched prescriptions for and representations of male music-making are revealing mirrors of attitudes that have become familiar to researchers of women's histories.

Men usually lacked even the most basic training that would have enabled appreciative listening; but the conditioned fascination with music as an erotically connotated spectacle kept their gaze on performances which only rarely held a musical interest for them. This visual focus is most evident in literary descriptions and – in certain periods, notably around 1800 – in those conduct books which explicitly denounce a regime of commodification. While women musicians are being set up and displayed as erotic objects, textual strategies of suppression and denigration in literary descriptions as well as gaps, overlaps and contradictions between prescription, representation and metaphor testify to an ineradicable uneasy fascination.

In its social practice and literary representations, domestic music embodies a number of weighted binaries which only just began to soften at the beginning of the twentieth century. Female and male are aligned with mind and body, visibility and visual control, with *melos* and *logos*, wordlessness and articulateness, divinity and humanity, metonymy and metaphor. Music itself – played on the drawing-room upright or on the poetic 'lyre' – can be seductive or redemptive, practical or theoretical, sensuous or geometrical, topical/modern or historical, alive or dead, physical or imaginary, sounding or silent, tactile or disembodied, enjoyed or understood, promoting sex or 'harmony', adultery or marriage. It may be a matter for the eye or the ear, for artisans or philosophers, queens or hired minstrels, for a young lady or for 'Woman' in general. But it is never fully real *and* morally acceptable, notwithstanding an increasing emotional leeway for music in the private sphere and a widening scope for the professional ambitions of both sexes. The literary and actual liberation of the piano that sets in after 1880 merely rounds off a narrative of restrictive ideologies and practices.

Most texts quoted in this study testify to a palpable *disregard* for – literally a 'looking away from' –the power of music. The literary tragedy of the piano is that it was mainly used to promote gender stereotypes and to record suppression although it would have made an eloquent representative of women's plights and joys. Even during its belated literary heyday, women were moving on from the newly available expressive relief of music to find readers and true listeners in actual rather than metaphorical language, now disregarding music in their turn. Gramophones, talkies and women's move into the workplace during the Great War completed the obliteration of the piano's domestic literary habitat. The instrument continues to figure in fiction up to the present day, but the typical twentieth-century pianist in novels is the male professional struggling to realize a personal potential for artistic and social success. Nostalgically historicizing or grotesque narratives that take the instrument to the swamps which Kipling had deemed it unsuitable for (see above 167) are as remote from mainstream reality as any nineteenth-century *Künstlerroman*, and romantic bestsellers exploit a mystique of pianist musicianship which earlier victims of piano mania could never have guessed at. Their success is based on a vague respect for centuries of fascination but they are as remote from ordinary experience as any eighteenth-century poem. For a brief moment, female *Bildungsromane* from the turn of the twentieth century brought the piano as close as it ever got to really speaking for its players; but even they only briefly transcend the pitfalls of performance.

References

1. Primary Works

1.1. Non-Fiction

"Agnes" (1851). "Woman: Her Position and Duty No. IV". *English-woman's Magazine* VI: 404-407.

Aïdé, Charles Hamilton (1863). "Amateur Music". *Cornhill Magazine* 8 (July-December): 93-98.

Allen, Charles (1769). *The Polite Lady, or A Course of Female Education in a Series of Letters, from a Mother to Her Daughter.* London: Newbery and Carnan.

Anon. ("A Lady of Distinction") (1997). *The Mirror of Graces, or The English Lady's Costume* (1811). London: B. Crosby & Co. Photographic reprint: Mendocino: R. L. Shep.

Anon. ("A Musical Man") (1892). "Women and the Piano". Letter to the Editor. *Musical Opinion & Music Trade Review* (October): 37.

Anon. ("Minimus") (1822). "On Church Music". *Quarterly Musical Magazine and Review* 4: 172-188.

Anon. [John Case?] (1586). *The Praise of Musicke.* Oxford: Joseph Barnes.

— (1616). *The Office of Christian Parents, shewing how children are to be gouerned throughout all ages and times of their life.* Cambridge: Cantrell Legge.

— (1696). *The Whole Duty of a Woman, or A Guide to the Female Sex from the Age of Sixteen to Sixty.* 2nd ed. London: J. Gwillim.

— (1778). "An Account [of Lady Anna Halkett's Life]". *Lady Anne Halkett. Meditations on the Twenty-Fifth Psalm. Also Meditations and Prayers upon the First Week: With Observations on Each Day's Creation. With Observations on Each Day's Creation. Likewise Instructions for Youth.* Edinburgh: Bayne and Mennons. 1-88.

— (1796). "Desultory Remarks on the Study and Practice of Music, Addressed to a Young Lady While under the Tuition of an Eminent Master". *European Magazine* 30 (July-December): 179-181.

— (1835). *The New Female Instructor, or Young Woman's Guide to Domestic Happiness* (1822). London: Thomas Kelly.

— (1823). "A Sketch of the State of Music in London". *Quarterly Musical Magazine and Review* 5: 241-275.

— (1825). "Private Concerts". *Quarterly Musical Magazine and Review* 7: 295-310.

— (1852). *Eliza Cook's Journal*. London: Charles Cook, Raquet Court, Fleet Street.

— (1899). "The Piano as a Cause of Neuroses". *British Medical Journal* 22 (April): 988.

Appleton, Elizabeth (1816). *Private Education, or A Practical Plan for the Studies of Young Ladies*. London: Henry Colburn.

Arthur, Timothy Shay (1855). *Advice to Young Ladies on Their Duties and Conduct in Life*. London: J. S. Hudson.

Ascham, Roger (1545). *Toxophilus*. London: [N. p.]

— (1570). *The Scholemaster, or Plaine and perfite way of teachyng children*. London: John Day.

Astell, Mary (1997). *A Serious Proposal to the Ladies, Part II: Wherein a Method is Offer'd for the Improvement of their Minds* (1694/1697). London: Pickering and Chatto.

Aster, Jane (1859). *The Habits of Good Society: A Handbook of Etiquette for Ladies and Gentlemen*. London: James Hoff.

Austen, Henry (1818). "Biographical Notice". Jane Austen. *Northanger Abbey: and Persuasion*. London: John Murray.

Baker, T. Herbert (1851). "Early Education". *British Mothers' Magazine* 7: 244-245.

Barnett, John Francis (1906). *Musical Reminiscences and Impressions*. London: Hodder and Stoughton.

Batchiler, John (1661). *The Virgins Pattern: In the Exemplary Life, and Lamented Death of Mrs. Susanna Perwich*. London: Simon Dover.

Becon, Thomas (1550). *The Jewel of Joye: Philemon, Eusebius, Theophile, and Christofer, talke togither*. London: John Day.

Berger, Francesco (1913). *Reminiscences, Impressions, Anecdotes*. London: Sampson Low, Marston & Co.

Berkenhout, Dr. John (1790). *A Volume of Letters from Dr. Berkenhout to his Son at the University*. Cambridge: J. Archdeacon.

Brittain, Vera (1988). *Testament of Youth: An Autobiographical Study of the Years 1900-1925* (1933). London: Virago.

Broadhurst, Thomas (1810). *Advice to Young Ladies on the Improvement of the Mind, and the Conduct of Life*. 2nd revised and corrected ed. London: Longman, Hurst, Rees, and Orme.

Burgh, Allatson (1814). *Anecdotes of Music, Historical and Biographical, in a Series of Letters from a Gentleman to his Daughter*. London: Longman, Hurst, Rees, Orme and Brown.

Burney, Dr. Charles (1935). *A General History of Music from the Earliest Ages to the Present Period* (1766-1784). London: G. T. Foulis.

Burton, Robert (1989-1994). *Anatomy of Melancholy* (1621). Oxford: Clarendon Press.

Busby, Thomas (1823). *A Dictionary of Music, Theoretical and Practical* (1787). London: Sir Richard Phillips & Co.

Butler, Samuel (1951). *Samuel Butler's Notebooks*. Geoffrey Keynes, Brian Hill, eds. London: Jonathan Cape.

Byrd, William (1613). *Parthenia, or The Maydenhead of the First Musicke that ever was Printed for the Virginalls*. London: Dorothy Evans.

Byron, George Gordon Noel, Lord (1973-1982). *The Complete and Unexpurgated Text of all the Letters Available in Manuscript and the Full Printed Version of all Others*. Leslie A. Marchand, ed. 12 vols. London: John Murray.

Carroll, David, ed. (1971). *George Eliot: The Critical Heritage*. London: Routledge and Kegan Paul.

Chapone, Hester (1773). *Letters on the Improvement of the Mind, Addressed to a Young Lady*. London: H. Hughs for J. Walter.

Chesterfield, Philip Dormer Stanhope, 4th Earl of (1774). *Letters Written by the Late Right Honourable Philip Dormer Stanhope, Earl of Chesterfield, to His Son, Philip Stanhope [...]*. Vol. 1. Dublin: G. Faulkner.

Cleland, James (1607). *ΗΡΩ–ΠΑΙΔΕΙΑ, or The institution of a Young Nobleman*. Oxford: Joseph Barnes.

Clerk, John (1892). *Memoirs of the Life of Sir John Clerk of Penicuik, Baronet, Extracted by Himself from His Own Journals 1676-1755*. Edinburgh: Edinburgh UP for the Scottish Historical Society.

Cobbe, Frances Power (1894). *Life of Frances Power Cobbe: By Herself. With Illustrations*. London: Richard Bentley and Son.

Cockle, Mary (1809). *Important Studies, for the Female Sex, in Reference to Modern Manners: Addressed to A Young Lady of Distinction*. London: C. Chapple.

Coleridge, Samuel Taylor (1836). *Letters, Conversations and Recollections of Samuel Taylor Coleridge*. London: Moxon.

Costeker, John Littleton (1732). *The Fine Gentleman, or The Compleat Education of A Young Nobleman*. London: J. Roberts.

Craven, Helen Emily (1897). *Notes of a Music Lover*. Guildford: Bentley and Son.

Crowest, Frederick James (1881). *Phases of Musical England*. Remington & Co.

Darrell, William (1704). *The Gentleman Instructed in the Conduct of a Virtuous and Happy Life*. London: E. Evets.

Darwin, Erasmus (1797). *A Plan for the Conduct of Female Education in Boarding Schools*. Derby: J. Drewry.

Defoe, Daniel (1697). *An Essay upon Projects*. London: Thomas Cockerill.

— (1728). "A Proposal to Prevent the Expensive Importation of Foreign Musicians, &c. by Forming an Academy of Our Own". *Augusta Triumphans, or The Way to Make London the Most Flourishing City in the Universe*. London: J. Roberts. 16-23.

Edgeworth, Maria (1995). *Practical Education* (1801). Reprint of 2nd ed. London: Routledge/Thoemmes Press.

Edwards, H. Sutherland (1875-1876). "The Literary Maltreatment of Music". *Macmillan's Magazine* 33 (November-April): 552-558.

Eliot, George (1954). *The George Eliot Letters*. Oxford: Oxford UP; New Haven, CT: Yale UP.

— (1963). "Silly Novels by Lady Novelists" (1856). Thomas Pinne, ed. *Essays of George Eliot*. London: Routledge and Kegan Paul. 301-324.

Ella, John (1869). *Musical Sketches Abroad and at Home*. London: Ridgway.

Ellis, Mrs. (1842). *The Daughters of England: Their Position in Society, Character and Responsibilities*. London: Fisher, Son & Co.

Elyot, Thomas (1531). *The Boke named the Governour*. London: Thomas Berthelet.

Essex, John (1722). *The Young Ladies Conduct, or Rules for Education, Under Several Heads; With Distinction upon Dress, Both Before and After Marriage*. London: Though Brotherton.

Evelyn, John (1955). *The Diary of John Evelyn: Now First Printed in Full from the Manuscripts*. Oxford: Clarendon Press.

Fanshawe, Ann, Anne Halkett (1979). *The Memoirs of Anne, Lady Halkett and Ann, Lady Fanshawe* (1670). Oxford: Oxford UP.

Farningham, Marianne (1869). *Girlhood*. London: James Clarke & Co.

Fellowes, Edmund (1946). *Memoirs of an Amateur Musician*. London: Methuen.

Fordyce, James, D. D. (1766). *Sermons to Young Women*. London: A. Millar et al.

Gisborne, Thomas (1974). *An Enquiry into the Duties of the Female Sex* (1797). Reprint. London/New York, NY: Garland Publishing.

Grey, Maria G., Emily Shirreff (1850). *Thoughts on Self-Culture, Addressed to Women*. London: Edward Moxon.

Grossmith, George (1888). *A Society Clown: Reminiscence by George Grossmith*. Bristol: Arrowsmith.

H. C. M. (1846). "A Concert of Amateurs". *The Connoisseur: A Journal of Music & the Fine Arts* 2.10/1 January: 7-9.

H. F. C. (1839). "The Pianoforte". *Westminster Review* 32: 306-356.

Hanway, Jonas (1765). *Thoughts on the Use and Advantages of Music, and Other Amusements*. London: J. Dodsley.

Haweis, The Reverend Hugh Reginald (1871). *Music and Morals*. London: Strahan.

— (1897). *Ideals for Girls*. London: James Bourden.

Haywood, Eliza Fowler (1755). *The Female Spectator*. London: A. Millar, W. Law and R. Cater.

Hoby, Thomas (1561). *The Courtyer of Count Baldessar Castilio [...] Done into Englyshe by Thomas Hoby*. London: William Seres.

Home, Henry, Lord Kames (1781). *Loose Hints upon Education, Chiefly Concerning the Culture of the Heart*. Edinburgh: John Bell.

Hooker, Richard (1593). *Of the Lavves of Ecclesiasticall Politie, Eyght bookes*. London: John Windet.

Hueffer, Francis (1977). *Half a Century of Music in England: 1837-1887: Essays towards a History* (1889). Reprint. Boston: Longwood Press.

Hullah, John (1877). *Music in the House*. London: Macmillan.

Hullah, Frances (1851). *A Few Words about Music, Containing Hints to Amateur Pianists to Which Is Added a Slight Historical Sketch of the Rise and Progress of the Art of Music*. London: Novello.

Huneker, James (1904). "The Eternal Feminine". *Overtones: A Book of Temperaments*. New York, NY: Charles Scribner's Sons. 277-306.

James I. (1599). *Βασιλικον Δωρον*. London: Robert Waldegrave.

Jarrold, Dr. Thomas (1819). "On Education". *Monthly Magazine* 1 (February): 11-14.

Keats, John (1958). *The Letters of John Keats*. Hyder Edward Rollins, ed. Cambridge: Cambridge UP.

Kermode, Frank and Anita, eds. (1995). *The Oxford Book of Letters*. Oxford: Oxford UP.

Knox, Vicesimus (1800). *Essays Moral and Literary*. Basil [sic]: James Decker.

Kuhe, Wilhelm (1896). *My Musical Recollections*. London: Richard Bentley.

Lister, Anne (1988). *I Know My Own Heart: The Diaries of Anne Lister*. Helena Whitbread, ed. London: Virago.

Locke, John (1968). "Some Thoughts Concerning Education" (1693). *The Educational Writings*. Cambridge: Cambridge UP. 109-325.

Macaulay Graham, Catherine (1970). *Letters on Education* (1790). London: C. Dilly; Oxford/New York, NY: Woodstock Books.

Mace, Thomas (1958). *Musick's Monument, or A Remembrancer of the Best Practical Musick, both Divine and Civil, that has ever been known, to have been in the World* (1676). Reprint. Paris: Editions du Centre National de la recherche scientifique.

Mansfield, Katherine, John Middleton Murry (1988). *Letters between Katherine Mansfield and John Middleton Murry*. London: Virago.

Mar, John Erskine, Earl of (1896). "Mar's Legacy to His Son". *The Earl of Mar's Legacies to Scotland and to His Son, Lord Erskine, 1722-1727*. Edinburgh: Printed at the University Press by T. and A. Constable for the Scottish History Society. 157-193.

Maurice, Frederick Denison (1898). "Introductory Lecture". Alec Tweedie, ed. *The First College Open to Women: Queen's College London. Memories and Records of Work Done 1848-1898*. London: [N. p.]

Melville, James (1842). *The Autobiography and Diary of Mr. James Melville: With a Continuation of the Diary*. Edinburgh: Woodrow Society.

Meredith, George (1970). *The Letters of George Meredith*. Oxford: Clarendon Press.

Montagu, Mary Wortley (1966). *Complete Letters*. Oxford: Oxford UP.

More, Hannah (1799). *Strictures on the Modern System for Female Education*. Dublin: William Porter.

Mulcaster, Richard (1581). *Positions Wherin Those Primitive Circumstances be Examined, which are Necessarie for the Training vp of Children*. London: Thomas Vautrollier.

Newman, Ernest (1879). "The Psychology of the Musician in Fiction". *The Musician* 2: 150-151.

Owen, Wilfred (1967). *Collected Letters*. Harold Owen, John Bell, eds. Oxford: Oxford UP.

Parry, Charles Hubert Hastings (1893). *The Art of Music*. New York, NY: D. Appleton.

Peacham, Henry (1622). *The Compleat Gentleman*. London: Francis Constable.

Pennington, Sarah (1761). *An Unfortunate Mother's Advice to her Daughters; in a Letter to Miss Pennington*. London: S. Chandler.

Pepys, Samuel (1972). *The Diary of Samuel Pepys: A New and Complete Transcription*. Robert Latham, William Matthews, eds. London: G. Bell.

Prynne, William (1633). *Histrio-Mastix: The Players Scourge, or Actors Tragœdie*. London: Michael Sparke.

Pullan, Matilda Marian (1855). *Maternal Counsels to a Daughter*. London: Darton.

Rose, Algernon (1895). *Greater Britain, Musically Considered: A Paper Read at the Annual Conference of the Incorporated Society of Musicians*. Dublin: [N. p.].

Ruskin, John (1903-1912). "Sesame and Lilies" (1871). *The Library Edition of the Works of John Ruskin*. Vol. 18. London: George Allen. 5-192.

Salter, Thomas (1578). *A Mirrhor mete for all Mothers, Matrones, and Maidens, intituled the Mirrhor of Modestie, no lesse profitable and pleasant, then necessarie to bee read and practised*. London: Edward White.

Saltonstall, Wye (1631). *Picturae Loquentes*. London: Thomas Co[a]tes.

Schmitz, Oscar A. H. (1925). *The Land without Music*. London: Jarrolds.

Scholes, Percy Alfred (1947). *The Mirror of Music 1844-1944*. Oxford: Oxford UP.

Shaw, George Bernard (1981). *Shaw's Music: The Complete Musical Criticism in Three Volumes*. Dan Laurence, ed. London: The Bodley Head.

Smart, Sir George (1907). *Leaves from the Journals of Sir George Smart*. London: Longmans, Green & Co.

Smith, Henry (1591). *A Preparative to Mariage: The summe whereof was spoken at a contract, and inlarged after.* London: R. Field for Thomas Man.

Southgate, T. L. (1896). "The Treatment of Music by Novelists". *Proceedings of the Musical Association.* 23-51.

Steele, Richard (1987). *The Tatler* (1709-1711). 3 vols. Oxford: Clarendon Press.

Stubbes, Phillip (1583). *The Anatomie of Abuses.* London: R. Jones.

Sullivan, Arthur (1899). "About Music: An Address Delivered at the Town Hall, Birmingham, on October 19, 1888". Arthur H. Lawrence, ed. *Sir Arthur Sullivan: Life-Story, Letters, and Reminiscences.* London: James Bowden. Chapter 14.

"Vetus" [Richard Mackenzie Bacon] (1820). "Music as a Pursuit for Men". *Quarterly Musical Magazine and Review* 2: 7-14.

Wakefield, Priscilla (1974). *Reflections on the Present Condition of the Female Sex* (1798). Reprint. London/New York, NY: Garland.

Walker, Bettina (1890). *My Musical Experiences.* London: Richard Bentley and Son.

Walker, Obadiah (1673). *Of Education, Especially of Young Men.* Oxford: At the Theatre.

Ward, Thomas Humphry, ed. (1887). *The Reign of Queen Victoria: A Survey of Fifty Years of Progress.* London: Smith, Elder & Co.

Weatherly, Frederic Edward (1926). *Piano and Gown.* London/New York, NY: G. P. Putnam's Sons.

West, Jane (1806). *Letters to a Young Lady, in Which the Duties and Character of Women Are Considered, Chiefly with a Reference to Prevailing Opinions.* London: Longman, Hurst, Rees and Orme.

Wilde, Oscar (2000). *The Complete Letters of Oscar Wilde.* New York, NY: Henry Holt & Co.

Wollstonecraft Godwin, Mary (1995). *Thoughts on the Education of Daughters* (1787). London: Thoemmes Press.

— (1792). *A Vindication of the Rights of Woman with Strictures on Political and Moral Subjects.* London: J. Johnson.

Woolf, Virginia (1978). *A Room of One's Own* (1929). London et al.: Granada Publishing.

— (1976). "Moments of Being" (1939). Jeanne Schulkind, ed. *Unpublished Autobiographical Writings.* London: Sussex UP. 61-138.

1.2. Prose Fiction

Aïdé, Charles Hamilton (1868). *The Marstons: A Novel*. Reprinted from *Forster's Magazine*. London: Chapman and Hall.

Allen, Grant (1995). *The Woman Who Did* (1895). Oxford: Oxford UP.

Amory, Thomas (1756-1766). *The Life of John Buncle, Esq.: Containing Various Observations and Reflections, Made in Several Parts of the World And Many Extraordinary Relations*. London: J. Noon.

Anon. (1693). *The Player's Tragedy, or Fatal Love, a New Novel*. London: Randal Taylor et al.

— (1915). *The Second Mrs. Tanqueray: A Novel Adapted from Sir Arthur Pinero's Play of That Name. Film Books Series*. London: William Heinemann.

Aubin, Penelope (1736). *The Life of Charlotta Du Pont, an English Lady: Taken from Her Own Memoirs*. London: A. Bettesworth and C. Hitch.

— (1973). *The Life and Adventures of Lady Lucy, the Daughter of an Irish Lord, Who Marry'd a German Officer [...]* (1726). Reprint. London/New York, NY: Garland Publishing.

Austen, Jane (1912). "Lady Susan" (1804). *The Novels of Jane Austen*, Vol. 11. Edinburgh: John Grant. 1-109.

— (2006). *Sense and Sensibility* (1810). Cambridge: Cambridge UP.

— (2006). *Pride and Prejudice* (1813). Cambridge: Cambridge UP.

— (2006). *Mansfield Park* (1814). Cambridge: Cambridge UP.

— (2005). *Emma* (1815). Cambridge: Cambridge UP.

— (2006). *Persuasion* (1817). Cambridge: Cambridge UP.

— (2006). *Northanger Abbey* (1818). Cambridge: Cambridge UP.

Bage, Robert (1985). *Hermsprong, or Man As He Is Not* (1796). Oxford: Oxford UP.

Baring-Gould, Sabine (1892). *In the Roar of the Sea: A Tale of the Cornish Coast*. London: Methuen & Co.

Barrett, Eaton Stannard (1927). *The Heroine, or Adventures of Cherubina* (1814). London: Elkin, Mathews and Marrot.

Barry, William Francis (1976). *The New Antigone: A Romance* (1887). Reprint. London/New York, NY: Garland Publishing.

Beerbohm, Max (1985). *Zuleika Dobson* (1911). Reprint. London/New Haven, CT: Yale UP.

Behn, Aphra (1689). *The History of the Nun, or The Fair Vow-Breaker*. London: A. Baskerville.

Bennett, Enoch Arnold (1976). *These Twain* (1916). London: Eyre Methuen.

Bentley, Edmund Clerihew (1915). *Trent's Last Case*. London/Edinburgh: T. Nelson and Sons.

Black, William (1871). *A Daughter of Heth*. Leipzig: Tauchnitz.

Bottome, Phyllis (1902). *Life, the Interpreter*. London: Longmans, Green & Co.

Braddon, Mary Elizabeth (1998). *Lady Audley's Secret* (1862). Harmondsworth: Penguin.

— (1998). *Aurora Floyd* (1863). Peterborough: Broadview Press.

Brontë, Anne (1988). *Agnes Grey* (1847). Oxford: Clarendon Press.

— (1992). *The Tenant of Wildfell Hall* (1848). Oxford: Clarendon Press.

Brontë, Charlotte (1969). *Jane Eyre* (1847). Oxford: Clarendon Press.

— (1979). *Villette* (1853). Harmondsworth: Penguin.

Brooke, Henry (1906). *The Fool of Quality, or The History of Henry Earl of Moreland* (1768). London: Routledge.

Broughton, Rhoda (1993). *Not Wisely, But Too Well* (1867). Stroud: Alan Sutton.

— (1883). *Belinda: A Novel*. Leipzig: Bernhard Tauchnitz.

Bulwer-Lytton, Edward George (1842). *Pelham, or The Adventures of a Gentleman* (1828). Leipzig: Tauchnitz.

Bunyan, John (1684). *The Pilgrim's Progress, from This World to That which is to come: The Second Part. Delivered under the Similitude of a Dream*. London: Nathaniel Parker.

Burney, Frances (1988). *Cecilia, or Memoirs of an Heiress* (1782). Oxford: Oxford UP.

— (1992). *Camilla, or A Picture of Youth* (1796). Oxford: Oxford UP.

— (1991). *The Wanderer, or Female Difficulties* (1814). Oxford: Oxford UP.

Butler, Samuel (1968). *The Way of All Flesh* (1903). The Shrewsbury Edition of the Works of Samuel Butler, vol. 17. New York, NY: AMS Press. Reprint of London edition 1923-1926.

Carswell, Catherine (1987). *The Camomile* (1922). London: Virago.

Cavendish, Margaret, Duchess of Newcastle (1656). "The Contract". *Natures Pictures Drawn by Fancies Pencil to the Life*. London: J. Martin and J. Allestrye. 22-54.

Coleridge, Mary Elizabeth (1906). *The Lady on the Drawing-Room Floor*. London: Edward Arnold.

Collier, Joel (1775). *Musical Travels through England: The Second Edition, with Additions*. London: G. Kearsly.

Collins, Wilkie (1994). *The Woman in White* (1860). Harmondsworth: Penguin.

— (1986). *No Name* (1862). Oxford: Oxford UP.

— (1989). *Armadale* (1866). Oxford: Oxford UP.

— (1966). *The Moonstone* (1868). Harmondsworth: Penguin.

— (1995). *Man and Wife* (1870). Oxford: Oxford UP.

— (1995). *Poor Miss Finch* (1872). Oxford: Oxford UP.

Conrad, Joseph (1987). *Heart of Darkness* (1902). New York, NY: Bantam Books.

— (1925). *The Secret Agent* (1907). The Works of Joseph Conrad, vol. 10. Edinburgh: John Grant.

— (1925). "Freya of the Seven Isles" (1912). *'Twixt Land and Sea*. The Works of Joseph Conrad, vol. 13. Edinburgh: John Grant. 147-238.

Coventry, Francis (1751). *The History of Pompey the Little, or The Life and Adventures of a Lap-Dog*. London: M. Cooper.

Craik, Dinah Maria Mulock (1975). *Olive: A Novel* (1850). Reprint. London/New York, NY: Garland.

Defoe, Daniel (1978). *The Fortunes and Misfortunes of the Famous Moll Flanders* (1722). Harmondsworth: Penguin.

Dickens, Charles (1966). *Oliver Twist* (1837-1838). Oxford: Clarendon Press.

— (1890). *Nicholas Nickleby* (1839). Dickens Memorial Edition. London: Chapman and Hall.

— (1974). *Dealings with the Firm of Dombey and Son, Wholesale, Retail and for Exportation* (1848). Oxford: Clarendon Press.

— (1981). *David Copperfield* (1849-1850). Oxford: Clarendon Press.

— (1979). *Little Dorrit* (1855-1857). Oxford: Clarendon Press.

— (1972). *The Mystery of Edwin Drood* (1870). Oxford: Clarendon Press.

Disraeli, Benjamin (1845). *Sybil, or The Two Nations*. Leipzig: Tauchnitz.

— (1975). *Lothair* (1870). Oxford: Oxford UP.

Dixon, Ella Hepworth (1895). *The Story of a Modern Woman*. Leipzig: Tauchnitz.

Dowie, Ménie Muriel (1995). *Gallia* (1895). London: J. M. Dent.

Doyle, Arthur Conan (1981). "The Adventure of the Solitary Cyclist"
    (1903). *The Complete Penguin Sherlock Holmes*. Harmondsworth:
    Penguin. 526-538.
Du Maurier, Gerald (1961). *Trilby* (1894). London/Glasgow: Collins.
Edgeworth, Maria (1801). *Belinda*. London: J. Thomson.
    http://lion.chadwyck.co.uk. Literature Online. University of Basel
    [22/01/2007].
— (1809). *Ennui* (1978). London: J. Johnson. Reprint: New York,
    NY: Garland.
— (1999). *Patronage* (1813). The Novels and Selected Works of
    Maria Edgeworth, vol. 6. London: Pickering and Chatto.
— (1999). *Helen: A Tale* (1834). The Novels and Selected Works of
    Maria Edgeworth, vol. 9. London: Pickering and Chatto.
Egerton, George (1894). *Discords*. London/Boston, MA: John Lane
    and Robert Brothers.
Eliot, George (1957). *The Mill on the Floss* (1860). Oxford: Oxford
    UP.
— (1986). *Middlemarch: A Study of Provincial Life* (1872). Oxford:
    Clarendon Press.
— (1984). *Daniel Deronda* (1876). Oxford: Clarendon Press.
Ferrier, Susan Edmonstone (1971). *Marriage: A Novel* (1818).
    Oxford: Oxford UP.
Field, Julian (1890). "A Waltz of Chopin". *Macmillan's Magazine*
    62/369 (July): 220-240.
Fielding, Henry (1975). *Tom Jones* (1749). Fredson Bowers, ed. The
    Wesleyan Edition. Oxford: Clarendon Press.
— (1983). *Amelia* (1752). Martin C. Battestin, ed. The Wesleyan
    Edition. Oxford: Clarendon Press.
Forster, Edward Morgan (1977). "[Old Lucy]" (1901-1903). *The Lucy
    Novels: Early Sketches for* A Room with a View. Oliver
    Stallybrass, ed. Abinger Edition, vol. 3a. London: Edward Arnold.
    1-85.
— (1990). *A Room with a View* (1908). Harmondsworth: Penguin.
— (1973). *Howards End* (1910). London: David Campbell.
— (1971). *Maurice* (1914). London: Edward Arnold.
— (1947). "Co-ordination" (1928). *Collected Short Stories of E. M.
    Forster*. London: Sidgwick and Jackson. 187-195.
Gallico, Paul (1959). *Too Many Ghosts*. New York, NY: Doubleday.
— (1964). *The Hand of Mary Constable*. London: Heinemann.

Galsworthy, John (1995). *Forsyte Saga* (1906-1921). Oxford: Oxford UP.

Galt, John (1978). *Annals of the Parish, or The Chronicle of Dalmailing during the Ministry of the Rev. Micah Balwhidder, Written by Himself* (1821). Reprint of 1895. London: Mercat Press.

— (1984). *The Entail, or The Lairds of Grippy* (1822). Oxford: Oxford UP.

Gaskell, Elizabeth (1994). *Mary Barton: A Tale of Manchester Life* (1848). London: Random House.

— "Uncle Peter" (1853). *Longmans, Green Fraser's Magazine* 48 (October): 434-445 and (November): 526-534. http://etext.lib.virginia.edu/modeng/modeng0.browse.html. The Oxford Text Archive. University of Basel [22/01/2007].

— (1973). *North and South* (1855). Oxford: Oxford UP.

— (1866). *Wives and Daughters: An Everyday Story*. London: Smith, Elder & Co.

Gissing, George Robert (1995). *The Odd Women* (1893). London: Virago.

— (1897). *The Whirlpool*. London: Lawrence and Bullen.

Godwin, William (1992). *Things as They Are, or The Adventures of Caleb Williams* (1794). Pamela Clemit, ed. Collected Novels and Memoirs of William Godwin, vol. 3. London: William Pickering.

— (1992). *Fleetwood, or the New Man of Feeling* (1832). London: William Pickering.

Gore, Catherine Frances (1836). *Diary of a Désennuyée*. Paris: Baudry's European Library.

— (1836). *Mrs. Armytage, or Female Domination*. Paris: G. W. M. Reynolds.

— (1841). *Cecil, or The Adventures of a Coxcomb: A Novel*. London: Richard Bentley.

Grand, Sarah (1994). *The Beth Book: Being a Study of the Life of Elizabeth Caldwell Maclure, a Woman of Genius* (1898). Reprint. Bristol: Thoemmes Press.

Graves, Richard (1774). *The Spiritual Quixote, or The Summer's Ramble of Mr. Geoffrey Wildgoose. A Comic Romance*. London: J. Dodsley.

Hanway, Mary Ann (1974). *Ellinor, or The World As It Is* (1798). Reprint. London/New York, NY: Garland.

Hardy, Thomas (1975). *A Pair of Blue Eyes* (1873). F. B. Pinion, ed. New Wessex Edition. London: Macmillan.

— (1975). *Far from the Madding Crowd* (1874). F. B. Pinion, ed. New Wessex Edition. London: Macmillan.

— (1975). *The Mayor of Casterbridge* (1886). F. B. Pinion, ed. New Wessex Edition. London: Macmillan.

— (1975). *The Woodlanders* (1887). F. B. Pinion, ed. New Wessex Edition. London: Macmillan.

— (1975). *Jude the Obscure* (1895). F. B. Pinion, ed. New Wessex Edition. London: Macmillan.

Hays, Mary (1995). (1996). *Memoirs of Emma Courtney* (1796). Oxford: Oxford UP.

— *The Victim of Prejudice* (1799). London: Routledge and Thoemmes Press.

Haywood, Eliza Fowler (1748). *The Fortunate Foundlings: Being the History of Colonel M – rs, and his Sister [...]*. 3rd ed. London: T. Gardner.

— (1753). *The History of Jemmy and Jenny Jessamy*. London: T. Gardner.

Head, Richard, Francis Kirkman (1671). *The English Rogue: Continued in the Life of Meriton Latroon, and Other Extravagants*. London: Francis Kirkman.

Heddle, Ethel Forster (1896). *Three Girls in a Flat*. London: Gardner, Darton & Co.

Holcroft, Thomas (1970). *Anna St. Ives* (1794). Oxford: Oxford UP.

— (1978). *The Adventures of Hugh Trevor* (1794-1797). Oxford: Oxford UP.

Howard, Keble (1906). *The Smiths of Surbiton*. London: Chapman and Hall.

Inchbald, Elizabeth (1988). *A Simple Story* (1791). Oxford: Oxford UP.

James, Henry (1969). "The Turn of the Screw" (1898). *The Turn of the Screw and Other Stories*. Harmondsworth: Penguin. 7-121.

— (1933). "The Beast in the Jungle" (1903). *The Altar of the Dead [...] and Other Tales*. London: Macmillan. 55-114.

Kingsley, Charles (1983). *Alton Locke, Tailor and Poet: An Autobiography* (1850). Oxford: Oxford UP.

Lennox, Charlotte Ramsay (1752). *The Female Quixote*. London: A. Millar.

Leverson, Ada Esther (1982). *The Little Ottleys* (1908-1916). New York, NY: The Dial Press.

Lister, Thomas Henry (1826). *Granby: A Novel*. London: Henry Colburn.

Lodge, David (1989). *Nice Work*. Harmondsworth: Penguin.

Mackenzie, Henry (1771). *The Man of Feeling*. London: Thomas Cadell.

— (1777). *Julia de Roubigné: A Tale in a Series of Letters*. Edinburgh: W. Creech.

Makower, Stanley Victor (1895). *The Mirror of Music*. London: John Lane.

Marshall, Emma (1888). *Alma, or The Story of a Little Music Mistress*. London: Wan, Sonnenschein, Lowry & Co.

Meredith, George (1914). *Beauchamp's Career* (1875) London: Constable.

— (1914). *The Ordeal of Richard Feverel* (1859/1878) London: Constable.

— (1885). *Diana of the Crossways: A Novel*. London: Chapman and Hall.

— (1919). *One of Our Conquerors* (1891). London: Constable.

Morgan, Lady Sydney (1807). *The Wild Irish Girl: A National Tale*. (1806). 3rd ed. London: Richard Phillips.
http://lion.chadwyck.co.uk. Literature Online. University of Basel [29/06/2006].

Moore, Frank Frankfort (1909). *The Food of Love*. Leipzig: Tauchnitz.

Moore, John (1965). *Mordaunt: Sketches of Life, Characters and Manners in Various Countries, Including the Memoirs of a French Lady* (1800). Oxford: Oxford UP.

More, Hannah (1800). *The Two Wealthy Farmers, or The History of Mr Bragwell. Cheap Repository*. London: J. Marshall.

— (1995). *Coelebs in Search of a Wife: Illustrated* (1809). Reprint. Bristol: Thoemmes Press.

Oliphant, Margaret (1986). *Salem Chapel* (1861). London: Virago.

Opie, Amelia (1974). *Adeline Mowbray, or The Mother and Daughter: A Tale* (1805). Reprint. London/New York, NY: Garland.

Peacock, Thomas Love (1963). "Melincourt, Or: Sir Oran Haut-Ton" (1817). David Garnett, ed. *The Novels of Thomas Love Peacock*, vol. 1. London: Rupert Hart-Davis. 91-344.

— (1963). "Nightmare Abbey" (1818). David Garnett, ed. *The Novels of Thomas Love Peacock*, vol. 1. London: Rupert Hart-Davis. 345-433.

— (1963). "Crotchet Castle" (1831). David Garnett, ed. *The Novels of Thomas Love Peacock*, vol. 2. London: Rupert Hart-Davis. 639-762.

Radcliffe, Ann (1995). *A Sicilian Romance* (1792). Reprint of 2nd ed. Poole/New York, NY: Woodstock Books.

— (1980). *The Mysteries of Udolpho* (1794). Oxford: Oxford UP.

Reade, Charles (1863). *Hard Cash: A Matter-of-Fact Romance*. London: Sampson Low, Son and Marston.

Richardson, Samuel (1928). *Familiar Letters on Important Occasions* (1741). London: Routledge and Sons.

— (1742). *Pamela, or Virtue Rewarded. In a Series of Familiar Letters From a Beautiful Young Damsel to her Parents [...]. The Third Edition, Corrected*. London: S. Richardson.

— (1985). *Clarissa, or The History of a Young Lady* (1751). Harmondsworth: Penguin.

— (1751). *Letters and passages restored from the original manuscripts of the history of Clarissa. To which is subjoined, a collection of such of the moral and instructive sentiments, [...] as are presumed to be of general use*. The 3rd ed. of Clarissa, vol. 8. London: printed for S. Richardson.

— (1972). *The History of Sir Charles Grandison* (1753-1754). Oxford: Oxford UP.

Robinson, Mary (1992). *Walsingham, or The Pupil of Nature: A Domestic Story* (1797). Reprint. London: Routledge and Thoemmes Press.

Rowson, Susanna Haswell (1794). *Mentoria, or The Young Lady's Friend*. Philadelphia, PA: Robert Campbell.

— (1794). *The Fille de Chambre*. Philadelphia, PA: H. and P. Rice.

— (1795). *Trials of the Human Heart*. Philadelphia, PA: Wrigley and Berriman.

Scott, Sarah Robinson (1986). *Millenium Hall* (1762). London: Virago.

— (1995). *The History of Sir George Ellison* (1766). Lexington, KY: The UP of Kentucky.

Scott, Sir Walter (1981). *Waverley, or 'Tis Sixty Years Since* (1814). Oxford: Clarendon Press.

— (1999). *Guy Mannering* (1815). The Edinburgh Edition of the Waverley Novels, vol. 2. Edinburgh: Edinburgh UP.

— (1995). *The Antiquary* (1816). The Edinburgh Edition of the Waverley Novels, vol. 3. Edinburgh: Edinburgh UP.

Shelley, Mary Wollstonecraft (1996). *Matilda* (1820). The Novels and Selected Works of Mary Shelley, vol. 2. London: Pickering and Chatto.

— (1996). *Lodore* (1835). The Novels and Selected Works of Mary Shelley, vol. 6. London: Pickering and Chatto.

— (1996). *Falkner: A Novel* (1837). The Novels and Selected Works of Mary Shelley, vol. 7. London: Pickering and Chatto.

Sheridan, Frances Chamberlaine (1995). *Memoirs of Miss Sidney Bidulph* (1761). Oxford: Oxford UP.

Sidney, Philip (1593). *The Covntesse of Pembrokes Arcadia. Written by Sir Philp Sidney, Knight. Now Since the First Edition Augmented and Amended.* London: William Ponsonbie.

Sinclair, Catherine (1841). *Modern Accomplishments, or The March of Intellect* (1837). Edinburgh: William Whyte & Co.

— (1855). *Jane Bouverie and How She Became an Old Maid.* London: Simpkin, Marshall & Co.

Sinclair, May (1907). *Audrey Craven* (1896). Edinburgh: William Blackwood and Sons.

— (1906). *The Divine Fire.* New York, NY: Henry Holt & Co.

— (1907). *The Helpmate.* London: Hutchinson & Co.

— (2002). *Mary Olivier: A Life* (1919). New York, NY: The New York Review of Books.

— (1924). *Arnold Waterlow: A Life.* Leipzig: Tauchnitz.

Smith, Charlotte Turner (1971). *Emmeline, the Orphan of the Castle* (1788). Oxford: Oxford UP.

Smollett, Tobias George (1988). *Ferdinand Count Fathom* (1753). London/Athens, GA: U of Georgia P.

— (2002). *Sir Launcelot Greaves* (1760-1762). London/Athens, GA: U of Georgia P.

— (1990). *The Expedition of Humphry Clinker* (1771). London/Athens, GA: U of Georgia P.

Somerville, Edith Anna Oenone, Martin Ross (1894). *The Real Charlotte.* London: Ward and Downey.

Swift, Jonathan (1959). *Gulliver's Travels* (1735). Oxford: Basil Blackwell.

Thackeray, William Makepeace (1908). "The Ravenswing" (1843). *The Memoirs of Barry Lyndon, The Fitz-Boodle Papers, Men's Wives Catherine. The Works vol. 4.* London: Smith, Elder & Co. 367-475.

— (1898). "The Book of Snobs" (1848). *Contributions to Punch etc.* The Works, vol. 6. London: Smith, Elder & Co. 303-466.

— (1900). *Vanity Fair: A Novel without a Hero* (1848). The Works, vol. 1. London: Smith, Elder & Co.

— (1898). *The History of Pendennis, His Fortunes and Misfortunes, His Fiends and His Greatest Enemy* (1848-1850). The Works, vol. 2. London: Smith, Elder & Co.

— (1899). *The Newcomes* (1848-1850). The Works, vol. 8. London: Smith, Elder & Co.

— (1909). *The History of Henry Esmond, Esq. Written by Himself* (1852). The Works, vol. 7. London: Smith, Elder & Co.

Toulmin, Camilla (1855). *Hildred: The Daughter.* London: G. Routledge.

Trollope, Anthony (1952). *The Warden* (1855). The Oxford Trollope. London et al.: Geoffrey Cumberlege; Oxford: Oxford UP.

— (1953). *Barchester Towers* (1857). The Oxford Trollope. London et al.: Geoffrey Cumberlege; Oxford: Oxford UP.

— (1980). *Framley Parsonage* (1861). Oxford: Oxford UP.

— (1936). *The Last Chronicle of Barset* (1867). London: J. Dent and Sons.

— (1950). *The Eustace Diamonds* (1872). The Oxford Trollope. London et al.: Geoffrey Cumberlege; Oxford: Oxford UP.

Trollope, Frances Milton (1840). *The Vicar of Wrexhill* (1837). New revised ed. London: Richard Bentley.

Vonnegut, Kurt (1952). *Player Piano.* New York, NY: Delacorte Press.

Walpole, Hugh (1931). *Jeremy* (1919). London: Macmillan.

Ward, Edward (1711-1712). *The Life and Notable Adventures of That Renown'd Knight, Don Quixote De la Mancha.* London: T. Norris.

Ward, Mrs. Humphry (1888). *Robert Elsmere.* Leipzig: Tauchnitz.

West, Jane (1974). *The Advantages of Education, or The History of Maria Williams* (1793). Reprint. London/New York, NY: Garland.

White, William Hale (1881). *The Autobiography of Mark Rutherford, Dissenting Minister: Edited by His Friend, Reuben Shapcott.* London: Trübner.

Wilde, Oscar (1988). *The Picture of Dorian Gray* (1891). London/New York, NY: W. W. Norton.

Willcocks, Mary Patricia (1912). *Wings of Desire.* London: John Lane, The Bodley Head.

Wollstonecraft Godwin, Mary (1788). *Mary: A Fiction*. London: J. Johnson.
— *The Wrongs of Woman, or Maria* (1798). London: J. Johnson.
Wood, Mrs. Henry (1861). *East Lynne*. Leipzig: Tauchnitz.
— (1901). *Mildred Arkell: A Novel* (1865). London: Macmillan.
Woolf, Virginia (1990). *Night and Day* (1919). London: The Hogarth Press.
Yonge, Charlotte Mary (1997). *The Heir of Redclyffe* (1853). Oxford: Oxford UP.
— (1861). *Hopes and Fears, or Scenes from the Life of a Spinster*. Leipzig: Tauchnitz.

1.3. Poetry

Anon. (1882-1898). "Fair Annie". J. F. Child, ed. *The English and Scottish Popular Ballads*. Boston, MA/New York, NY: Houghton Mifflin & Co. 77-79.
Bacon, Phanuel (1722). *The Kite: An Heroi-Comical Poem in Three Canto's*. Oxford: L. Lichfield.
Bailey, Philip James (1877). *Festus*. London: Longmans, Green & Co.
Baker, Henry (1725). "On Mrs. – S–'s Playing on the Harpsicord, and Singing". *Original Poems Serious and Humorous*. London: Printed for the Author. 66-67.
Barlow, George (1902-1914). "The Marriage in Music". *The Poetical Works*, vol. 2. London: Henry T. Glaisher. 92.
Bennett, William Cox (1862). "Sketches from a Painter's Studio: A Tale of Today". *Poems*. New Edition. London/New York, NY: Warne and Routledge. 71-74.
    http://lion.chadwyck.co.uk. Literature Online. University of Basel [22/01/2007].
Bloomfield, Robert (1827). "May-Day With the Muses". *The Poems, in Three Volumes*, vol. 3. London: Longman et al. 177-200.
Breton, Nicholas (1582). "[Amid my ioyes]". *A Floorish vpon Fancie: As gallant a Glose, ypon so trifling a text as euer, was written*. London: Richard Jones. Giii[r].
Brown, Jones (Arthur Joseph Munby) (1891). "The Heroine". *Vulgar Verses*. London: Reeves and Turner. 1-2.
    http://lion.chadwyck.co.uk. Literature Online. University of Basel [22/01/2007].

Browne, William (1631). "The Fifth Song" (1616). *Britannia's Pastorals*. London: George Norton. 126-151.

Byron, Lord (1986). *Don Juan* (1824). The Complete Poetical Works, vol. 5. Oxford: Clarendon Press.

Calverley, Charles Stuart (1901). "Play" (1872). *The Complete Works*. London: George Bell and Sons. 89-90.

Chocke, A. (1710). "[Celia Learning on the Spinnet]". (Three-voice catch with music by John Isum). Microfilm. London: British Library. 1 reel (575fr.): negative; 35mm. Mus. Mic. 1400. Microfilm, positive. Mus. Mic. A. 1420.

Clough, Arthur Hugh (1974). "The Bothie of Tober-na Vuolich" (1848). *The Poems*. 2nd ed. Oxford: Clarendon Press. 44-93.

— (1974). "Amours de Voyage" (1849). *The Poems*. 2nd ed. Oxford: Clarendon Press. 94-136.

Colvill, Robert (1789). "Extempore at a Concert. Where L*** B**** C***** performed on the Harpsichord". *The Poetical Works of the Rev. Mr Colvill of Dyasart*. London: J. Dodsley et al. 100.

— (1789). "To the elegant Seraphina, performing on the piano forte, at a private concert". *The Poetical Works of the Rev. Mr Colvill of Dyasart*. London: J. Dodsley et al. 97-99.

Combe, William (1816). *The English Dance of Death: From the Designs of Thomas Rowlandson with Metrical Illustrations, by the Author of "Doctor Syntax"*. London: J. Diggens.

Croly, George (1827). *May Fair in Four Cantos*. London: William M. Ainsworth.
   http://lion.chadwyck.co.uk. Literature Online. University of Basel [22/01/2007].

Cunningham, Alan (1813). "Fashionable Sin". *Songs: Chiefly in the Rural Language of Scotland*. London: Smith and Davy et al. 43-45.
   http://lion.chadwyck.co.uk. Literature Online. University of Basel [30/05/2006].

Dibdin, Charles (1804). *The Harmonic Preceptor: A Didactic Poem In Three Parts*. Edinburgh: The Author.
   http://lion.chadwyck.co.uk. Literature Online. University of Basel [22/01/2007].

Dobson, Austin (1913). "An Autumn Idyll". *Collected Poems*. London: Kegan Paul, Trench, Trübner & Co. 83-89.

— (1913). "Incognita". *Collected Poems*. London: Kegan Paul, Trench, Trübner & Co. 383-386.

Dyer, George (1801). "Ode XXVIII: The Musicians: Two Amiable Young Women Playing Successively on the Harpsichord". *Poems*. London: Longman and Rees. 138-139. http://lion.chadwyck.co.uk. Literature Online. University of Basel [22/01/2007].

— (1812). "Ode VI: The Charm of Music. Written in Worcestershire". *Poetics, or a Series of Poems, and Disquisitions on Poetry*, vol. 1. London: J. Johnson. 207-208.

E. C. (1595). *Emaricdulfe: Sonnets Written by E. C. Esquier*. London: Matthew Law.

Eliot, George (1989). "Armgart" (1870). *Collected Poems*. London: Skoob Books Publishing. 115-151.

Gale, Norman Rowland (1896). "Aunt Jan". *Songs for Little People*. Westminster: Archibald Constable & Co. 69-70.

— (1912). "The Old Piano". *Song in September*. London: Constable and Company. 78-80.

Gray, John (1988). "Sound". Ian Fletcher, ed. *The Poems of John Gray*. Greensboro, NC: ELT Press University of North Carolina. 46.

Hardy, Thomas (1982). "To a Lady Playing and Singing in the Morning" (1884). *The Complete Poetical Works*, vol 2. Oxford: Clarendon Press. 344-345.

Havergal, Frances Ridley (1884). "The Moonlight Sonata". *The Poetical Works*, vol. 2. London: James Nisbet & Co. 14-31.

Hayley, William (1781). *The Triumph of Temper: A Poem in Six Cantos*. London: J. Dodsley.

Hill, Aaron (1753). "Bellaria, at Her Spinnet". *The Works of the Late Aaron Hill*, vol. 3. London: Printed for the Benefit of the Family. 141-145.

— (1753). "To Celinda, Complaining that Her Harpsichord Was out of Tune". *The Works of the Late Aaron Hill*, vol. 3. Printed for the Benefit of the Family. 13-16.

Henry, William Henry (1807). *Stultifera Navis, or The Modern Ship of Fools*. London: William Savage.

Hood, Thomas (1878). "Ode for St. Cecilia's Eve". *The Poetical Works of Thomas Hood. With Memoir, Explanatory Notes, &c.* London/New York, NY: Fredrick Warne & Co. 250-252.

Kipling, Rudyard (1990). "The Song of the Banjo" (1894). *The Complete Verse*. London: Kyle Cathie Ltd. 82-84.

Langhorne, John (1760). "To Miss – In return for a Set of Reading-Ribbands". *Poems on Several Occasions*. London: W. Wood. 98-102.

Lawrence, D. H. (1986). "The Piano" (1910). M. H. Abrams, ed. *The Norton Anthology of English Literature*, vol. 2. London/New York, NY: W. W. Norton. 2508-2509.

Leapor, Mary (1748). "Song to Cloe, Playing on Her Spinet". *Poems upon Several Occasions*. London: J. Roberts. 120-122.

Locker-Lampson, Frederick (1865). "The Castle in the Air". *A Selection from the Works of Frederick Locker*. London: Edward Moxon. 112-118.

Lyte, Henry Francis (1829). "Tale Fourth: Edward Field". *Tales in Verse Illustrative of the Seven Petitions of the Lord's Prayer*. 2nd ed. London: Marsh and Miller. 91-118. http://lion.chadwyck.co.uk. Literature Online. University of Basel [30/06/2006].

Macneill, Hector (1811). *Bygane Times, and Late Come Changes, or a Bridge Street Dialogue, in Scottish Verse*. Edinburgh/London: William Blackwood.

Meredith, George (1978). "Marian". *The Poems of George Meredith*, vol. 1. London/New Haven, CT: Yale UP. 174.

Milton, John (2005). *Paradise Lost* (1674). Gordon Teskey, ed. London/New York, NY: Norton.

Moncrieff, William Thomas (1850). "Cupid's Cookery Book". *An Original Collection of Songs*. London: John Duncombe. 147-148.

Patmore, Coventry (1921). "The Angel in the House" (1854). *Poems*. London: G. Bell and Sons. 3-145.

Praed, Winthrop Mackworth (1864). "Sir Lidian's Love". *The Poems of Winthrop Mackworth Praed*. 2nd ed. London: Edward Moxon & Co. 207-221.

Rossetti, Dante Gabriel (1911). "During Music". *The Works of Dante Gabriel Rossetti*. William M. Rossetti, ed. Rev. and enlarged ed. London: Ellis. 195.

Rowson, Susanna Haswell (1804). "Women as They Are". *Miscellaneous Poems*. Boston, MA: Gilbert and Dean. 105-115.

Sewell, George (1728). "Upon Mr. Addison's Cato". *Posthumous Works of Dr. George Sewell*, vol. 2. London: Henry Curll. 15-17.

Shakespeare, William (1974). "Sonnets". *The Riverside Shakespeare*. Boston, MA: Houghton Mifflin. 1745-1780.

Shelley, Percy Bysshe (1960). "Julian and Maddalo". Thomas Hutchinson, ed. *The Complete Poetical Works*. Oxford: Oxford UP. 189-203.

Sladen, Douglas Brooke Wheelton (1884). *A Summer Christmas and a Sonnet upon the S. S. Ballaarat*. London/New York, NY: Griffith, Farran, Okeden and Walsh.
http://lion.chadwyck.co.uk. Literature Online. University of Basel [22/01/2007].

Smith, John (1713). "To a Young Lady Singing and Playing upon Her Spinet". *Poems upon Several Occasions*. London: H. Clement. 218-221.

— (1713). "To a Jilting Mistress". *Poems upon Several Occasions*. London: H. Clement. 294-301.

Smith, James (1840). "The Two Sisters". *Memoirs, Letters and Comic Miscellanies in Prose and Verse, of the late James Smith*, vol. 1. London: Henry Colburn. 243-245.

Smith, Walter Chalmers (1902). "Hilda". *The Poetical Works*. London: J. M. Dent. 159-216.

Spenser, Edmund (1932-1949). "Iambicum Trimetrum". *The Works of Edmund Spenser: A Variorum Edition*, vol. 2. Baltimore: The Johns Hopkins Press. 267.

Steele, Richard (1952). "To Celia's Spinet" (1703). *The Occasional Verse of Richard Steele*. Oxford: Clarendon Press. 21.

Stephen, James Kenneth (1891). "Of W. W. (Americanus)". *Lapsus Calami*. Cambridge: Macmillan and Bowes. 43.

Stevenson, Robert Louis (1950). "To Himself at the Piano" (1886). *Collected Poems*. London: Rupert Hart-Davis. 548.

Sylvester, Josuah Du Bartas (1641). *Hus Diuine Weeks and Workes [...] Translated and written by ye famous Philomusus, Iosuah Sylvester, Gent* (1605). London: Robert Young.

Thelwall, John (1787). "On a Dog laying his Head in the Lap of a Lady, while she was playing on an Harpsichord, and singing". *Poems on Various Subjects*, vol. 2. London: Printed by the Author. 179.
http://lion.chadwyck.co.uk. Literature Online. University of Basel [22/01/2007].

Thompson, William (1757). "The Conquest". *Poems on Several Occasions*, vol. 1. Oxford: Printed at the Theatre. 109.

Tollet, Elizabeth (1755). "To Mrs. Elizabeth Blackler, Playing on the Harpsichord". *Poems on Several Occasions*. London: John Clarke. 30-32.

1.4. Drama

Arnold, Edwin (1856). *Griselda: A Tragedy, and Other Poems*. London: D. Bogue.

Barrie, James M. (1931). "The Twelve-Pound Look" (1912). *The Works of J. M. Barrie: The Peter Pan Edition*, vol. 14. New York, NY: AMS Press. 223-254.

Colman, George (1762). *The Musical Lady: A Farce*. London: T. Becket and P. A. Dehondt.

Dekker, Thomas, Thomas Middleton (1605). *The Honest Whore*. [Part I]. London: John Hodgets.

Gough, John (1640). *The Strange Discovery: A Tragi-Comedy*. London: E. G.

Holyday, Barten (1618). *Technogamia, or The Marriages of the Arts: A Comedie*. London: William Stansby for John Parker.

Hook, Theodore Edward (1808). *Music-Mad*. London: G. Sidney.

Lee, Nathaniel (1689). *The Princess of Cleve: As it was Acted at the Queens Theatre in Dorset-Garden*. London: [N. p.].

Lyly, John (1592). *Midas*. London: Thomas Scarlet.

Macdonald, George (1855). *Within and Without: A Dramatic Poem*. London: Longman, Brown, Green, and Longmans.

Marmion, Shackerley (1633). *A Fine Companion*. London: Augustine Matthews.

Mayne, Jasper (1639). *The Citye Match: A Commedye*. Oxford: Leonard Lichfield.

Middleton, Thomas (1607). *Michaelmas Term: As it hath been sundry times acted by the Children of Paules*. London: A. I.

— (1630). *A Chast Mayd in Cheape-side: A Pleasant Conceited Comedy*. London: Francis Constable.

Pinero, Arthur Wing (1995). "The Second Mrs Tanqueray" (1893). *Trelawny of the Wells' and Other Plays*. Oxford: Oxford UP. 141-212.

Reynolds, John (1623). *The Triumphs of Gods Revenge, against the Crying and Execrable sinne of Murther*. London: Augustine Matthews.

Rowley, Samuel (1634). *The Noble Sovldier, or A Contract Broken, Justly Reveng'd. A Tragedy*. London: Nicholas Vavasour.

Shadwell, Charles (1773). *The Fair Quaker, or The Humours of the Navy. Formerly written by Mr. Charles Shadwell, and now alter'd with great additions and a new character. London: F. T. Lownds.*

Shadwell, Thomas (1673). *Epsom-Wells: A Comedy, Acted at the Duke's Theatre*. London: Henry Herringman.

— (1691). *The Scowrers: A Comedy, Acted by Their Majesties Servants*. London: James Knapton.

Shakespeare, William (1974). "The Second Part of Henry VI" (1592). *The Riverside Shakespeare*. Boston, MA: Houghton Mifflin. 630-670.

— (1974). "The First Part of Henry IV" (1596-1597). *The Riverside Shakespeare*. Boston, MA: Houghton Mifflin. 842-885.

— (1974). "The Merchant of Venice" (1596-1598). *The Riverside Shakespeare*. Boston, MA: Houghton Mifflin. 250-285.

— (1974). "Much Ado About Nothing" (1598-1599). *The Riverside Shakespeare*. Boston, MA: Houghton Mifflin. 327-364.

— (1974). "Hamlet" (1600). *The Riverside Shakespeare*. Boston, MA: Houghton Mifflin. 1135-1197.

— (1974). "Othello" (1603-1604). *The Riverside Shakespeare*. Boston, MA: Houghton Mifflin. 1198-1248.

— (1974). "Coriolanus" (1607-1608). *The Riverside Shakespeare*. Boston, MA: Houghton Mifflin. 1392-1440.

— (1974). "Pericles" (1607-1608). *The Riverside Shakespeare*. Boston, MA: Houghton Mifflin. 1479-1516.

— (1974). "The Winter's Tale" (1610-1611). *The Riverside Shakespeare*. Boston, MA: Houghton Mifflin. 1564-1605.

— (1974). "Troilus and Cressida" (1613). *The Riverside Shakespeare*. Boston, MA: Houghton Mifflin. 443-498.

— (1974). "Two Noble Kinsmen" (1613). *The Riverside Shakespeare*. Boston, MA: Houghton Mifflin. 1639-1682.

Shaw, George Bernard (1972). "The Music-Cure: A Piece of Utter Nonsense" (1913). *Collected Plays with Their Prefaces*, vol. 4. London et al.: The Bodley Head. 875-894.

Southerne, Thomas (1693). *The Maid's Last Prayer, or Any Rather Than Fail. A Comedy*. London: R. Bentley.

Wager, Lewis (1566). *A new Enterlude, neuer before this tyme imprinted, entreating of the Life and Repentaunce of Marie Magdalene*. London: John Charlewood.

Wilde, Oscar (1986). "The Importance of Being Earnest" (1895). *The Importance of Being Earnest and Other Plays*. Harmondsworth: Penguin. 247-313.

2. Secondary Works

2.1. Word-and-Music Studies

Asbee, Sue, Tom Cooper (2006). "Music and Kate Chopin's *The Awakening*". Delia Gwendolen da Sousa Correa, ed. *Phrase and Subject: Studies in Music and Literature*. Oxford: Legenda. 125-134.
Austern, Linda Phyllis (1989). "'Sing Againe Syren': The Female Musician and Sexual Enchantment in Elizabethan Life and Literature". *Renaissance Quarterly* 42/3: 420-448.
— (1991). "Love, Death and Music in the English Renaissance". Kenneth R. Bartlett et al., eds. *Love and Death in the Renaissance*. Ottawa: Dovehouse. 17-36.
— (1993). "'Alluring the Auditorie to Effeminacie': Music and the Idea of the Feminine in Early Modern England". *Music and Letters* 74/3 (August): 343-354.
— (1994). "'No Women Are Indeed': The Boy Actor as Vocal Seductress in Late 16th- and Early 17th-Century English Drama". Leslie C. Dunn, Nancy A. Jones, eds. *Embodied Voices: Representing Female Vocality in Western Culture*. Cambridge: Cambridge UP. 83-102.
— (1998). "'For, Love's a Good Musician': Performance, Audition and Erotic Disorders in Early Modern Europe". *Musical Quarterly* 82/3-4 (Fall/Winter): 614-653.
Barthes, Roland (1982). "The Reality Effect" (1968). Zvetan Todorov, ed. *French Literary Theory Today: A Reader*. Cambridge: Cambridge UP. 11-17.
— (1977). "The Grain of the Voice". *Image/Music/Text*. New York, NY: Hill and Wang. 179-189.
Berley, Marc (2000). *After the Heavenly Tune: English Poetry and the Aspiration to Song*. Pittsburgh, PA: Duquesne UP.
Binstock, Lynn Ruth (1985). "A Study of Music in Victorian Prose". PhD thesis Oxford University.

Burgan, Mary (1989). "Heroines at the Piano: Women and Music in 19th-Century Fiction". Nicholas Temperley, ed. *The Lost Chord: Essays on Victorian Music*. Bloomington, IN: Indiana UP. 42-67.

Clapp-Itnyre, Alisa Marie (2002). *Angelic Airs, Subversive Songs: Music as Social Discourse in the Victorian Novel*. Athens, OH: Ohio UP.

Da Sousa Correa, Delia Gwendolen (2003). *George Eliot, Music and Victorian Culture*. Basingstoke: Palgrave Macmillan.

Dunn, Leslie C. (1994). "Ophelia's Songs in *Hamlet*: Music, Madness and the Feminine". Leslie C. Dunn, Nancy A. Jones, eds. *Embodied Voices: Representing Female Vocality in Western Culture*. Cambridge: Cambridge UP. 50-64.

Fuller, Sophie (2005). "'Cribb'd, cabin'd and confined': Female Musical Creativity in Victorian Fiction". Sophie Fuller, Nicky Losseff, eds. *The Idea of Music in Victorian Fiction*. Aldershot: Ashgate. 27-56.

Hollander, John (1961). *The Untuning of the Sky: Ideas of Music in English Poetry 1500-1700*. Princeton, NJ: Princeton UP.

— (1970). *Images of Voice: Music and Sound in Romanticism*. Cambridge: Heffer.

Law, Joe (2004). "The 'Perniciously Homosexual Art': Music and Homoerotic Desire in *The Picture of Dorian Gray* and Other *fin-de-siècle* Fiction". Sophie Fuller, Nicky Losseff, eds. *The Idea of Music in Victorian Fiction*. Aldershot: Ashgate. 173-196.

Leppert, Richard D. (1993). *The Sight of Sound: Music, Representation and the History of the Body*. Berkeley, CA: U of California P.

Losseff, Nicky (2000). "Absent Melody and *The Woman in White*". *Music and Letters* 81/4 (November): 532-550.

Lustig, Jodi (2004). "The Piano at Play in the Victorian Novel". Sophie Fuller, Nicky Losseff, eds. *The Idea of Music in Victorian Fiction*. Aldershot: Ashgate. 83-104.

Pollack, Janet (2005). "Princess Elizabeth Stuart as Musician and Muse". Thomasin LaMay, ed. *Musical Voices of Early Modern Women: Many-Headed Melodies*. Aldershot: Ashgate. 399-423.

Schafer, R. Murray, ed. (1977). *Ezra Pound and Music*. New York, NY: New Directions.

Smith, D. J. (1963). "Music in the Victorian Novel". *The Kenyon Review* 25: 517-532.

Stevens, John (1979). *Music and Poetry in the Early Tudor Court*. Cambridge: Cambridge UP.

Sutton, Emma (2005). "'The Music Spoke for Us': Music and Sexuality in *fin-de-siècle* Poetry". Phyllis Weliver, ed. *The Figure of Music in Nineteenth-Century British Poetry*. Aldershot: Ashgate. 213-229.

Vorachek, Laura (2000). "'The Instrument of the Century': The Piano as an Icon of Female Sexuality in the 19th Century". *George Eliot-George Henry Lewes Studies* 38-39 (September): 26-43.

Weliver, Phyllis (2004). "Music, Crowd Control and the Female Perfomer in *Trilby*". Sophie Fuller, Nicky Losseff, eds. *The Idea of Music in Victorian Fiction*. Aldershot: Ashgate. 57-82.

2.2. Literary and Cultural Studies

Adorno, Theodor W. (1980). *Minima Moralia* (1951). Frankfurt am Main: Suhrkamp.

Armstrong, Isobel (1974). "Browning and Victorian Poetry of Sexual Love". Isobel Armstrong, ed. *Writers and Their Background: Robert Browning*. London: G. Bell and Sons. 267-298.

Armstrong, Nancy (1987). "The Rise of the Domestic Woman". Nancy Armstrong, Leonard Tennenhouse, eds. *The Ideology of Conduct: Essays in Literature and the History of Sexuality*. London/New York, NY: Methuen. 96-141.

Auerbach, Nina (1982). *Woman and the Demon: The Life of a Victorian Myth*. Cambridge, MA: Harvard UP.

Bal, Mieke (1993). "His Master's Eye". David Michael Levin, ed. *Modernity and the Hegemony of Vision*. Berkeley, CA: U of California P. 379-404.

Ballaster, Ros, et al. (1991). *Women's Worlds: Ideology, Femininity and the Woman's Magazine*. London: Macmillan.

Belsey, Catherine (1994). *Desire: Love Stories in Western Culture*. Oxford/Cambridge, MA: Blackwell.

Booth, Stephen, ed. (1977/1978). *Shakespeare's Sonnets*. London/New Haven, CT: U of Yale P.

Bové, Paul (1995). "Discourse". Frank Lentricchia, Thomas McLaughlin, eds. *Critical Terms for Literary Studies*. Chicago, IL: Chicago UP. 50-65.

Coveney, Peter (1967). *Image of Childhood: The Individual and Society: A Study of the Theme in English Literature*. Harmondsworth: Penguin.

Crookes, David Z. (1985). "Shakespeare's Sonnet 128". *Explicator Washington DC* 43/2 (Winter): 14-15.

Dever, Carolyn (2005). "Everywhere and Nowhere: Sexuality in the Victorian Novel". Francis O'Gorman, ed. *A Concise Companion to the Victorian Novel*. Oxford: Blackwell. 156-179.

Drew, Elizabeth (1926). *The Modern Novel: Some Aspects of Contemporary Fiction*. London: Jonathan Cape.

Dubrow, Heather (1999). "'Incertainties now crown themselves assur'd': The Politics of Plotting Shakespeare's Sonnets". James Schiffer, ed. *Shakespeare's Sonnets*. London/New York, NY: Garland. 113-134.

Easthope, Antony (1991). *Literary into Cultural Studies*. London: Routledge.

Edmondson, Paul, Stanley Wells, eds. (2004). *Shakespeare's Sonnets*. Oxford: Oxford UP.

Edwards, Philip (1968). *Shakespeare and the Confines of Art*. London/New York, NY: Methuen.

Fineman, Joel (1986). *Shakespeare's Perjured Eye: The Invention of Poetic Subjectivity in the Sonnets*. Berkeley, CA: U of California P.

Foucault, Michel (1980). *The History of Sexuality. Vol. I: An Introduction*. New York, NY: Vintage Books.

Friedman, Michael (1990). "'Hush'd on Purpose to Grace Harmony': Wives and Silence in *Much Ado About Nothing*". *Theatre Journal* 42: 350-363.

Gilbert, Sandra M., Susan Gubar (1979). *The Madwoman in the Attic*. London/New Haven, CT: Yale UP.

Gorham, Deborah (1982). *The Victorian Girl and the Feminine Ideal*. Bloomington, IN: Indiana UP.

Hellerstein, Erna Olafson, et al., eds. (1981). *Victorian Women: A Documentary Account of Women's Lives in 19th-Century England, France and the United States*. Stanford, CA: The Harvester Press.

Hohl Trillini, Regula (2006). "The Dear Dead Past: The Piano in 19th Century Poetry". Delia Gwendolen da Sousa Correa, ed. *Phrase and Subject: Studies in Music and Literature*. Oxford: Legenda. 112-124.

— (2007). "Tom, Dick and … Jack in the *OED* and in Sonnet 128". *Shakespeare-Jahrbuch* 143: 177-179.

— (2008). "The Gaze of the Listener: Shakespeare's Sonnet 126 and Early Modern Discourses of Music and Gender". *Music and Letters* 89/1 (February): 1-17.

Innes, Paul (1997). *Shakespeare and the English Renaissance Sonnet: Verses of Feigning Love*. Basingstoke: Macmillan; New York, NY: St. Martin's Press.

Irigaray, Luce (1985). *Speculum of the Other Woman*. Ithaca, NY: Cornell UP.

Janson, Dora Jane (1971). *From Slave to Siren: The Victorian Woman and Her Jewellery, from Neoclassic to Art Nouveau*. Durham, NC: The Duke University Museum of Art.

Kitson, P. R. (1987). "Virginal Jacks". *Notes and Queries* 34/2: 204-205.

Kosofsky Sedgwick, Eve (1985). *Between Men: English Literature and Homosocial Desire*. New York, NY: Columbia UP.

Kristeva, Julia (1980). "The Bounded Text". *Desire in Language: A Semiotic Approach to Literature and Art*. New York, NY: Columbia UP. 36-63.

Langland, Elizabeth (1995). *Nobody's Angel: Middle-Class Women and Domestic Ideology in Victorian Culture*. London/Ithaca, NY: Cornell UP.

Lausberg, Heinrich (1998). *Handbook of Literary Rhetoric: A Foundation for Literary Study*. Leiden et al.: Brill.

Lipking, Laurence (1970). *The Ordering of the Arts in 18ᵗʰ-Century England*. Princeton, NJ: Princeton UP.

Mitchell, Sally (1981). *Fallen Angel: Chastity, Class and Women's Reading 1835-1880*. Bowling Green, OH: Bowling Green Univ. Popular Press.

— (1995). *The New Girl: Girls' Culture in England 1880-1915*. New York, NY: Columbia UP.

Mueschke Paul, Jeannette Fleisher (1933). "Jonsonian Elements in the Comic Underplot of *Twelfth Night*". *PMLA* 48/3: 722-740.

Mulvey, Laura (1989). "Visual Pleasure and Narrative Cinema". *Visual and Other Pleasures*. Bloomington, IN/Indianapolis, IN: Indiana UP. 14-26.

Peterson, Mildred Jeanne (1984). "No Angels in the House: The Victorian Myth and the Paget Women". *American Historical Review* 89/3: 677-708.

Raitt, Suzanne (2000). *May Sinclair: A Modern Victorian*. Oxford: Clarendon Press.

Robbins, R. H. A. (1967). "A Seventeenth-Century Manuscript of Shakespeare's Sonnet 128". *Notes and Queries* 14: 137-138.

Rowbotham, Judith (1989). *Good Girls Make Good Wives: Guidance for Girls in Victorian Fiction*. Oxford: Basil Blackwell.

Sadleir, Michael, Morris Longstreth Parrish (1931). *Bulwer: A Panorama. Part I: Edward and Rosina, 1803-1836*. London: Little, Brown and Co.

Schwartz, Robert (1990). *Shakespeare's Parted Eye*. New York, NY et al.: Peter Lang.

Sennett, Richard (1976). *The Fall of Public Man*. Cambridge: Cambridge UP.

Sobba Green, Katherine (1991). *The Courtship Novel 1740-1820: A Feminized Genre*. Lexington, KY: The UP of Kentucky.

Stone, Lawrence (1992). *Uncertain Unions: Marriage in England 1660-1753*. Oxford: Oxford UP.

Stubbs, Patricia (1979). *Women and Fiction: Feminism and the Novel 1880-1920*. Brighton: Harvester Press.

Trotter, David (1993). *The English Novel in History 1895-1920*. London: Routledge.

Wilson, Katharine (1974). *Shakespeare's Sugared Sonnets*. London: George Allen and Unwin.

Wright, Eugene Patrick (1993). *The Structure of Shakespeare's Sonnets*. Lewiston, ME: The Edwin Mellen Press.

2.3. Musicology

Blom, Eric Walter (1969). *The Romance of the Piano* (1928). New York, NY: Da Capo Press.

Boyd, Morris Comegys (1940). *Elizabethan Music and Music Criticism*. Philadelphia, PA: U of Pennsylvania P.

Burgess, Anthony (1981). "The Well-Tempered Revolution: A Consideration of the Piano's Social and Intellectual History". James Gaines, ed. *The Lives of the Piano*. New York, NY: Holt, Rinehart and Winston. 3-40.

Chappell, William (1961). *Old English Popular Music*. A New Edition with a Preface and Notes, and the Earlier Examples Entirely Revised. New York, NY: Jack Brussel.

Closson, Ernest (1944). *Histoire du piano*. Bruxelles: Les Presses de Belgique (Éditions universitaires).

Ehrlich, Cyril (1975). "Social Emulation and Industrial Progress: The Victorian Piano". *New Lecture Series* 82. Belfast: Queen's Univ.

Gaines, James (1981). *The Lives of the Piano*. New York, NY: Holt, Rinehart and Winston.

Gellrich, Martin (1992). *Üben mit Lis(z)t: Wiederentdeckte Geheimnisse aus der Werkstatt der Klaviervirtuosen*. Frauenfeld: Waldgut.

Gillett, Paula (2000). "Ambivalent Friendships: Music-Lovers, Amateur and Professional Musicians in the Late Nineteenth Century". Christina Bashford, Leanne Langley, eds. *Music and British Culture, 1785-1914: Essays in Honour of Cyril Ehrlich*. Oxford: Oxford UP. 321-340.

— (2000). *Musical Women in England, 1870-1914*. London: Macmillan.

Green, Lucy (1997). *Music, Gender, Education*. Cambridge: Cambridge UP.

Harding, Rosamond E. M. (1989). *The Piano-Forte: Its History Traced to the Great Exhibition of 1851* (1933). Cambridge: Cambridge UP.

Irving, Howard (1990). "'Music as a Pursuit for Men': Accompanied Keyboard Music as Domestic Recreation in England". *College Music Symposium* 30: 126-137.

Johnson, David (1972). *Music and Society in Lowland Scotland in the 18th Century*. Oxford: Oxford UP.

Kopelson, Kevin (1996). *Beethoven's Kiss: Pianism, Perversion and the Mastery of Desire*. Stanford, CA: Stanford UP.

Loesser, Arthur (1990). *Men, Women and Pianos: A Social History* (1954). New York, NY: Dover.

McVeigh, Simon (1993). *Concert Life in London from Mozart to Haydn*. Cambridge: Cambridge UP.

Pearsall, Roland (1973). *Victorian Popular Music*. Newton Abbot: David and Charles.

Raynor, Henry (1972). *A Social History of Music from the Middle Ages to Beethoven*. New York, NY: Taplinger.

Scott, Derek B. (1989). *The Singing Bourgeois: Songs of the Victorian Drawing Room*. Milton Keynes: Open UP.

Shepherd, John (1993). "Difference and Power in Music". Ruth Solie, ed. *Musicology and Difference: Gender and Sexuality in Music Scholarship*. Berkeley, CA et al.: U of California P. 46-65.

Solie, Ruth A. (2004). *Music in Other Words: Victorian Conversations*. Berkeley, CA et al.: U of California P.

Young, Percy M. (1965). *The Concert Tradition: From the Middle Ages to the 20th Century*. London: Routledge and Kegan Paul.